THE
VIKING
SETTLEMENTS
OF
NORTH AMERICA

BOOKS BY FREDERICK J. POHL

When Things Were New (nine plays, privately printed) 1928
Brittle Heaven (play, with coauthor Vincent York)
Amerigo Vespucci, Pilot Major
The Sinclair Expedition to Nova Scotia in 1398
The Lost Discovery
The Vikings on Cape Cod
Atlantic Crossings Before Columbus
The Viking Explorers

THE
VIKING
SETTLEMENTS
OF
NORTH AMERICA

BY FREDERICK J. POHL

 Clarkson N. Potter, Inc./Publisher NEW YORK

DISTRIBUTED BY CROWN PUBLISHERS, INC.

ACKNOWLEDGMENTS

First I wish to acknowledge the help received through more than thirty years of reading-desk and field research into the Viking voyages to Vinland. I have named a host of helpers in previous books. Here my naming, or renaming, only a few is to emphasize the varied directions from which help has come.

I wish to pay respect to those who have added to our knowledge of the Viking penetration of our continent—to archaeologists like Thomas E. Lee of Centre d'Etudes Nordiques, Université Laval, Quebec.

My gratitude goes to many librarians in America and in Europe, such as Gerard Alexander of the Map Division of the New York Public Library.

Great assistance has come from museum personnel, as for example Bjarni Vilhjálmsson, Director of the National Archives in Reykjavík, and his predecessor, Dr. Kristján Eldjárn, who became Premier of Iceland.

Good advice came from many friends, among them Hjalmar R. Holand.

Dr. Robert K. Zuck, Chairman of the Department of Biology at Drew University, and other professors in various subjects have given invaluable information.

Practical assistance came from members of the Massachusetts Archaeological Society, from Dr. Maurice Robbins, and from Charles E. White of North Attleboro, who was in the group that discovered the shoring for a viking ship.

Essential help came from fellow members of the Ship Lore Club—men with special knowledge of ships and how early mariners sailed them—such men as Captain Bob Bartlett, of Arctic fame, and Captain George H. Seeth, onetime president of the New York Harbor Pilots' Association.

Correspondents in America like Dr. Wallace W. Nelson of

Grand Forks, North Dakota, have prodded me with queries and suggestions. Similar stimuli have come from correspondents abroad, especially in Scandinavia, as from Arth J. Tonnesen of Stavanger, Norway. Gloria Farley (Mrs. J. Ray Farley), of Heavener, Oklahoma, is an active investigator, who has generously shared her knowledge of numerous important discoveries.

I am deeply appreciative of the work of Paul N. Jago of North Quincey, and others who have labored on their own initiative; and I cannot resist mentioning William A. Turner of Needham, Massachusetts, after whose name in my address book are the words: "a boy who wants to help dig."

My thanks go to those who have accompanied me in the field: Thomas Carr, Moulton H. Farnham, Albert E. Snow, William L. Smyth, Ralph C. Urban, John C. Mobyed, George McGrath, June N. and Robert D. Barnes, F. Newton Miller, and Richard L. Mearns.

I am indebted to the perceptive editor, Clarkson N. Potter, for a most helpful suggestion in the reshaping of the manuscript of *The Viking Settlements of North America*.

Finally, I thank my wife, Josephine, who with a writer's understanding of a writer's needs, has given me constant encouragement.

CONTENTS

LIST OF ILLUSTRATIONS

FOREWORD

What Frederick Pohl has done in this book is an achievement
indeed. He tells the story of what happened in the Viking voyages
in Vinland in plain language and plain terms worked out by himself from his own translations. By his indefatigable detective work,
in the geographical sense, he has identified eighty-nine locations,
many of them mentioned confusingly or vaguely in such sources as
have survived. In this he has been helped by his intimate acquaintance with the geography of the eastern half of North America,
and with the meteorological conditions and weather variations
even between sites a few miles apart, not forgetting those important features, the tides and river currents. His treatment, too,
of Thorfinn Karlsefni amounts practically to a biography of the
strange man who explored over 3,000 miles of the North American

coast back in the early eleventh century. For good measure, he gives us an appendix, a brief but well-evidenced summary of the Viking settlements in North America which are not directly traceable from any of the sagas which have survived. In short, Mr. Pohl makes sense of the Sagas, and that in itself is no slight achievement in these days.

There are some who are inclined still to brush the idea of the Viking achievements aside as if they had never been made, or if made, added up to little or nothing. Some even seem to doubt all such voyages. The Sagas have been regarded as vague and contradictory, uncertain accounts of events and voyages not proven. A generation which has seen the Atlantic crossed single-handed by a young woman in a large yacht, an odd crew in a reconstruction of a reed boat, a man in a dugout canoe, and others in a raft or a war-surplus old jeep, yachts old and new of all sorts and sizes from fourteen feet upwards, racing, drifting, or just having fun, and a couple of British paratroopers rowing an unsatisfactory small boat without any sail at all, can have no real difficulty in accepting the voyages of the Vikings. These Norsemen were professional seamen, rough, tough, and headstrong: competent, used to the acceptance of hardship at sea and ashore. They had reasonable craft for voyage-making and keeping the sea. They faced the Western Ocean at its least breadth and greatest vulnerability; from western Norway to eastern Iceland, from western Iceland to eastern Greenland, from western Greenland to the coasts of Labrador and Newfoundland—these are all comparatively short crossings. Currents and winds are frequently favorable; and here up north east winds often blow when there are wild west storms farther to the south'ard. Whoever could reach Newfoundland had the whole coasts of North America to range along in the summers, at leisure.

If proof were needed that these westward Western Ocean passages could be taken in the Vikings' competent stride, there is the voyage made by Magnus Andersen from Marstein, near Bergen in Norway, to Newfoundland in the late spring of 1893, in a reconstruction of the famous Gokstad ship. This is a *real* Viking ship, recovered in Norway: the replica was a *precise* copy. There was no nonsense about it: there were no "improvements" either insisted upon by competent maritime authorities or taken along for convenience, or publicity, or any other reason. Magnus Andersen was a professional seaman. He hadn't even a contract to write a book. The object of the exercise was to demonstrate just what it did—that a standard type of larger Viking vessel could take a westbound crossing of the North Atlantic in those comparatively high latitudes in her stride. The reconstruction sailed on April 30, 1893, and was at Newfoundland on May 27, despite more than enough bad weather. The rig was the standard rig of the Gokstad ship without refinements—just the single great mast and sail. Steering was the Viking way by "steer board" attached to the starboard quarter manipulated by a small piece of wood, a sort of 'thwartships tiller.

Just as we found when we sailed the replica *Mayflower* from Plymouth, Devon, to Plymouth, Massachusetts, in 1957, those old shipwrights and craft-builders knew what they were at. The apparently weak rigging of the *Mayflower II* bothered us: but we learned that in a real seaway with the little bark jumping and leaping about, the very give of the hemp and lanyards in the rigging took care of the stresses aloft: she was all right. What seemed weakness was in fact a sort of strength. Magnus Andersen noted that the bottom of his Viking boat—lashed with withies to the simple ribs—worked in a seaway, breathing like the skin of a whale: nothing gave way. There were no leaks. And the vessel could run a nice ten knots. She was all right.

The case for the voyages is proven. Remembering this, I have studied what Mr. Pohl had to say here with great interest, and profit.

Oxford,
September 3, 1971   Captain Alan Villiers

PART ONE

The Narrative

THE SEARCH FOR
VINLAND

The vikings[1] shortly before and after A.D. 1000 voyaged to a land to which Leif Erikson gave the name "Vinland." Centuries later, when direct contact had ceased and Vinland had faded from the

[1] The vikings were those men from the fjords (*viks*) of Scandinavian countries and of the islands in the North Atlantic (Faeroes, Hebrides, Iceland, etc.) who went out to other lands first as raiders and later as traders for a period of three centuries ending about A.D. 1075. The word "vik-men" or "viking" is not capitalized, since the vikings were not a nation, but individuals who engaged in organized plunder or merchant trading. In Iceland and Greenland there were "great vikings," in use of the term contemporary with Leif Erikson, who went out as traders, not raiders. As the Norsemen became Christianized, they turned from marauding and gained wealth by carrying merchandise or valuable raw materials in their oceangoing ships.

3

sight of all Norsemen, historians questioned what land Vinland was. They did much guessing, but the general opinion was that it was the continent of North America. Since the first viking of record who landed in Vinland appeared to have a claim to being the discoverer of America, everyone asked, "Where in Vinland did Leif Erikson go ashore?" But with awareness that other vikings after Leif Erikson explored the country extensively, the question now being asked is "How far did the vikings penetrate our continent?"

The answer lies in the sagas (tellings) of the viking voyages to Vinland, and in identifications of the geographical observations stated or implied in those narratives.

Here is the story of those voyages. The identifications and the detective work and the archaeological discoveries that unraveled the puzzle are in the second section of this book, and they in turn are followed by the author's translation of the Vinland sagas.

[To make it easy for the reader to check on the author's geographical observations, each geographical observation stated or implied in the sagas, and each identification is marked in the margins with a letter and a number throughout. Bjarni Herjulfsson's geographical observations are numbered B 1 to B 7; those by Leif Erikson, L 1 to L 20; those by Thorvald Erikson, T 1 to T 14; and those by Thorfinn Karlsefni, K 1 to K 45. Those that bear upon the voyage by the Icelandic brothers Helgi and Finnboge and by Leif's half-sister Freydis are marked F 1 to F 3.]

THE MAN WHO MISNAMED
A GREAT ISLAND

Erik the Red never sailed to Vinland, but he cannot be omitted from the story of Vinland because the first sighting of that land occurred as a direct result of something he did. The explorers of Vinland were also motivated by reactions to one of Erik's less creditable achievements.

Erik was born in Norway. In a brawl, his father Thorvald committed manslaughter and was exiled. He sailed with his infant son to Iceland. There, all the good land had already been settled, and he was compelled to take up residence near the northwestern corner of Iceland on the inhospitable Hornstrands, a coast where fishing and whale and walrus hunting were impeded by pack ice.

It looked as though his son would not have a fair chance in life, but young Erik grew to manhood the stronger for having had to face and overcome difficulties and dangers. After his father died, Erik left Hornstrands, and married Thjodhild, whose family held land in Haukadale. He went to Haukadale, acquired and cleared land and had his own farm, Erikstead. There he begat three sons and an illegitimate daughter.

Like his father, Erik got into a brawl. He directed his thralls to modify the local geography. They were almost as effective as an earthquake, for they caused a landslide that destroyed a neighbor's farm. In revenge, a kinsman of that landscaped neighbor slew Erik's thralls. To avenge this, Erik slew two men whose appalling names, Eyolf the Foul and Hrafn the Dueller, suggest that their departure to Valhalla was good riddance, but it was against the law, and Erik was banished from Haukadale.

He went to an island in the great fjord of western Iceland, and since he had no house for the moment, he loaned the carved posts and boards of his sleeping platform to Thorgest of Breidabol-stead. But when he had a house and asked for the return of his furniture, Thorgest unwisely refused. Erik promptly went to Thorgest's house and seized the boards. Thorgest, lacking in good judgment, pursued Erik, and they fought a battle in which two sons of Thorgest and several other men were slain. Then there was an open feud, inviting to all who wished to participate. Erik and Thorgest each maintained a force of fighting men at home. The affair was brought before the Thorsness Lawthing, the public council of landowners and priests, and judgment went against Erik. He and his men were outlawed from Iceland for three years.

Erik secretly left his son Leif and presumably his other sons in the care of a foster-father, the German-born Tyrker. Disregarding the legal decision, Thorgest and his men were searching for Erik and his men to kill them. While a friend on Svin Island kept him in hiding, Erik had his ship made ready, and when it was ready, his loyal friends accompanied him out beyond the islands in Breidafjord. There was an emotional parting. Erik vowed that, at the risk of his own life, he would give his friends a safe hiding place if they ever had need of one. He had to stay out of Iceland for three years. He was going to sail into unknown seas to the west. To where? He could not survive three months on the ocean, to say nothing of three years. He must find land to the west. But what land? He told his friends he would search for the land which Gunnbjorn had sighted when, driven, off course to the west, he had discovered some small rocky islets, the Gunnbjorn Skerries. Erik's final words to his friends were terse and grim, with fateful implications, "If I find this land, I will return to visit you."

If he did not find land, he would never see them again. Putting to sea, he held in sight Snaefellsjökul, the snow peak of over 4,700 feet in altitude at the western tip of the cape on the south side of Breidafjord. Snaefellsjökul was visible at sea for ninety-one miles, and so long as Erik had it within sight he could steer a straight course.

He made a landfall near a glacier later called Black Sark. He found he was off a coast where landing was forbidden to him by pack ice jammed along the shore. Up above was an ice cap from which many a glacier descended, and from the fringe of each glacier an immense block almost the size of a mountain would sometimes break off without warning, with a noise like thunder, and cause huge waves as it splashed into the sea to become an iceberg.[2] He could find no place to venture ashore, and he looked in vain for pastureland. He sailed for hundreds of miles in company with many icebergs being swept southward in a swift current, and then around the southern end of the great land. And when the current swept him and the menacing icebergs northward along the western coast of the land, he had to steer clear of many rock islets drenched with spray. Above them he heard the beating wings and watched the flight of thousands of eider ducks, gulls, and guillemots. But here and there was an open seaway into the mouth of a fjord, and so he sailed into each fjord, looking for grassland, and he was

[2] The Greenland ice cap covers 715,000 square miles. The ocean level was about $2\frac{1}{2}$ feet higher then than now. Some of the Greenland (and Antarctic) ice had melted to make the ocean level higher. How much had melted? The Greenland ice cap is thousands of feet thick, much of it a mile thick. It is a fair estimate that there was about fifty feet less of thickness to the Greenland ice cap in Erik the Red's day, and so the glaciers and numbers of icebergs were about the same as now.

happy to find thin patches of brown moors with touches of emerald green, and at the inner end of each fjord a few narrow green meadows.

He spent the first of the three winters of exile on what he called Erik Island, near the middle of a fjord. In the next sailing season he sailed into that fjord, and at its inner end selected a site for his farmstead that had the best pastureland in all the country. That same summer he explored fjords farther to the northwest, and, with a great plan forming in his mind to establish a colony over which he as founder would preside, he gave names everywhere, to islands, headlands, and fjords. He no doubt either drew a chart to show the various fjords that had habitable lands to which he would assign colonists, or he raised stone beacons at the mouth of each such fjord to identify it. He spent the second winter at what he called Hrafnsgnipa, and the next sailing season in further exploration of fjords, always to the inner end of each. He spent the third winter on Erik Island, from which he probably sent men in to lay the stone foundations and erect the sod walls of his permanent house at the inner end of Eriksfjord.

He had explored a thousand miles of coastline, and now he was to become a land promoter. He cast about in his mind for a name for the country that would induce settlers to come to it, for from his boyhood he had known the problem of land hunger and the keenest desires of land seekers. And he hit upon a name for the ice-hooded country—a dishonest name, or at best an exaggeration of its few and slender grassy areas, for he said, "Men will be more readily persuaded to go there, if the land has an attractive name." So when he sailed back to Iceland in the fourth summer and landed in Breidafjord, he told the folk of the land to the west and made it sound wonderful by giving it a name which appealed irresistibly to them—Greenland.

He was in Iceland one winter, stirring up a desire in many hearts to leave home and settle in Greenland. The next season, in the year 985, twenty-five (some said thirty-five) ships, each crowded with from twenty-five to forty men, women, and children, and with domestic animals, set sail out of Breidafjord and Borgarfjord. Some were driven back and some were cast away. Only fourteen of the ships made it. The leaders of those who arrived in Greenland gave their names to some of the fjords, though it seems that Erik had made various assignments in advance.

BJARNI HERJULFSSON'S
TELLING

The first sighting of Vinland happened because a young man, Bjarni, was determined to spend the winter with his father. As a boy Bjarni loved sea voyaging, and he naturally took to merchant trading across the Atlantic, from his home in Iceland to Norway and back. He was a success at it, and acquired wealth enough to become a shipowner. The ocean crossing was in one direction only each sailing season, and so it was Bjarni's custom to spend one winter in Norway and the next at home. Now in the summer of the year 985, Bjarni set sail from Norway, but while his ship plowed the waves westward something happened in Iceland that was to change all his future life. For when Bjarni steered his ship into his home port, Eyrarbakki, on the southwest coast of Iceland, he was confronted with the news that his father Herjulf had decided to accompany Erik the Red to a new country called Greenland, and had departed from his home. Bjarni was greatly surprised and deeply upset. He did not give his crew the expected order to unload the ship, and so the men asked what he intended to do. He replied that it was his purpose to hold to his custom and to spend the winter with his father. He told his shipmates he would take the ship to Greenland if they would go with him. They all replied that they would follow him wherever he decided to go. Then Bjarni warned them: "Our voyage into the Greenland Sea may be regarded as foolhardy, since none of us has ever been in those waters."

Nevertheless, when they had taken on fresh water and food and wood for cooking fires, they put to sea and sailed around the southwestern corner of Iceland to a position off Breidafjord where Bjarni wanted to set the same course that Erik the Red and the many colonists had taken from Snaefellsjökul. But when the land fell below the horizon, the fair (following) wind failed and changed into north winds and fogs, and they had no idea in which direction they were carried. This uncertainty lasted many days. When the sun came forth again, they were able to establish direction from the sun, and at night from the stars, and they hoisted sail. The wind was no longer from the north or east, but from the south, veering as it does in the northern hemisphere. With a southerly wind and sail swung to the starboard, Bjarni sailed toward the west or northwest. They sailed a day before they sighted land. They wondered what land it could be. Bjarni doubted that it was Greenland. His shipmates asked whether he wished to sail to the land, but he proposed that they merely sail close to it, and as they did so, they perceived that the land was mountainless and wooded, with low hillocks. This land is known today as Cape Cod.

They left the land on their starboard with their sail swung over toward it, and so sailed away toward the northeast. They sailed for two days before they sighted another land. The men asked Bjarni whether he thought this was Greenland, but he said

B 1

B 2

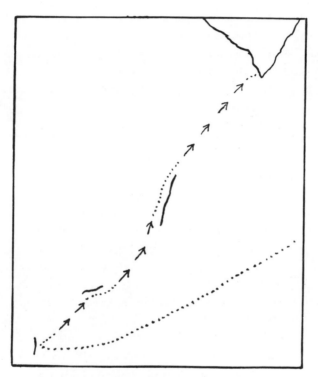

BJARNI'S SIGHTING OF NEW LANDS
Arrows indicate the number of day's sailing between them

this was no more like Greenland than the first, because he had been told that in Greenland there were mountains with very large glaciers. When they drew near this second land, somewhere near the future site of Halifax, Nova Scotia, or within thirty miles to **B 3** the east of it, the land as they saw it from their ship was extensively forested and appeared level. In the lee of a promontory the wind failed them, and they lowered sail. The crew thought it prudent to go ashore for wood and water, but Bjarni refused. The men protested that they might need wood and water in the continuing voyage, and when Bjarni said they had enough of both, his crew began to criticize his judgment. However, they obeyed when he ordered them to raise the sail. As they turned from the shore they picked up the wind, which was now of gale force from the southwest, and sailed away on the high seas out of sight of land, since with such a wind it was safer far out than close to land.

B 4   After three days' sailing, they saw a third land, which was **B 5** high and mountainous, with what looked to be glaciers. This was the long western coast of Newfoundland. When the men asked if he wished to go ashore, Bjarni, realizing that this was not Greenland, said: "No. This land looks unprofitable." His refusal was only in part motivated by the appearance of the land. It was late in the sailing season, and he was anxious to reach Greenland and rejoin his father before winter set in. Without lowering their sail, they coasted along this land to the northward, and eventually per- **B 6** ceived that it was an island, for they passed through a strait and, leaving this land astern, found themselves again on the open ocean, upon which they sailed with the same southwesterly wind. The wind rose mightily, and Bjarni had the sail reefed to reduce speed and ease the ship and the rigging.

They now sailed toward the northeast out of sight of land for **B 7** four days, and then, on the fifth day sighted a fourth land. This time Bjarni without hesitation said, "This looks like Greenland, according to all I have been told about it, and here we may steer to the land." This they did, and that evening they reached the shore at the base of a headland where they saw a boat. Happy to relate, it was there on that very cape at the mouth of the first habitable fjord near the southern end of the western side of Greenland that Bjarni's father Herjulf had settled, and for whom that cape was named Herjulfsness. Bjarni joined his father that very evening. He gave up voyaging and resided with his father as long as Herjulf lived, and remained at Herjulfsness for years thereafter.

BJARNI'S ACTUAL
LAND SIGHTING

LEIF ERIKSON
COMES OF AGE

Erik the Red was an ardent worshipper of Thor, the god of thunder and rainstorms, and hence the god of farmers and fishermen. He rejoiced in his red hair and beard, because they were the same color as Thor's. At Brattahlid, on his spacious farmstead, he kept up family worship and brought up his sons religiously, as well as intelligently, for they understood the spiritual value of religion. Erik's worship of Thor was practically monotheistic. He did well with his sons but not so well with his daughter Freydis, perhaps because of the attitude of his wife Thjodhild toward her and toward himself for having begotten Freydis out of wedlock. Freydis was a large girl who appeared marriageable very early, and so Erik married her off against her wishes to Thorvard, who though physically small and despised by Freydis was rich—a shipowner.

Erik's sons were most promising young men, so everyone said. Thorstein was less adventurous than most, but had mental qualities that compensated. Thorvald was liked by everyone. Leif was a very large and strong fellow, with an imposing look, but he was very understanding of folk, and while he had great initiative he also had a touch of proper caution. Leif was a natural leader, and so when he came of age, his wanderlust was no surprise to his father. Leif asked permission to sail a ship to Norway.

It was sixteen winters after Erik had first envisioned the Greenland Settlements and had explored far to the north in preparation for them, taking count of the pastureland in each fjord, and shaping a mental picture of how he would parcel out the land to settlers. The sixteen winters were those of 983 through 998. Leif set sail for Norway early in the summer of 999.

He was driven off course and landed in the Hebrides. There he promptly fell in love with a woman of noble ancestry named Thorgunna. He soon had reason to learn that she was a woman who knew more than he did about some things. Toward the end of that instructive summer, when he was about to sail away to Norway, Thorgunna asked him to take her in the ship with him. Leif foresaw opposition and asked if her kinsmen would consent to it. She replied, "I do not care whether they will or not." With some wariness Leif said, "It is not advisable to abduct a woman of such noble kin in what is to me a foreign country, the more since I have so few men with me." Thorgunna had an answering argument, "You may discover you are making a mistake." Leif replied, "I shall put it to the proof, notwithstanding." "Then you must hear it," said Thorgunna. "I no longer have only myself to consider; for I am pregnant, and the responsibility is yours." And then she added with an apparent certainty that expectant mothers do not generally have, "I foresee that I shall give birth to a male child." She told Leif that even though he abandoned her, she would rear the boy (not expose him or drown him as an unwanted child, as was religious custom). She would send the boy to Leif in Greenland as soon as he was old enough to go as a member of a ship's crew. Thorgunna said with sarcasm: "I guess you will not relish having a son by me anymore than this our parting implies. Furthermore, I intend to come to Greenland myself eventually."

Leif's better nature came to the surface, and he gave her a gold finger ring, by heathen custom practically making her his wife. He also gave her a mantle woven of wool from Greenland sheep, and a belt of walrus ivory. The boy, for it was a male, was called Thorgils. When he later arrived in Greenland, Leif publicly acknowledged his paternity. But while Thorgils eventually inherited Leif's Greenland farmstead, he was not a man like his grandfather or father, for it was said there was something not quite right about him.

Leif sailed his ship from the Hebrides to Trondheim in Norway, reaching it in the autumn after King Olaf Tryggvason had arrived there. Leif put into port at Nidaros, and went immediately to visit King Olaf. The king esteemed Leif greatly and considered him a very capable man—the very man to serve the king's purpose in Greenland. And so the king, who was one of the fanatic new Christians in Norway, expounded the Christian faith to Leif as well as to other heathen men. Leif found no difficulty in becoming a Christian, although he may have been influenced by what he knew would happen to him if he did not, for King Olaf was holding heathen men from Iceland as hostages, to pressure Icelanders into declaring Christianity their official religion. Leif and all his shipmates were christened. Then the king asked Leif whether it was his intention to return to Greenland the next sailing season. Leif said it was, but added diplomatically, "if the king is willing." Then King Olaf said, "You are to go there on a mission for me, to preach Christianity there." Leif, alarmed by the thought of how his Thor-worshipping father would react, said, "It is for the king to decide, but I firmly believe it would be difficult to be a successful Christian missionary in Greenland." The king replied that there was no man better fitted for the task, and to cheer Leif, who showed dismay, he said, "Your good luck will give you success." "That can only be," said Leif, "if I am supported by the grace of your protection."

Leif abode with the king that winter, and was royally treated.

In the summer of the year A.D. 1000, the same year in which Iceland formally denounced heathen practices, renounced the
heathen gods, and set up Christianity as the only legal religion of
that island, Leif landed in Eriksfjord and went home to Brattahlid
where he was warmly welcomed. He began at once to preach the
Christian faith throughout the country, giving the people King
Olaf's message, and showing them, as the saga puts it, "the value
and the glory of this religion."

Leif had been Erik's pride, a chip off the old block, for as soon
as he got away from home to the Hebrides, had he not fathered a
natural son? The story of Leif's infatuation and begetting of the
child and his parting from the mother was on many men's lips.
Leif presumably was reticent about the details of his love affair
after he got home, but his men talked of it with affectionate
amusement. Remembering his own natural daughter, Erik ap-
proved of Leif's affair. But Erik disapproved of everything else
Leif had done and of what he was now doing. He was disgusted
with Leif for changing his religion—for his repudiating Thor and
switching to Christ, who to Erik's thinking was too gentle a god, a
tenderizer, a weakener, who made strong men soft. Leif's brothers
Thorvald and Thorstein became Christians, and so Erik was wor-
ried about all his sons. Thjodhild was immediately a convert, and
she wanted a church built on the farm, conveniently close to the
house. Erik did not want it. In a sort of compromise, Thjodhild
had a church built "not too near the house." It was called Thjodhild's Church, and there she worshipped with many other new
believers.[3]

Thjodhild did her best to convert Erik, but when he stub-
bornly held to Thor, she refused to have sexual relations with
him, a deprivation which greatly vexed him.

Erik was practically isolated from his whole family. Only a
few conservative friends stood with him—those who valued free-

---

[3] When archaeologists looked for the site of Thjodhild's Church, they supposed
they had found it when they unearthed foundations of a church within about a
hundred feet of the house. But that church dated long after Thjodhild's time. When
they later found the site of Thjodhild's Church two hundred yards from the house,
they realized how precise was the saga statement as to its location.

dom. Against them was the argument that the King of Norway would encourage the sending of more trading ships to Greenland only if the Greenlanders became Christians. The quick spread of the new religion in Greenland looked to old Erik like an epidemic. Leif's bringing a priest home to Greenland was in Erik's eyes a frightful mistake. Everyone had heard the story of how Bishop Poppo got King Harold of Denmark to accept the Christian faith. The king had not been won over by the bishop's teaching, but by his performance of sorcerer's magic. "The bishop bore redhot irons in his hands, and exhibited the unscorched hands to the king, and therefore King Harold allowed himself to be baptized, and also the whole Danish army." Everyone knew to what Erik referred when he said that the priest Leif had brought to Greenland was a "trickster."

LEIF'S THREE
LANDINGS

Greenlanders were becoming acutely aware of the need for more merchant traders willing to carry goods between Norway and Greenland, if the Greenland Settlements were to prosper. Leif had let them know that King Olaf would encourage such traders only if the Greenlanders became Christians. Now that Christianity was spreading throughout the Greenland fjords, it seemed wise to keep up as many contacts as possible with the king, and this was probably one of the reasons why the next summer after Leif Erikson came home, Bjarni Herjulfsson sailed to Norway. But Bjarni did not meet King Olaf Tryggvason, for the king had been slain in battle a half year after Leif said farewell to him. The ruler in Norway was now Earl Eric, and he warmly welcomed Bjarni. That winter Bjarni told of the voyage on which he had sighted three new lands far to the southwest of Greenland. When the Earl and the worshipful people in Norway asked Bjarni to give them detailed descriptions of these lands, he could not do so. Asked why not, he said he had not gone ashore on any of them. For this, everyone thought Bjarni was singularly lacking in curiosity, and they slandered him. When they asked with asperity why he had not told of these new lands at the time he sighted them, he said he had told of them at once at the end of the voyage, as soon as he arrived at his father's home in Greenland, but it was then only three months after the Settlements had been started, and the Greenland folk had been so concerned with the labors of settling that they had paid no attention to his telling. They were building houses and barns and making all snug—too busy finding food and fuel for the winter to give heed to his sighting of far-off lands. His telling in Greenland, Bjarni said, did not cause more than a ripple of talk. No Greenlanders had sought to visit those lands.

Now, sixteen years later, his telling of them in Norway started much talk. Rumor of the existence of three new lands began to spread in Norway, and when Bjarni, who had become the Earl's Man, arrived back in Herjulfsness in 1002, talk of the new lands spread through the Greenland fjords. The Greenlanders gave ear to the talk, the more because they heard how the leaders in Norway had reacted.

And so, Leif Erikson, no doubt combining a missionary trip south of Eriksfjord with curiosity to hear about the new lands from Bjarni Herjulfsson's own lips, went to visit Bjarni at Herjulfsness. Leif was so stirred by Bjarni's telling that he bought Bjarni's sizable ship, for Bjarni was old and had no further desire to use it. Leif now planned to visit the three lands. When he brought the ship into Eriksfjord, he assembled a crew of thirty-five men, and while he was making preparations, he begged his father to lead the expedition. But Erik excused himself, saying he was too old and was no longer able as of yore to endure the hardships of the sea. Leif then used a bit of flattery, saying that Erik might be a better commander. Erik yielded to Leif, and when all was ready, he rode from the house to the ship, though it was only a little way, about 600 yards. The horse stumbled, or Erik said it stumbled, and Erik fell off and hurt his foot. Then Erik declared, "It is not my fate to find more lands than this where now we dwell." He thus showed his sensitivity to criticism of himself for having mis-named Greenland, and his awareness and his fear that new lands far to the southwest might prove to be more attractive than Green-land. Erik said further, "You, my son, and I may no longer follow together." He meant that he and Leif must henceforth go separate ways not only in crossing water, but in religion.

Erik went back to the house, and Leif went to the ship with his thirty-five men. They had with them Leif's foster-father, Tyr-ker. They made ready the ship and put to sea.

Leif had only Bjarni's sailing directions to point him to the three lands, and he followed those directions.[4] Bjarni's ship had been carried out of sight of land from waters near the south end of Greenland to the farthest of the three lands by currents which had a southward set in the open ocean. On his return northward he perceived that he had been carried east of the coast of the nearest of those three lands, an island. Since after sighting the other two lands Bjarni had experienced following winds which had pro-pelled his ship northward along the west coast of the great island, the preferable sailing routes were thus indicated. Leif made use of them. Furthermore, since he planned to land on each of the three lands and to inspect each, and since Bjarni had seen the west coast of the great island but had not seen its east coast, Leif realized that by visiting its east coast he would be adding to the knowledge of viking mariners. That he did in fact land on the east coast of New-foundland is made certain by three geographical observations which he made.

Leif and his men found first that land which was the last one Bjarni had sighted. They sailed to the land and anchored in a shel-tered cove or harbor, put out the boat, and went ashore. From the

L 1

---

[4] Leif's historic voyage in 1003 was a long time ago, but a long arm reaches back. I have met a member of a family which preserves the tradition that one of their an-cestors was one of the thirty-five men who sailed with Leif Erikson.

shore they had an easy climb. up a brook to an altitude of a thousand feet. The slopes up from the shore were forested, and because trees naturally preclude meadow grass, it would not have occurred to Leif to make a critical comment on the absence of grass. After the climb he found himself in a vast treeless area which was not a meadow suitable for grazing cattle, but was to his surprise infer-

L 2 tile. From his lookout position, he gazed upon what he called ice mountains far away. From where he stood he saw what appeared to be a level stone field—ten miles of tableland of rocks, which as far as he could tell, extended all the way to the mountains. Such a land was good for nothing. Then Leif said, "Unlike Bjarni, we have stepped ashore on this land, and I will now give it a name. I

L 3 call it *Helluland* [Flat Rock Land]."

Afterward they returned to the ship, and sailed away on the open ocean. They found another land, and sailed to it and cast anchor, put out the boat, and went ashore. As far as they saw it, that

L 4, L 5 land was level and completely wooded, with broad stretches of white sand. Wherever they went the shore region did not slant steeply. Then Leif said, "This land shall have a name in keeping with its nature. I call it *Markland* [Forestland]."

Leif's men grinned and then laughed when they heard "in keeping with its nature," for the words were an obvious slam at Erik's misnaming of Greenland.

After that they went back to the ship as fast as possible, to take advantage of a wind that was blowing from the northeast. They were out of sight of land for two days. Then they saw land,

L 6 and sailed to it. They found shelter in the lee of an island (Great Point of Nantucket) which seemed to lie north of the land.

Early in the morning they went to the highest point on that island to look around. It was a fair day. They found water in the

L 7 grass, which they called dew, and when they wet their fingers with the dew and brought their fingers to their mouths, they thought they had never tasted anything so sweet. Afterward they went to

L 8, L 9 their ship and sailed into a sound (Nantucket Sound) that lay between the island and a cape (Cape Cod) which extended to the north from the land. They steered in to the west of the cape.

It was very shallow there at ebb tide, and their ship was

grounded. From there it was a long distance to look to the ocean **L 10** from the ship.

Yet they were so eager to go ashore that they could not wait for the tide to rise under the ship, but ran a boat to the land, into a river (Bass River) that flowed down from a lake. But as soon as the tide rose under the ship, they took the boat and rowed to the ship and conveyed the ship up the river and to the lake and there **L 11** cast anchor. They carried their sleeping bags ashore and built temporary shelters.

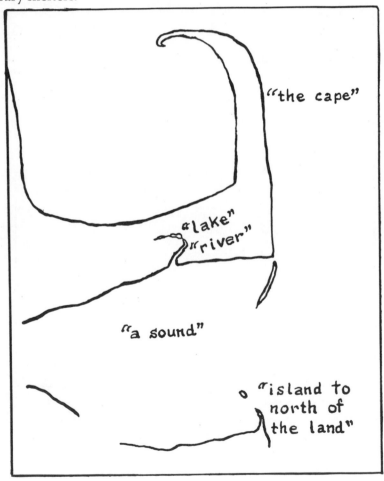

VINLAND AS LEIF SAW IT

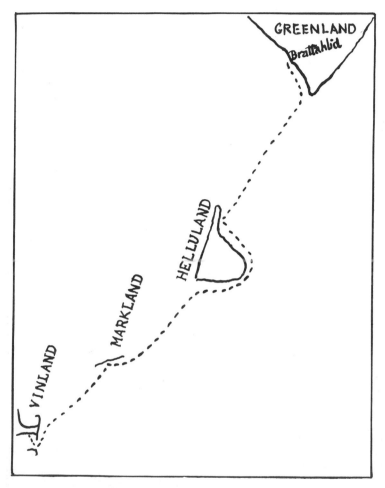

HOW LEIF ADDED TO THE MAP

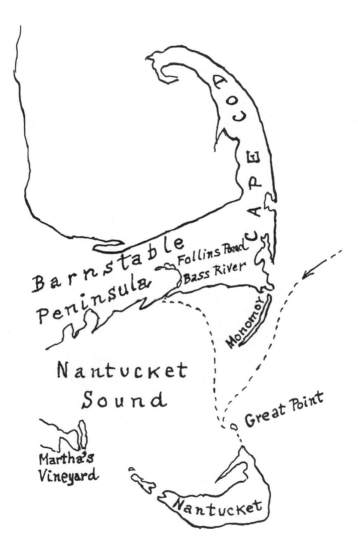

MODERN MAP OF LEIF'S VINLAND

LEIF'S VINLAND CAMPSITE

Leif had been undecided as to whether he would return home that sailing season, or spend the winter in the new land. But when he looked around and saw that he had luckily found an area (the south shore of Follins Pond) that was ideally suited for their wintering, he decided to remain. The terrain had everything needful. It had convenient access to a plentiful supply of good drinking water. It was a strong defensive position, almost an island, surrounded by water on three sides. It had trees growing to the water's edge so that they could be cut into logs which could be rolled down to where they could be loaded on the ship. Timber would be a most valuable cargo to take home. Leif remembered that when

L 12

his father had first brought him to Brattahlid as a boy, there had been some dwarf birches and willows in the hollows, but those small trees had long since all been used, and also the driftwood, and now Greenland's greatest need was timber. A shipload of logs in Greenland would make its owner a rich man. Also Leif observed a site at the top of a hill which, with some trees cut away, would command a view of all the lake and of the river approach to it, and from that hill they could keep watch against possible ene-

L 13   mies. Realizing all these factors, Leif had his men build a large house at that site. They called the house "large" because it was of a size to provide sleeping platforms for all of them—thirty-six men. It was about eighteen feet wide and fifty feet long. Like the house at Brattahlid, it was sod-walled.

They called their campsite "Leif's Booths" or "Leif's Shel-ters," using the word *buda* ("booths") in the plural because there

L 14   were two buildings—the house and the ship shed. The two were only 250 feet apart. Leif and his men wanted the house close to where there was a good place for a ship shed, since the ship upon

L 15   which their lives depended had to be shored and under cover, pro-tected against snow and ice.

They had arrived late in August, and their first activity was to

L 16   catch all the salmon they needed—larger salmon than they had ever seen—in the river and in the lake, until the salmon ceased running about the tenth of September. They preserved the salmon for winter eating, some dried in the sun, and some smoked. With an eye to opportunities for dairy farming, they were pleased to note that the extensive meadows of marsh grass in the lake and

L 17   along the river promised plenty of cattle fodder. Since no frost came in the winter—none that Greenlanders would call frost—and since there was slight withering of the grass, all of it remaining a good shade of green, they concluded that cattle could graze out of doors all winter in this new country.

Being knowledgeable mariners, Leif and his men ascribed the mildness of the winter to their being so far south. They noted that the days and nights were more nearly of equal length than in Greenland or Iceland. They made an astronomical observation

L 18   that on the shortest day of winter, at *Eyktarstad* (afternoon mealtime), which their appetites timed with some accuracy, the sun touched the horizon, and that it rose at *Dagmalastad* (morning mealtime or breakfast time).

When they had finished building the house (*skala,* literally "the hall"), Leif said to his fellows, "Now I will let our company be divided into two parts, and I will let them explore the land, and one-half of the company shall remain at home, while the other half shall explore the land, but go no farther away than they can return in the evening, and not be separated." Now they did so for a while. Leif alternately went out with them and stayed at home in the hall.

One evening came the tidings that a man was missing from the company. It was Tyrker, the Southerner. Leif was very much troubled by this because Tyrker had been with his father and himself for a long time, and had loved Leif much in his childhood. Leif severely blamed his companions and immediately ordered an expedition in search of him, taking twelve men with him. But when they had gone but a short way from the hall, Tyrker came to meet them. He was well received. Leif perceived at once that his foster-father was excited. Tyrker had a large forehead and restless eyes, and small freckles on his face. Though he was a puny, insignificant-looking fellow, he was a leader in martial sports. Leif asked him, "Why are you late, my foster-father, and separated from your comrades?"

For a long time Tyrker talked in his southern tongue, rolling his eyes and making wry faces, and they could not understand him. Then he explained in Norse, "I did not walk far beyond the others, but I have big news for you. I have found withy vines [*vin vid*] and wine berries [*vin ber*]." "Is it truly so, foster-father?"   **L 19** Leif asked. "Most certain," said he, "for I was born where there is   **L 20** no lack of withy vines and wine berries."

This discovery of wine berries (grapes) made a lasting impression on Leif and his men. They could not themselves have discovered them, for the growing of grapes was outside their experience as men from Scandinavia, Iceland, and Greenland. They did not know the taste of fresh grapes, but some of them were familiar with wine, for they knew currants and some other berries from which wine could be made. They had probably observed the grapes on Cape Cod as a fruit unknown to them, and may have feared to taste them lest they be poisonous. Tyrker from boyhood memories in Germany recognized the grapes by the shape of the grape leaves. The grapes were ripe (in mid-September) when he found them, and he verified his discovery by tasting them.

After a night's sleep, Leif said to his shipmates, "From now on we have two things to do. Every day we shall either gather wine berries, or cut withy vines, and chop down trees to make a lading for my ship." This they did, and they got their after-boat filled with grapes. The after-boat, the size of a whaleboat, usually carried athwart on board ship, was their only large receptacle. It made a convenient winepress. The grapes were pressed and the juice, some of it no doubt before it was properly fermented, went down their throats then and there. They had no bottling facilities. Leif and his men had several drinking sprees.

The name Leif coined for the land fitted both of the products Tyrker had discovered—the withy vines and the grapes. Leif called the country *Vinland*, which meant both Vineland and (more appealingly) Wineland.

LEIF'S VOYAGE
HOME FROM VINLAND

Very early in the spring, as soon as Leif and his men were sure there would be no chance of snow or ice, they raised the ship off the bearings in the shed, got her onto rollers, and down into the water. Then they carried the mast to the ship and restepped it. Next they hung the sail, which they had kept rolled up and dry all winter. It was essential to relaunch the ship at the earliest possible moment, for with exposure to air the hull could suffer from dry rot, whereas immersion in water would keep the outside planks swollen and the joints tight. Every mariner knew this. And so they expeditiously got the ship ready for sailing early in the spring, but they took their time in loading the withy vines and timber. They did not set sail for home until the wild grapes were again ripe, in mid-September, and they could again press grape mash in the after-boat and enjoy more drinking. They knew that late in the summer there would be little or no pack ice left along the Greenland coast to impede and imperil their entrance into Eriksfjord. Also, they counted on having a fair wind to waft them home swiftly in early September or early October, as had been Bjarni Herjulfsson's experience. With a fair wind it would be a voyage of only about ten days. And so, their bellies full of grape juice, they took the ship out of the lake, down the river, and eastward in the sound to the lee of Monomoy, there ready to put to sea as soon as a strong west wind blew.

Their voyage home followed Bjarni's route from Cape Cod to within sight of Nova Scotia, then into the Gulf of St. Lawrence and along the west coast of Newfoundland, and out through the Strait of Belle Isle and across. As it had with Bjarni, the fair wind lasted all the way to Greenland, where they could see the moors under the glaciers. Then one of the men spoke to Leif, "Why do you steer the ship so much into the wind?" Leif's steering, when he had a perfect fair wind, was unaccountable, and the man thought Leif foolish for apparently trying to beat back against a wind that would carry them into the home fjord. Leif gruffly replied, "I am taking care of the rudder, but of more than that besides, or what do you see that is remarkable?" The men answered that they saw nothing remarkable. Leif then explained his steering. "I do not know," he said, "whether I see a ship or a skerry [rock islet]." Now the men saw it, and said it was a skerry, but Leif had better eyesight than they did, for he saw men on the skerry. "Now I want to beat against the wind," said he, "so as to get near to them upwind and see if they want to be picked up by us, and whether they need our assistance." The men on the skerry were waving frantically to them. Leif said, "If they are not peacefully inclined, then we shall have the superior position." If the men on the skerry were laying a trap, Leif's ship could take instant advantage of the wind and sail rapidly and safely away. But as they drew close to the skerry, it became obvious that the men on it had suffered a real shipwreck and were in desperate straits. And so Leif and his men lowered the sail and dropped anchor. They put out the little boat which they had with them, not the after-boat with the precious mash. The little boat was a skiff, capable of holding three persons at most.

Tyrker and Leif got into the skiff and came near enough to parley with the men on the skerry. It is an interesting revelation of Leif's character that in the skiff he deferred to Tyrker.

Then Tyrker asked, "Who is the leader of your party?" The leader said, "I am called Thorer, and am of northern kin. But what is your name?" Leif told his name. Thorer asked, "Are you the son of Erik the Red of Brattahlid?" Leif replied that he was, and said, "Now I make you this offer. I will take you all on my ship, and all the goods that the ship will hold." They accepted those terms.

The exchange of identities between Leif and Thorer established confidence on both sides. Thorer was probably a distant kinsman of Erik's. By custom of salvage, whatever cargo Leif rescued from the shipwreck became his property. He could not take much on board his ship, for the only available space was that which had been emptied by the consumption of firewood, food, and water on his voyage from Vinland. But he risked overloading now that he was close to home.

And so they sailed to Eriksfjord with the cargo, until they came to Brattahlid. They unloaded the ship, and then Leif invited Thorer and his wife Gudrid and three other men to dwell with him. He also provided dwellings for the other men, both Thorer's and his own. With the wood in the cargo and hull of Thorer's ship, which he soon had brought to him, in addition to the shipload of withies and timber from Vinland, Leif became the richest man in treeless Greenland. He had fame as well for his voyage of discovery, and he was given the nickname "Lucky." Men felt that Leif was not only lucky himself, but a bringer of luck to others. And, Leif was lucky in having rescued the shipwrecked party of fifteen men and the woman since he thereby saved the life of Gudrid, who later married one .of Leif's brothers and then another very distinguished man. But he did not bring luck to everyone around him. That winter there was much sickness among Thorer's men. Weakened from exposure to cold on the skerry, Thorer and a good part of his crew died. Erik the Red also died that winter, very likely of the infirmities which had been creeping up on him for a long time, though he may have caught an infection, possibly pneumonia, from Thorer.

The death of Erik the Red placed upon Leif's shoulders responsibility for the management of the Brattahlid farm and the burden of leadership in the councils of the Greenlanders. Tied down to his many duties, Leif could not expect to take time off ever again to revisit the distant land where he had spent a winter. Yet he felt that Vinland in a sense belonged to him. He had been the first to step on its shores and claim possession and build there. He believed that his Shelters—his house and the ship shed—were a beginning for a settlement, of which he would be titular head. Others must carry on from his beginnings. That is why he welcomed questioning about Vinland, and that is why he did not resent his brother Thorvald's implied criticism that he had not sufficiently explored Vinland.

How large was Vinland? Thorvald wanted to know. Leif of his own knowledge had no idea of its size. All Leif could tell was what he had seen from hilltops within a mile or two of his Shelters —evidence of land to the south of the sound (treetops on Nantucket island); and land to the southwest (Martha's Vineyard); and to the north, the cape and the bay (Cape Cod Bay) ; and on the west side of the bay, slightly more than twenty miles of coast extending to the north. The land might be of any size. Yes, Leif admitted, the country had not been sufficiently explored.

It was easy for those who enjoyed the comforts of home to feel critical of those who lived through the dangers of a voyage and the hardships of a winter in an unknown wilderness. Leif had been wisely cautious in the new country. He had let his men explore in the forest only as far as they could on foot in daylight hours. But he had kept his men from getting lost in a tangle of vines. It had taken only a few steps for Tyrker to get temporarily lost. Obviously, the proper way to explore Vinland would not be on foot through the woods but by ship, along the ocean shore and by after-boat into sounds and fjords and rivers. This was what Leif's brother Thorvald proposed to do. And so Leif said to Thorvald, "You shall go out with my ship, brother, if you will go to Vinland. However, I want the ship to go first to fetch the wood which Thorer had on the skerry." And so it was done.

THORVALD ERIKSON'S
KEEL CAPE AND
CROSS CAPE

On Leif's advice, Thorvald took a crew of only thirty men. That
would mean fewer mouths to feed in the wilderness and yet more
than enough to shore the ship. There seemed to be no reason to fear
human enemies in Vinland, even if Leif's men had found evidence
of natives, such as a path through the forest and the smoke of distant campfires.

Thorvald and his men prepared the ship and put to sea, and
there is nothing to be said of their voyage until they arrived at
Leif's Shelters. "Nothing to be said of their voyage" was the vi-

king way of saying that the voyage was smooth and swift. Thorvald
and his men shored the ship in the shed and on the same keel bearings Leif had provided. They busied themselves drying and smoking the fish they caught, laid up fuel for the hearth and cooking
fires, and "kept quiet that winter." In the spring they made the
ship ready—standard procedure, even though Thorvald did not intend to use the ship that summer.

Thorvald's plan was to explore the coast in each direction
from Leif's Shelters. It would require two sailing seasons and
three winterings in Vinland, a long stay for which they would
need vegetables as well as fish and flesh food. Therefore, Thorvald
kept a majority of his men at Leif's Shelters the first summer to
plant crops. They had brought seeds for such vegetables as broc-
coli, cabbage, carrots, chervil, kale, lettuce, parsley, rhubarb, sor-
rel, spinach, and turnips, all of which could grow in Greenland.
He also wanted the men to cut timber and stack the logs on rocks
for two years of seasoning in the sun. Since the set of tides in Nantucket Sound indicated that it led into inland waterways to the west,
where a small boat would serve more handily than the ship, Thorvald ordered some men to go in the after-boat to explore the western part of the land during the summer. The after-boat had room
for a crew of ten or twelve men, and had a sail and oars.

The after-boat party found a pleasing, well-wooded country,
with forests near the salt water and the white sands. There were
many islands and shoals. They found no dwellings of men or lairs
of beasts. On one of the islands to the west, however, they did find
a corncrib of wood. They found no other works of man. They returned to Leif's Shelters in time to take part in the harvesting of
crops.

Their report was notably lacking in distinctive details. They
were unimaginative men, with little vision of possibilities beyond
their noting the obvious advantage of quantities of trees growing
near the salt water. They found many islands and shoals in Buzzards Bay, Narragansett Bay, and along the coast of the northern
side of Long Island Sound. They did not mention having seen
hills and bays and rivers with good land for thousands of farmsteads.

T 1

But there was something more interesting to tell of Thorvald's explorations of the next summer, even though this part of the telling also came, not from Thorvald himself, but from the men who sailed with him.

While on one side of Leif's Shelters the coast ran to the west, on the other side it ran to the north with open ocean. Exploring via the ocean necessitated use of the ship. And so, the second summer, in 1007, Thorvald left some ten men at Leif's Shelters with the after-boat, and sailed with the rest on the ship eastward to the ocean and then northward along the land.   **T 2**

They had coasted northward for about thirty-five miles from the southern end of Monomoy to that part of the eastern shore of Cape Cod which is under high dunes. That northward coasting took six or seven hours, at the end of which they were caught by a sudden onshore blow.   **T 3**

The merchant ship was planned to carry cargo for most of its length, so that there was room for no more than three oars on each side at each end. With a dozen oars, the men could propel the ship at a speed of only four knots; thus even a very moderate onshore breeze spelled disaster.

The ship was blown up on a shore that was sandy, not rocky. From the nature of the damage, we know what happened. The ship was driven over a sandbank a little distance offshore, and in crossing the top of that bank, the keel broke. Inside the sandbank the waves were less violent, and Thorvald and his men were able to beach the ship. They were lucky, for storms off Cape Cod have made total wrecks of many ships.

Thorvald and his men had to erect temporary shelters for themselves and for the food and gear that they took out of the ship. They could not move the ship any considerable distance from the water, for the dunes above the beach were cliffs, some of them rising to 150 feet in height. Thorvald and his men therefore made a shoring on the beach just clear of the high-tide line. They probably used stones for keel bearings and jacked the ship up until its keel was more than two feet above the sand.

Their next task was to plant enough posts or piles of stones under the garboards (the strakes next to the keel) and the other lower strakes to support the weight of the ship. After that they were able to remove the bearings under the keel. Only then could they begin to release the broken section of keel by getting it free of its attachments to the garboards and the deadwood knee (solid timber at the bow or stern). Afterward they could lower the keel down from the bottom of the ship. The original keel was likely all one piece, about sixty feet long. The break was, of course, amidships, and the section of keel removed was necessarily nearly two-thirds of the original length. Where the keel had broken there were broken garboards.

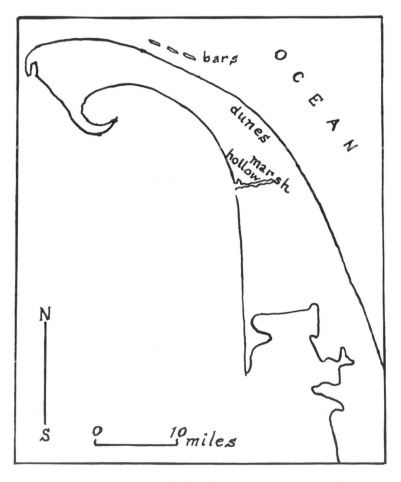

KEEL CAPE

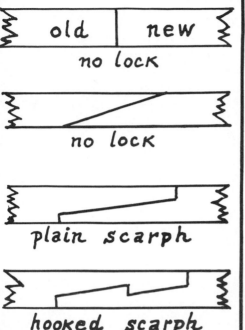

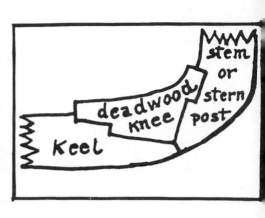

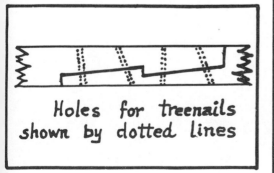

SCARPHING, TREENAILS, DEADWOOD TREES, ETC.

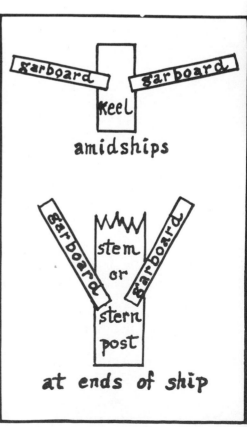

While some of Thorvald's men were removing the major portion of the keel, others searched the country to find a tree of an acceptable kind with a straight trunk tall enough to make a new section of keel nearly forty feet in length.

The locality where the broken section of keel was removed and the new section fitted in was in all probability near Truro. It was in that region of Cape Cod that trees tall enough for Thorvald's need grew in the hollows. The profusion of freshwater springs just under the sands, eight feet and more below, kept roots so moist that trees grew to prodigious height and girth. Most of the Cape was covered with forest. One hollow in the Truro area was a freshwater postglacial lake with great trees at its shores: oak, cedar, hickory, cypress, and pine.

Having found and felled a big tree, the men trimmed the log with axes to the desired dimensions, and carried the new section of keel to the ship, dragging it into position under the ship. They also had to cut down one or two other trees to fashion planks to replace the broken garboards.

In shaping the new section of keel to fit properly into the frame of the ship, they knew it must not be placed end-to-end with the old section with a straight crosscut or slanting cut, neither of which would lock the old and new together. They knew that in anything so important as a keel, they must join the two by scarphing, and not by a plain scarph but by a hooked scarph that would hold the two sections together. The shaping of the ends to a hooked scarphing had to be achieved by chipping with axes and paring with knives. And the planks that were to replace the broken garboards had to be properly curved or bent. For this, the green wood was an advantage since it was pliable. The cutting of rabbets, or grooves, in the new section of keel to receive the edges of curved and twisted garboards was extremely complicated carpentry and called for painstaking labor by the men most skilled in woodworking.

After the new section of keel had been jacked up to fit into the bottom of the frame, the hooked scarphing of the keel sections was firmly fastened with treenails (pegs of a hard wood like oak that would be driven into a bored hole and would swell when wet). When the new sections of garboards were rabbeted in with the keel and with adjacent strakes, all the new jointures and seams had to be calked. Resin to make tar with which to impregnate the oakum for calking had to be collected from pine trees.

The work kept Thorvald and his men busy for at least one month.

While the repairs were being completed, Thorvald looked at the old section of keel lying nearby on the sand and thought of a use to which it might be put. It would make a handsome beacon that would stand nearly thirty-five feet in the air, about as high as his ship's mast. If he planted it vertically at the top of the highest dune it would be a notable monument. Since it had been the keel of Leif's ship, Thorvald knew it would be a memorial to his brother's landing in Vinland as well as to the labor that his own crew had expended in replacing it. And so with the planting of the old keel on a high dune, Thorvald named the cape *Kialnar Nes* (Keel Cape).

From Keel Cape, Thorvald sailed away and continued to explore the coast. He and his men soon found themselves sailing eastward along the land. They sailed down east off the coast of Maine, keeping well out in the offing to avoid the sharp-fingered capes and rock-belted islands. They sailed into the mouths of a fjord that was near there. The fjord was in mountainous land that extended far out and was therefore near the course of the ship. The mountain range on Mt. Desert Island was visible to Thorvald and his men for more than fifty miles. After sighting those mountains, it took them ten hours of sailing to reach and enter Somes Sound through one of its four mouths. As they looked northward toward the inner reaches of the fjord, they saw in the middle of the picture a hill or low mountain (Flying Mountain) about half the height of the mountains that flanked the fjord, and it was covered with trees.

There at the base of that headland they found something which nature rarely furnishes, a proper berthing site for a ship. It was so extraordinary that the men remembered and spoke of it years afterward. On the east side of the headland, a tumble of granite blocks shelved off into deep water so that they were able to

T 4

T 5

T 6
T 7

bring the ship sideways close to the bank. It rose so steeply that their gangplank resting on the gunwale about three and a half feet above the water reached out to the rocks and was not too far from horizontal.

They were delighted to find the berthing site, for they had left the after-boat with the men at Leif's Shelters and had only the skiff with them. If they had been compelled to anchor or moor the ship, the skiff would have had to make ten trips from ship to shore to disembark all the crew, and another ten trips to fetch them aboard again. The berthing site was a great convenience.

The berthing site was slightly longer than the ship, but less than a hundred feet in length. Immediately to the north of it, the shelf steepened to a vertical cliff where no one could possibly step ashore with or without a gangplank. Immediately to the south of it, the shelf leveled out and the water close to shore was too shallow for the ship.

T 8   Thorvald and all his companions went up on the land. This was an extraordinary thing to do, but Thorvald would not have permitted all to go ashore with no one left on board to guard the ship had he not observed that the ship could safely be left unguarded for a little while. He saw that no human being could approach the ship from the north or west, for directly above the landing shelf and to the north, the forested side of the headland rose precipitously. The only overland approach to the berthing site was by the rocky beach to the south of it. With assurance that no stranger or enemy could get to the ship behind their backs, he let the entire crew accompany him along that beach.

From the beach they scrambled up a fifteen-foot bank to an open meadow that rose to a slight elevation, and there they admired the view and the natural advantages. Thorvald then re-
T 9   marked, "Here it is fair."

The land to which Thorvald and his men climbed and upon which he stood when he pronounced it "fair" had been cleared by centuries of Indian use. The Indians used it either for agriculture, or as a camping site when they came from the Penobscot down to the seashore in the summers and fished and dug clams and had clambakes, using the trees for firewood. Testifying to this is an ancient shell heap containing arrowheads and shards. The open land is called Jesuit Field because when the Jesuits first arrived in 1613, they found it cleared land ready for their use.

The modern visitor to Jesuit Field is likely to feel that he can point to the precise spot where Thorvald wanted to build his permanent home. Halfway along the western side of the cleared land and near the edge of the forested slopes is the highest elevation in the field. That eminence commands the best view. It was probably there, where a house now stands, that Thorvald said, "Here I should like to set up my residence."

Thus far Thorvald's party had seen no natives or native boats in the fjord, but they were soon to meet them. From the field they returned to the ship and sailed farther into the fjord, skirting the almost vertical cliff which forms the east side of Flying Mountain. The moment they came abreast of the end of that cliff, every eye was drawn to the spectacular scenery that dramatically opened to the west. They looked into a sensationally beautiful cove tucked snugly "within the headland" or between the headland and the sheer rock wall of a mountain. On the curving boulder-studded shore of the cove, about 125 yards from the near point at the base of the headland, Thorvald and his men saw a tiny beach of sand. On that sand were three "mounds." Thorvald steered the ship to **T 10** larboard toward these objects, and he and his men soon saw that they were "boats with three men under each."

When the ship drew close to the sands, half of the crew silently slipped overboard and waded ashore. When the ship had glided past the sands, the other half of the crew performed the same maneuver. The vikings closed in from both sides upon the reclining men, who were probably all asleep. The vikings captured all except one who escaped in his canoe.

Thorvald had only twenty men with him. Sixteen of these had their hands full holding eight captives. They probably did not have ropes enough to tie them up. All but four of Thorvald's crew were thus immobilized. They had to do something with the captives. What could they do? Go on holding them? To release them would have appeared tactically unwise. Thorvald's men solved their problem quickly—they killed them.

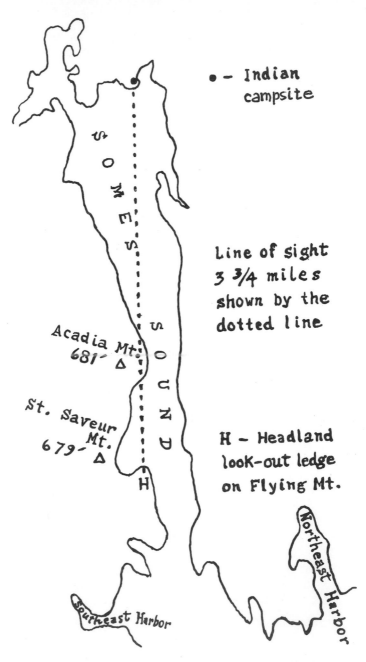

• – Indian campsite

Line of sight 3 ¾ miles shown by the dotted line

H – Headland look-out ledge on Flying Mt.

LINE OF SIGHT FROM FLYING MOUNTAIN TO INDIAN CAMP

Considering the numbers involved in seizing and overpowering the Skraelings (meaning "Shriekers" or "War-Whoopers," a term the vikings applied to Greenland Eskimos and to American Indians alike), it was not surprising that one had managed to escape. Perhaps he was wounded in one foot, and Thorvald's men saw him limp or hop on one foot down to the water with one canoe. Anyhow, some five years later when the crew of a viking ship came sailing past this region where Thorvald's men had killed the eight Skraelings, they called it the Land of the One-Legged (Uniped Land).

Their blood stirred by the killing of the eight Skraelings, Thorvald and his men may have been too excited to examine the material of which the two canoes in their possession were made. They assumed they were "skin boats," though they were most likely made of birchbark, a material with which Greenlanders were not familiar.[5]

From the tiny beach into the woods was the beginning of a trail. In half a minute Thorvald's men saw that this ascended toward the summit of the headland. It was Thorvald's purpose to explore Vinland, and he was doing so by every means at his disposal, by waterways and by observation from elevations to which there was easy access from a waterway. And so he and his men ascended the headland by the Skraelings' trail.   T 11

It was a climb of 284 feet, and took them less than fifteen minutes. They went up a steepening slope under evergreen trees for two-thirds of the way, and then had a bit of a scramble over broken granite outcroppings. From the summit they had views in every direction: a magnificent panorama of islands in the Great Harbor of Mt. Desert with the ocean beyond, an eagle's eyrie view down into the cove where their ship was anchored, and a long

---

[5] They may actually have been skin boats, with which Greenlanders were familiar from contacts with Eskimos and the Irish. The Irish, in their curraghs, made of oxhide stretched over light frames, had very likely crossed the ocean to Newfoundland ("Ireland the Great"), and the idea of using animal skins for canoes may have spread from Newfoundland to some of the near continental shores. Since no birchbark or skin coverings of canoes could have survived for archaeological investigations, we can only surmise.

view toward the north end of the fjord. From granite ledges close to the summit they saw some hillocks within the fjord. Their view of these was in a line just clear of the side of a mountain which was a mile from them at the north end of the cove, and the hillocks were nearly four miles away, so that Thorvald and his men at that distance could not with certainty identify them. But they guessed correctly. They "surmised" that these were human habitations.

The native who had escaped the massacre at the sands had paddled out of sight around the base of the mountain one mile to the north of the sands. If the distant hillocks were human habitations, it was to them that the escaped man carried his tale of the killing of his companions. Thorvald and his men should have anticipated a probable retaliatory attack. But their walk from the berthed ship to the attractive field, their wandering over the field, the walk back to the ship, and the melee at the sands, and then the climb up the headland and back down to the shore of the cove, all unusual exertions on a hot summer's day, had made them as somnolent as the Skraelings had been. Such great weariness befell them that they could not keep awake and all fell asleep.

The words "all fell asleep" have to be understood within the frame of the circumstances. The escape of the native who had seen his eight companions killed almost certainly meant to Thorvald and his men that his tribesmen would be aroused to avenge. Having reason to expect an attack, it would have been incredibly reckless of Thorvald not to leave a watchman on the sands or on board the ship. The "all" meant all who had ascended the headland. And, having seen or assumed that they had seen from the top of the headland where the tribesmen of the slain natives lived, it is the more certain that Thorvald thought that at least one man would be alert while the others slept.

Thorvald and his men napped in the comfortable coolness of the woods back of the sands, close enough to the ship to feel assured that if an emergency arose they would reach the ship in good time. The escaped Skraeling had about four miles to paddle to reach the summer habitation of his tribe. This took him about three-quarters of an hour. Allowing time for the gathering of many warriors, the planning of their attack, and the speed of their

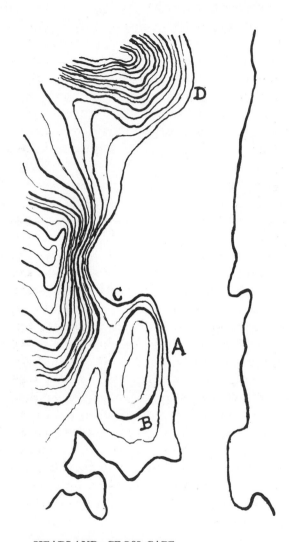

HEADLAND—CROSS CAPE

A—Berthing site
B—Dwelling site chosen by Thorvald
C—Canoes on sands in Valley Cove
D—Where war canoes appeared

canoes, it was somewhat less than two hours after the massacre that
the avenging party was first sighted by the ship's watchman, or by
one of Thorvald's men who happened to have awakened. Thorvald and his men had spent about one hour on the headland in
climbing, discussing what they saw from the summit, and in descending. They had about one hour of uninterrupted sleep.

The many canoes that suddenly came into sight as they
rounded the base of the mountain a mile distant were less than
eight minutes away. The watchman or the first man awake shouted
his warning.

T 13

Some of the men were already awake, or drowsily half-con-
scious. The frantic call they heard roused them swiftly, and they
awakened those who were still asleep. The shouted warning came
to their ears not as the recognizable voice of any of themselves, not
as the voice of an individual, but louder than human, magnified
from on high, like the voice of a god on a mountain.

The call said, "Awake, Thorvald, and all your men, if you
would save your life, and go to your ship, you and all your men,
and get clear of the land with all speed!"

Thorvald and his men had time to dash into the water and
wade out to the anchored ship, scramble on board, raise the sail,
and weigh the anchor. Then Thorvald ordered, "We will put the
shields outboards and defend ourselves as best we may, but attack
only a little." So they did. The "countless" native boats soon encircled the ship. The war whoops of the enraged Skraelings made so
continuous and piercing a sound that Thorvald's men did not observe the echoes. When any of the savages attempted to board the
ship, they were cut down by viking swords. The encirclement of
the ship by the war boats lasted until the Skraelings had shot all
their arrows.

Then Thorvald asked his men whether they were in any way
wounded, and they replied, "None wounded." "I have received a
wound in my armpit," Thorvald said. "An arrow flew between the
side of the ship and the shield and under my arm, and here is the
arrow. If this leads to my death, I advise you to prepare to sail as
soon as possible on your return passage, but carry me to that headland which seemed to be most habitable. It may be that a true

word came out of my mouth, when I said I might dwell there for a while. There you shall bury me and set a cross at my head and at my feet, and call it *Krossanes* [Cross Cape] forever after."   **T 14**

Retribution for the massacre had been swift, and it struck the leader who had been responsible. Realizing that he was dying, Thorvald's mind reverted to that attractive field where he had wanted to set up his permanent residence.

Thorvald died and his men did everything that he had told them to do, burying him with two crosses. Then they rejoined their comrades at Leif's Shelters, and exchanged such tidings as they had. They dwelt there that winter and gathered grapes and vinestocks for their ship.

The year after Thorvald was killed, his men sailed home from Leif's Shelters. When they steered through Eriksfjord and to Brattahlid without their leader and told why he was not with them, the Erikson brothers Leif and Thorstein were deeply affected. They felt not only grief but consternation. Leif's happy view of the potential of Vinland was now impaired. There as elsewhere, death could be swift and merciless. He had thought it a fair land where life was easy. As the leading man in Greenland, he had been holding out hopes to his fellow Christians of someday planting a colony in the warmer country. Bleak Greenland had been his father's choice, a heathen man's choice. Vinland had promised to be the kind of country good Christians deserved. As confirmed and devout Christians, Leif and Thorstein and their mother Thjodhild agonized because Thorvald's body was lying in the wilderness in unhallowed ground. While some believed that a cross at one's head and a cross at one's feet made a Christian burial, it was distressing that Thorvald's grave was not in a churchyard properly consecrated by a priest. The missionary priest Leif had brought to Greenland was emphatic in telling the family that Thorvald's burial had not been in keeping with the customs of the Church. No exceptions should be allowed. None had hitherto been permitted, for when the father of the family, Erik the Red, had died unconverted, he had been denied burial inside the graveyard of Thjodhild's Church. To preserve the religious significance of that exclusion from consecrated ground, any infringement of the prescribed practice of the Church should at all costs be rectified. The family must bring Thorvald's body home for churchyard burial. The family must set a proper example and maintain Christian teachings, which were just beginning to take hold of the people in Greenland. Since it was impracticable for the priest to go to Cross Cape and there consecrate the ground around Thorvald's grave, when there was as yet no church in all that land, someone else must go there to bring home Thorvald's body. Bound by his responsibilities in Greenland, Leif could not be expected to go. But his brother Thorstein, with only himself and his wife Gudrid to consider, could and should undertake the voyage. Thus Thorstein Erikson was motivated.

THORSTEIN ERIKSON IN THE WESTERN SETTLEMENT

Thorstein Erikson had married Gudrid, Thorbjorn Vifilsson's daughter, who had been the wife of Thorer the Eastman, as was mentioned before. Thorstein desired to go to Vinland for the body of his brother Thorvald. And so he set sail, taking Gudrid with him. It was not his fault that he floundered around all summer lost at sea until he landed in the Western Settlement of Greenland. There, in his death room, his wife Gudrid experienced superstitious terror of corpses that sat up and talked, and tried to put on shoes, and made prophecy as to her third marriage. But when

Thorstein died Gudrid was comforted in her grief, and saved from embarrassment and shame by her host, Thorstein the Swarthy, who arranged, by bringing in other persons, that she and he would not spend the winter alone together in his house. The next summer he brought her, along with Thorstein Erikson's body, to the house of her brother-in-law Leif, and himself lived out his life in Eriksfjord, highly respected—one of nature's gentlemen.

The story of Thorstein Erikson in the Western Settlement is shocking, and to the modern mind, most amusing. It is so delightfully told in the original Icelandic that at this point it is recommended that the reader turn to page 278 of the translation.

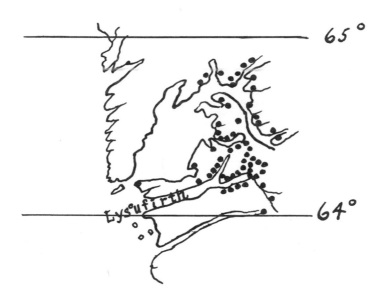

WESTERN SETTLEMENT OF GREENLAND

THORFINN KARLSEFNI'S
DECISION

In the autumn of that same year of Gudrid's return to Eriksfjord, Thorfinn Karlsefni and three other Icelandic traders, two of them in each of two ships, put to sea from Iceland for Greenland. They followed the course that Erik the Red had taken—from the snow peak Snaefellsjökul, the mariners' landmark, straight across to Black Sark on Greenland's east coast. As they pursued Erik's route southward along the perilous coast, Thorfinn felt unbounded pride in his fellow Icelander Erik the Red for having dared so courageously, amid ice flows and icebergs, to search a thousand miles of the forbidding Greenland coast in his determination to find pastureland. When he steered into Eriksfjord, the most habitable of the fjords in Greenland, Thorfinn saw on what stingy ground shrewd old Erik had coined the lying and alluring name—how he had called the whole country Greenland on the basis of a few meadows below the moors in a strip along the sides of this inner fjord, more of them to larboard than starboard, and the best of them narrow. And over the prow Thorfinn caught a glimpse of the broadest meadows and best grazing land in all Greenland, which Erik the Red had chosen for himself. At the head of the fjord on the larboard side was Brattahlid, as Erik had named it, a large farm extending nearly half a mile along the shore, with numerous buildings. It seemed to have everything—meadows, a running stream, and upland pastures enclosed by a ridge in back of them. There was a landing place, to which folk wearing hoods and close-fitting woolens were hastening from all directions, those on horseback loping ahead of those on foot, while others rowed across from the opposite side of the fjord, all in a rush to get to where they knew the trading ships would land. At the landing slope was a broad slide cleared of rocks, where ships could be beached or drawn up on shore without damage to their planking. Thorfinn told his men to stand close-packed at the stern so as to raise the prow to nose it up on the slide.

Thorfinn and the masters and men of the two ships brought out their cargo: malt to make drinks; wheat, which Greenlanders could not grow in their half-frozen land; colored cloth which women would fancy; spears and swords for the men; belt buckles, bracelets, and rings for both men and women; honey from Norway; nuts and dried fruits. In exchange for the ship merchandise, the Greenlanders offered furs, sealskins, walrus ivory, eiderdown feathers, and soapstone dishes. The ships were a thrilling emporium. Thorfinn and the other owners inquired whether any of the folk had falcons and polar bear cubs, for such were most desired abroad.

The eagerness with which the Greenlanders sought the goods confirmed Thorfinn's guess that too few trading ships had come to Greenland, and that while the people there had many furs and much ivory, they lacked many needful things. Being generous of heart, he felt sorry for them.

BRATTAHLID

Isafjord

Breidafjord

Eriksfjord   GARDAR

Einarsfjord

N

S

EASTERN SETTLEMENT
of
GREENLAND

showing farms and
church sites

Herjulfsness

CAPE FARVEL

The trading had scarce begun when a tall commanding man strode to the landing place, and with him an attractive young woman of remarkable bearing. Folk whispered to Thorfinn that the man was Leif, son of Erik, and the woman was Gudrid. For a moment Thorfinn thought her Leif's wife. However, when he was told that the charming woman at Leif's side had no husband, but was the widow of Leif's brother Thorstein, Thorfinn looked at her again and was deeply moved. In his eyes she was most beautiful. Along with the other shipowners, he heard himself saying to her, "We invite you to help yourself to whatever of our wares you desire." If Thorfinn had then had the wit to question himself as to what he was saying and why, he would have felt that he had forgotten why he had come to Greenland. Indeed at that moment he did not know whether he was a trader or a charity giver—or something else.

A VIKING MERCHANT SHIP

Leif, not to be outdone in generosity, "offered the hospitality of quarters for the crew of both ships." The cargoes were stored in warehouses near the landing place. Leif invited the four merchants to be his houseguests for the winter in Brattahlid.

Leif escorted his guests to the hall his father Erik had built. When they saw its walls of turf eight feet thick, they knew it would be winter-snug. And the hall inside was ample—forty-eight feet long and fifteen feet wide. The floor was of neat fieldstones, and Leif showed them where there was a cistern underneath, and fireplaces above the cistern, and conduits to keep the water from freezing. When he took his guests on a tour of the farmstead, he pointed with pride to an outside well fifty feet from the entrance to the hall, the only well in Greenland that did not freeze in winter. He showed his barns and his byres with stalls for thirty cows, and his summer milking pen. He boasted of having salmon in the stream that crossed his meadows, and near the stream he showed them the church his mother Thjodhild had built. South of the stream, he showed them his smithy and a warehouse that was huge inside, sixty-five feet long and twenty-five feet wide. It was end-on to shore, and Thorfinn thought it might be used as a ship shed and still have room for a whole ship's cargo in storage.

Leif inquired of each of his guests where his home was. Bjarni Grimolfsson was from Breidafjord on the west coast of Iceland, and with him in the same ship, Thorhall Gamlason was from the East-fjords. In the ship with Thorfinn, Snorri Thorbrandsson was from Alptafjord, one of the Eastfjords. Thorfinn Karlsefni was from Skaga Fjord on the north coast. Thus from the east, west, and north of Iceland, Leif was happy to note, shipowners had seen the chance of profitable trading in Greenland.

These four houseguests were called "great vikings." This was a term of high honor since it meant the master of a ship who had crossed the wide ocean and become wealthy by trading voyages. A hundred years before it would have meant a man who had gained wealth by raiding monasteries and churches. But most of the gold and silver treasures near seacoasts had been seized by viking raiders, and the old ways were no longer profitable. The old ways were frowned upon anyway, for Christianity had been legally adopted

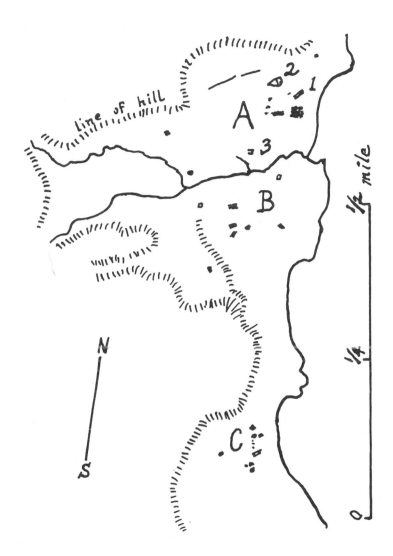

BRATTAHLID

A—Home farm with byres and barns
  1—Erik the Red's house
  2—Milking pen
  3—Thjodhild's Church. A later
    church and churchyard shown in
    dotted lines south of house.

B—Second farm
C—Storehouses and meeting place of
    Lawthing. Presumed landing place.
    Ship sheds have been obliterated by
    the grinding of shore ice. A third
    farm was a half mile south of C.

in Norway, Iceland, and Greenland. Also, there seemed to be no more good unoccupied land for the taking. Norsemen had settled and filled all the known islands in the North Atlantic—the Faeroes, Shetlands, Orkneys, Hebrides—and had overrun Ireland. And so it was only by trading voyages that a viking could now honorably become rich. He had to be a shrewd bargainer to acquire wealth enough to buy a ship, and a shipowner had to have courage to venture the stormy sea crossings. He had to endure, and have Thor's luck, or as men now said, Christ's help.

Thorfinn Karlsefni was the most distinguished of the great vikings. He was descended from an illustrious line of Danish, Swedish, Norwegian, Irish, and Scottish ancestors. Among them were kings of Norway, and kings like Kjarval, Norse king of the Irish, and Olav Hvite, who had been king of the Norse in Scotland. He was a blood relative of all the great land takers in the northern ocean. He shared some of the same ancestry as Naddod, who 150 years before was the first of the Norsemen to sight Iceland, which because of its great snowfields Naddod had called "Snowland." Thorfinn was likewise related to Floki Vilgerdsson, who, seeing the ice choking one of Iceland's northern fjords, renamed the island "Iceland." Floki was the first settler in Iceland. Thorfinn was more closely related, something like a fourth cousin, to Erik the Red, the discoverer and namer of Greenland. And so Thorfinn Karlsefni and Leif Erikson were cousins. In a later century, they were to have a distant cousin named George Washington.

When an owner of a merchant ship made a successful trading voyage "abroad" (to Norway) in one sailing season, and back to Iceland with a full cargo the next, he was amply rewarded for his hardships and perils. The profits were large enough to satisfy any ordinary man. But Thorfinn, having an active imagination, saw beyond other merchant-ship owners who were content with their trading. He realized the greater opportunities that would come to a shipowner who, like old Erik the Red, could lead colonists to some land not yet settled, if such land there were.

In Iceland he had heard a rumor of the existence of such land. A recently confirmed report had it that Bjarni Herjulfsson, setting out from his home port at Eyrarbakki, had sighted three

**ICELAND, SHOWING FJORDS FROM WHICH
THE "GREAT VIKINGS" CAME**

new lands. It was now said that some Greenlanders had recently followed Bjarni's sailing directions and had visited those lands and had wintered in one of them and found it fair. It was a wilderness in which they had encountered only a few savage inhabitants. They had brought home from it withy vines and timber. Two of the three lands were said to be heavily forested. Icelanders needed timber, and therefore Thorfinn, as an Icelander, wanted to learn all he could of the new unsettled lands. But it was only from Greenlanders who had been to those lands that he could learn the sailing directions to them. This was the real reason why he had come to Greenland.

As it drew near Christmas, Leif began to be silent and Thorfinn observed that he seemed to be less happy than before. Thorfinn directly questioned Leif, "Have you any sorrow, Leif, my friend? Everyone thinks you are less cheerful than you used to be." Shrewdly guessing what was causing Leif's depression, Thorfinn said, "You have entertained us with the greatest splendor, and we are bound to return it to you with such service as we can command. Say now, what troubles you?" With his inmost thoughts thus exposed, but sensing Thorfinn's kindness of intention, Leif unburdened his heart. "You have accepted my hospitality with courtesy and good grace, and I cannot think that our relationship will bring you any discredit. On the other hand, I fear that when you are a guest anywhere else it will be said that you never passed a worse Yule than that which now approaches, when Leif the son of Erik entertained you at Brattahlid, in Greenland."

"It shall not be so, Householder!" said Karlsefni. "We have in our ship both malt and corn [wheat]. Take as much of it as you desire, and make ready a feast as grand as you like!" This Leif accepted. Preparations were made for the feast of Yule, and it was so good that people thought they had hardly ever seen the like in a poor land.

After Yule, Karlsefni approached Leif and asked for the hand of Gudrid, whom he regarded as being under her brother-in-law's care. Thorfinn said he thought her a lovable and capable woman. Leif replied that he would speak to her in favor of the suit. He said, "She is worthy of a good match. It may be that it is her destiny to marry you." He added that he had heard good reports of Karlsefni. When Gudrid heard the proposal, she said she would accept Leif's advice. Not to make a long story of it, she followed Leif's counsel, and so there was another feast at their betrothal and still another when their bridal was toasted.

By Church rule, banns had to be announced several weeks before the wedding. What with Yule preparations and celebration, betrothal feast, and wedding feast, with malt drinks at all of them, that winter was convivially memorable.

During that joyful winter, Leif told Thorfinn all he knew or had heard of the new lands. Thorfinn listened attentively, and thought of what he should do. Should he himself make a voyage to Vinland? The tellings had stated the hazards. Leif's brother Thorvald had been killed in Vinland by an arrow shot by a Skraeling. Their brother Thorstein had been lost in fog and unknown currents and had never reached Vinland. Leif was the only one of the sons of Erik who remained alive. A voyager to Vinland must face grave dangers. But it would be a great adventure!

As he listened to the tellings, Thorfinn was particularly observant of an important fact, about which, so far as the records show, he said nothing to Leif. It did not escape Thorfinn that the explorations undertaken by Thorvald in the after-boat to the west and in the trading ship to the north and east, though each had extended for many miles, had neither of them found the end of the coast of Vinland in either direction. Vinland therefore must be an immensely long land. Surely, Thorfinn thought to himself, in so huge a country there must be many good farmstead sites, places where many people could dwell. A man would be wise to seize any opportunity to take land in that great country.

With thoughts like this, Thorfinn gave ear to his wife Gudrid, to Leif and Leif's mother, to their priest, to old Tyrker, to Thorstein the Swarthy, and to Leif's half-sister Freydis, and to the men in Eriksfjord who had been to Vinland. All were saying that another voyage to Vinland should be undertaken. And now they began to say that he should be its leader. He listened to them in silence and at first did not tell them what he thought. They did not suspect that he had already made up his mind. He knew that the man who appears to be the last to be persuaded is held to be the man of surest judgment.

The talk at Brattahlid had filled him with a great ambition, which was to do as Erik the Red had done, to establish settlements. He could plant a colony in Vinland. He saw the opportunity of becoming the father of a new country. And so, after due deliberation, he announced his decision. He would lead an expedition to Vinland with the intention of starting a permanent settlement there, if they were able to do so. He knew he would be the leader of a large expedition of several ships. To meet the menace of the Skraelings, he hired sixty fighting men (one saga says sixty-five men and five women).

The colony would be a communal enterprise. He made a compact with his crew that they should have equal shares in everything of value that they obtained.

THORFINN KARLSEFNI
AT LEIF'S SHELTERS

Thorfinn asked Leif for his buildings in Vinland, but Leif replied that he would lend him the buildings, not give them.

On board the ships, in addition to men and women, were all kinds of domestic animals, an apparently intolerable jamming. But domestic animals then were by no means so large as now. Selection by breeders through the past 2,500 years has steadily increased the size of cattle, sheep, and pigs. A thousand years ago these were about half the length and height of livestock today, and about one-quarter the weight.[6] The ships of the Karlsefni Expedi-

---

[6] By the fourteenth century, as shown by bones from a medieval slaughterhouse in Paris, cattle were a third of the weight and two-thirds the length of present live-

tion were as crowded as could be, but within reason. They put to sea and arrived safely at Leif's Shelters, and there the men carried up their leather bags, which were combination tote bags and waterproof sleeping bags.

Soon they had plenty of good food, for a large and excellent whale was driven ashore. They went to where it was and cut into it, and so had no shortage. The domestic animals were turned out to graze, but the males soon became frisky and wild. They had brought one bull with them.

Karlsefni had trees cut down and shaped into timbers to make a shipload, and this wood was stacked upon a rock for drying. They gathered a supply of all the good things that the country produced, grapes and game and fish.

During the summer following their first winter, they became aware of the presence of the Skraelings, a great band of whom came out of the forest, hoping to trade their wares. The cattle were near at hand and the bull bellowed and roared mightily. This frightened the Skraelings and they fled with their bundles of gray fur and sable and all kinds of skin wares. They turned toward Karl-sefni's abode and tried to enter the buildings, but Karlsefni and his men held the doors to keep them out. Neither side understood the language of the other. Then the Skraelings put down their packs and loosened them and offered their wares in trade, showing especial eagerness for weapons. Karlsefni forbade his companions to trade any weapons, but got the idea of having the women carry milk out to them. The moment the Skraelings saw the milk, they wanted nothing else. Thus the Skraelings carried their goods away in their stomachs, while they left their bundles of fur skins with Karlsefni and his men.

K 1   Following this occurrence, Karlsefni had a strong fence of pal-ings erected around his abode and made all ready there. The pali-sade around the house was the largest construction at Leif's Shel-ters—about 115 feet long and 85 to 90 feet wide. The entrance to it

stock in France. Horses in Iceland and Greenland tended to be the size of Shetland ponies. This explains reports of prodigious feats of eating in ancient times, as for example a Greek warrior devouring a whole leg of lamb at one sitting.

was opposite the doorway to the house, logically on the east side at the north end, at the corner nearest to the ship shed. The fence did not consist of contiguous posts, but rather, its posts were planted in a zigzag pattern, with tree branches and briers interwoven and twisted in and out between the posts. It was a withy fence built with a minimum of effort. An occasional larger post or a tree stripped of its branches was incorporated into it for greater strength.

At this time Gudrid gave birth to a male child, who was called Snorri.

Early in the second winter the Skraelings came again, in larger numbers, with the same wares as before. Karlsefni then told the women to trade milk as they had before, and nothing else. When the Skraelings saw the milk, they threw their bundles in over the palisade. While Gudrid was seated inside the doorway beside the cradle of her infant son, Snorri, a shadow fell upon the door and a woman in a narrow black kirtle entered. She was a short woman, with a band about her head, and light chestnut hair, pale skin, and such large eyes as had never been seen in a human head. The woman went to where Gudrid sat and with sign language asked, "What is your name?" or so Gudrid understood her. Gudrid replied, "Ek heiti Gudridr [My name is Gudrid]." The five syllables were not too many for the native woman, hearing them spoken, to pronounce perfectly, and so when Gudrid asked, "What is your name?" the Skraeling woman repeated, "Ek heiti Gudridr."

At this, the housewife Gudrid pointed with her hand to a seat beside her. But at that instant there was a great crash, and the woman disappeared. One of the Skraelings had tried to seize some weapons and had been slain by one of Karlsefni's men. Instantly the Skraelings fled, leaving garments and goods behind them. No one save Gudrid had seen the woman.

"Now we shall have to plan against them," said Karlsefni, "for I think they will return a third time to attack us in great force. This is what we shall do. Let ten of our men go out upon this cape and show themselves."   K 2

The palisade could be reached by savages coming out of the for-

est on foot only from the southwest. Karlsefni realized that it was
from that direction that the attack must come. He assumed that a
half-mile away along the water's edge, due south of the palisade,
many enemy eyes were keeping watch. They would be looking for
such an opportune time as he proposed to simulate. They would
see the men sent out upon the cape, the land between Follins Pond
and Dinah's Pond. This cape was three-quarters of a mile long. If
it appeared to the savages that the men on the cape were a much
larger number then they actually were, and seemed to be scattered
over the cape, the Skraelings would think it a favorable moment to
attack. The ten men out on the cape would make believe they were
working there. Karlsefni no doubt instructed them to call loudly
to each other to make certain that their presence there was observed by Skraeling watchers. By voice and gesture they were to
make it appear that many others were working with them. Then
while three or four remained on the cape to keep up the illusion
of a large working party, the others were to hasten to join with
those of Karlsefni's men who were prepared to fall upon the flank
of the Skraeling attackers.

In preparing for the battle, Karlsefni's men had built an enclosing fence to keep his cattle from
running away into the wilderness, and, naturally, he built it where
the shortest length of fence would serve the purpose. It was a fence
only 1,000 feet long, and it enclosed the more than 250 acres of
"this cape." It made the whole area a tidy farm. It no doubt en-
K 3   closed the shore spring, and since the cattle would come to that
spring regularly to drink, Karlsefni's men did not have to round
them up at milking time.

In preparing for the battle, Karlsefni's men had to cut
through the enclosing fence to hew a passage for the cattle. When
they drove the cattle out before them upon the flank of the Skraelings, one of the men no doubt twisted the bull's tail to make him
bellow.

The site Karlsefni chose for the battlefield was directed by the
terrain. It was to the west of the palisade—ground over which the
Skraelings must come and ground which had been cleared of trees
by Leif Erikson's and Thorvald Erikson's men, and by Karlsefni's

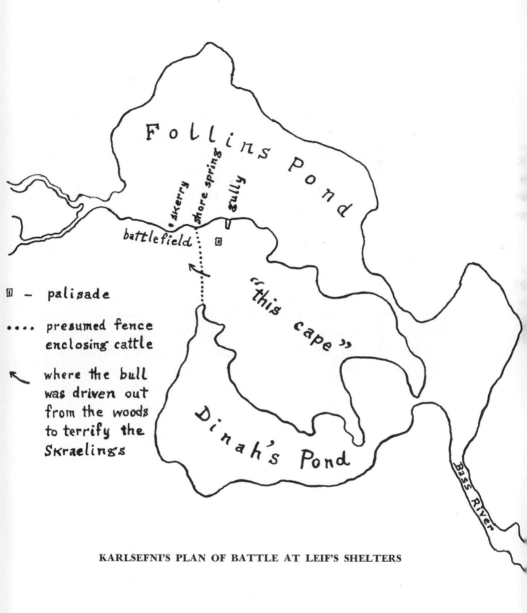

KARLSEFNI'S PLAN OF BATTLE AT LEIF'S SHELTERS

men in getting posts for the palisade. It was there outside the cattle enclosure that garden crops had been planted.

Karlsefni's plan was the logical one. While the ten men went out on the cape and showed themselves, Karlsefni and the rest of his men slipped into the woods and hewed a passage for the cattle. When the savages advanced from the forest, Karlsefni drove the cattle and the bull out ahead of them. The Skraelings were caught between the terrifying bull and Karlsefni's men on the one side, and the shore of Follins Pond on the other side. It followed that in the fight many Skraelings were killed. Among the Skraelings was a tall man, fair to behold (*vaem*—"beautiful," "fine"), whom Karlsefni believed to be their chieftain. One of the Skraelings picked up an ax and examined it. Then he lifted it against a comrade and struck at him, and he was instantly felled. The tall man seized the ax, and after looking at it for a while, hurled it into the salt water with all his might. Then they all fled into the forest. Thus the battle ended.

Karlsefni stayed at Leif's Shelters throughout that second winter, but in the spring decided to remain no longer, and to return to Greenland. He and his men made ready for the voyage and took with them great quantities of withies, berries, and skin wares. They set sail upon the ocean and arrived at Eriksfjord with the ship in good condition. They spent the winter there.

THORFINN EXPLORES
TO STREAM FJORD

The telling of Thorfinn's voyage to Leif's Shelters was by Greenlanders who were admirers and friends of Leif, and desirous of
preserving his fame. They gave no details of Karlsefni's voyage,
made no mention of any ship in the expedition except his, and
said nothing of his having had experiences in Vinland outside of
Leif's Shelters or after his two winters there. But the telling in Iceland that originally came from Karlsefni's own lips specifies five
ships and implies a sixth, avoids mention of Leif's Shelters, and
goes into fascinating details of Karlsefni's doings in various places
outside of Leif's Shelters. We now follow that telling.

In Brattahlid people began to talk about Vinland the Good,

and said it should be explored *(skyldu leita)*. Karlsefni and Snorri made ready their ship to explore the land in the spring. With them went also the before-named men called Bjarni Grimolfsson and Thorhall Gamlason with their ship. There was a man named Thorvard, who was Erik the Red's son-in-law, for he was the husband of Freydis, the natural daughter of Erik the Red. He also went with them. It seems clear that Thorvard went in his own ship.

"So also did Thorvald, the son of Erik."

The name Thorvald here may be a scribe's error, just as in this saga Leif is frequently erroneously called Erik. Or it may mean that the ship that had last been to Vinland with Thorvald Erikson (Leif's ship) was part of the Karlsefni Expedition.

The next person who had a ship in the expedition was Thorhall, who was called the Huntsman. Thorhall had long been with Erik, serving him as huntsman in summer and steward in winter. He was a large fellow, strong, swarthy, and uncouth. He was habitually taciturn, but when he did speak he was annoyingly offensive. He always egged on Erik to the worst. He was forever an irritant. He had very little to do with religious faith after it came to Greenland. He was a bad Christian. Useful as a man who had wide experience with uninhabited places, he went on his own ship.

The description of Thorhall the Huntsman reflects the social disapproval of a man who spoke his own mind in defiance of his neighbors' opinions, and it shows religious prejudice against him. One variant of the saga says that Thorhall went on a ship "along with Thorvald," and the other variant says "along with Thorvard and Thorvald." Since the implication is that these two went on separate ships, the words "on a ship along with" probably meant on a separate ship. In the later story of the expedition, Thorhall the Huntsman had a ship.

The saga also says, "They had the ship which Thorbjorn (Vifilsson) had brought out from Iceland." In this sentence, if "they" refers to the whole expedition, as it probably does, then there may have been six ships. Thorbjorn Vifilsson was Gudrid's father, and since Gudrid was going to Vinland, he understandably would have made his ship available to his son-in-law's expedition.

Hitherto, a widely accepted estimate of the size of the Karl-sefni expedition to Vinland has been three or four ships with 160 men and five women. But the saga practically identifies six ships: Karlsefni's, Bjarni Grimolfsson's, Thorvard's, Thorvald's, Thorhall the Huntsman's, and the ship which had been brought to Greenland by Thorbjorn Vifilsson. It is only in respect to Karlsefni's hiring of sixty ship soldiers and five women that any women are mentioned, aside from Gudrid and Freydis. Since the expedition planned a permanent settlement, it must have included a considerable number of women. There would have been several women on each of the ships just to do the cooking. The work of cooking for a large ship's crew would be too much for one woman. Freydis was undoubtedly on her husband's ship, not Karlsefni's. Four years later when the ship belonging to her husband Thorvard was one of two preparing to sail to Vinland, there were meant to be five women in each, though the agreement was violated. It seems a safe assumption that the Karlsefni Expedition had about thirty women in addition to the 160 men. Such a number plus livestock would have required at least five ships, as is demonstrable: Karlsefni's ship and the ship of Bjarni Grimolfsson had brought to Greenland forty men each, and that was presumably their comfortable capacity. Surely neither of them carried more than that number of men when about five women and "all kinds of domestic animals" were also taken on board. Thorvard's ship probably carried thirty men and five women, the same number which Thorvard and Freydis announced it would carry on a later occasion. This left fifty men and presumably about fifteen women, whose numbers required at least two other ships.

Karlsefni had spent a whole winter, five months, with men who had been to Vinland and knew the sailing directions to it. For him there was no question of how to get most directly from Greenland to Vinland. Clearly, therefore, the words *skyldu leita* in his telling cannot mean, as some have thought, "should search for" or "should go in search of," in the sense of hunting for something which is undetermined or lost; but they have the alternative and acceptable meaning of "should be inquired into," "should be explored." Karlsefni understood that he would have no difficulty in finding Leif's Shelters, and that understanding was implicit in the statement that Leif "loaned" Karlsefni the buildings at Leif's Shelters.

While preparing for the expedition, Karlsefni thought of all the tellings. Leif's brother Thorvald had not found the end of Vinland in either direction. How far did Vinland extend to the west, and how far to the east beyond the fjord where Thorvald had been killed? It did not escape Karlsefni's thoughts that Thorvald Erikson's sailing around Keel Cape to the north and afterward to the eastward was the following of a great bend of the coast to the north and east. How far did this bend of coast extend? Also, how large was Markland? He would find out.

The telling, by Gudrid and by Thorstein the Swarthy, of Gudrid's second widowing at Lysufirth had often turned her third husband's thoughts to the Western Settlement of Greenland. Everyone from the Western Settlement who met Karlsefni told of land only a day and a half's sail to the west from the Western Settlement. Many fishermen of the Western Settlement had sighted that land.

Is that land also a part of Markland? Karlsefni asked himself. It was his plan to find out. He would sail his ship to the Western Settlement, and then across to the other land, and south along that land to see if it were a part of Markland. The route was recommended because of what fishermen told of the current that flowed along the west coast of Greenland and past the Western Settlement and then across to the west and south along that other land. There is no hint in the record, however, that his plan was shared with anyone except his fellow shipmaster, Snorri. Either he did not speak of his plan to the Greenlanders, or if they heard of it, it did not impress them, and in their telling they chose to say nothing of it. We are left guessing as to whether all the ships sailed in convoy with Karlsefni's or whether the other ships sailed directly to a rendezvous in Vinland. That rendezvous was of course Leif's Shelters. Because of the overcrowding of people and cattle on board, the shipmasters would wish to reach Vinland as quickly as possible, so in all probability the other ships sailed directly to Leif's Shelters.

It is likely that Karlsefni's ship alone "sailed first to the West-

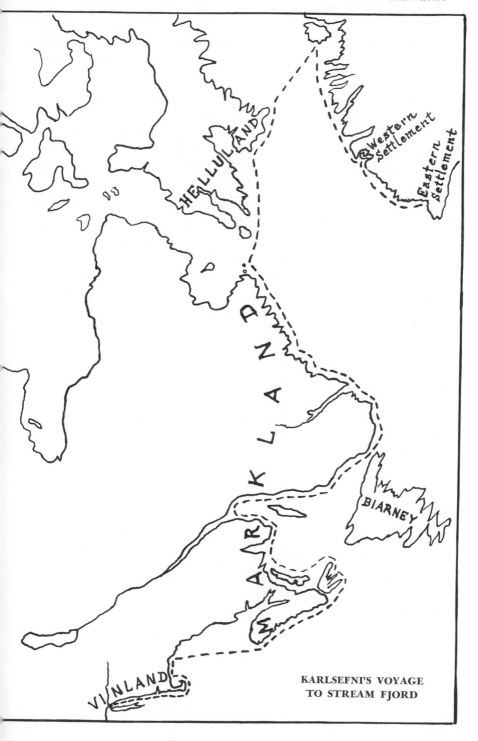

KARLSEFNI'S VOYAGE
TO STREAM FJORD

ern Settlement and from there to Bear [Disco] Island and thence across the open sea to the southward for two days' sailing distance, and saw land."

Because Karlsefni began his voyage from Eriksfjord to Vinland by steering to the northwest, some commentators have assumed that he was hunting for Vinland, and did not know the sailing directions for the direct route. The only reasonable explanation for his following the route he did is that he was a man of large imagination who was pursuing an intelligent plan.

Karlsefni went as far north as Disco Island off the west coast of Greenland, to take advantage of currents that the Greenland fishermen said would carry his ship across to the southwest. He did not know that the land he next saw was an island; for it seems a safe assumption that no Greenlander had circumnavigated Baffin Land, which is a thousand miles long, and extends to $73\frac{1}{2}°$ North.

When he went ashore, he saw foxes and found large flat rocks, many of them twelve ells broad. Many of the stones were so broad that two men could stretch out on one rock with their soles touching. Karlsefni gave the country the same descriptive name that Leif had given to Newfoundland—*Helluland*.

K 4

We can appreciate each step of Karlsefni's voyage when we keep in mind his purpose of exploring and especially of ascertaining the extent of continuous coastline of Markland and of Vinland. From his Helluland (the Cumberland Peninsula of Baffin Land) he sailed with northerly winds two days' sailing distance, or three hundred miles. This is the precise distance from the southern tip of Cumberland Peninsula out of sight of land across to the northern tip of Labrador. Whether or not fishermen of the Western Settlement had told him of the great gap (the entrance to Hudson Strait) which he had to cross, he did cross that gap in the last third of his three hundred miles of sailing, and then he saw a well-wooded land ahead. This northern tip of Labrador was a most significant landfall in his explorations, since eventually he would demonstrate that it was the northern end of the eastern seaboard of Vinland. He found the land well wooded all along the east coast of Labrador and around the south end of Labrador,

K 5

K 6

and west inside the Gulf of St. Lawrence, and south along the coast of New Brunswick and Nova Scotia.

When he followed the coast on the northwest side of the Strait of Belle Isle, there was an island (Newfoundland) off to the southeast of this land. The island and the wooded land were both within sight at the same time, for the Strait of Belle Isle at its narrowest is only twelve miles wide. He crossed the straight to that island, and because his men found a bear there they called it Bear Island *(Biarney)*. They called the wooded land *Markland,* that is, they called all the continuous wooded land from Labrador to Nova Scotia *Markland.*

Karlsefni knew that Bjarni Herjulfsson and Leif Erikson had sailed from the southwestern shore of Markland out of sight of land for two days to Vinland, and so he followed their sailing directions. But it appears that the wind carried him to a landfall a considerable distance to the north of Cape Cod, and from there he sailed southward for a long time, probably slowed by southern winds, before he came to a cape. The land was off to the starboard as they crossed over to the northeastern side of the cape.

On the cape they found long beaches and sand dunes. They rowed ashore there and saw the keel of a ship—unquestionably the keel Thorvald Erikson had left as a monument. Karlsefni and his men called it Keel Cape.

They called the beaches *Furdustrands* ("Astonishing Strands") because they took so long to sail by—much longer than any they had ever seen. Beyond these Astonishing Strands, the country was indented with bays, into one of which (obviously Nantucket Sound) they sailed. This is as near as Karlsefni's telling comes to saying that they went in to rendezvous with the other ships at Leif's Shelters.

It is here that the saga emanating from Karlsefni's explorations dovetails in with the saga of Leif and the Greenlanders. Karlsefni's sailing into a bay beyond the Keel Cape beaches allows us to correlate it with the previously narrated experiences of Karlsefni at Leif's Shelters. It seems likely that, having met at the rendezvous, the united expedition remained at Leif's Shelters the first

K 7

K 8

K 9

K 10

winter. To obviate confusion, we note that the Karlsefni Expedition spent four winters in Vinland. The Greenlanders' saga tells us that Karlsefni spent the first two winters at Leif's Shelters, where his son Snorri was born during or after "the summer following their first winter." The saga that originated from Karlsefni and Gudrid's telling informs us that the boy Snorri was "three winters old" when he left Vinland with his parents, who surely knew his age. Neither saga tells where the rest of the expedition spent their first winter, but the saga that originated from Karlsefni's lips tells where most of the members of the expedition spent their last three winters.

The soil at Leif's Shelters was sandy. The men of Thorvald Erikson's after-boat exploring party, everyone remembered, had reported that there was good land to the west of Leif's Shelters. Most members of the expedition felt there would be satisfactory conditions for a permanent settlement in that land to the west. They could not help it if Leif Erikson would be disappointed by their leaving Leif's Shelters and going elsewhere to settle. The telling mentions another Astonishing Strands, obviously on the way to the west. Karlsefni had encountered the first such strands on the cape, before he came to the bay. The second Astonishing Strands were beyond the bay. They were the eastern half of the north shore of Long Island—a virtually unbroken stretch of sand beaches forty-five miles long beginning at Orient Point.

We know with practical certainty where Karlsefni next landed. It was at the base of the first high ground the Karlsefni party came to, at the western end of the long beaches, or the east end of the Long Island moraine. The high ground is on the west side of Mt. Sinai Harbor. Having an elevation of 180 feet, this was visible to the men on Karlsefni's ship for twenty-five miles before they reached it. This high ground is called Belle Terre. Karlsefni's party undoubtedly ascended it. High ground always lured an explorer, for two reasons. It afforded a quick means of surveying the surrounding country more extensively than from the deck or mast of a floating ship. Also, where high ground is, freshwater springs are almost invariably found.

From Belle Terre Karlsefni and his men saw to the south a

K 11

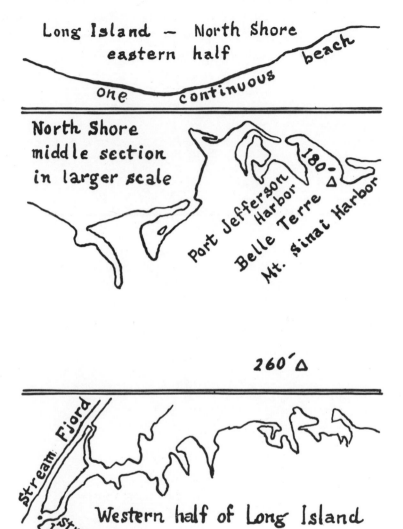

LONG ISLAND—NORTH SHORE

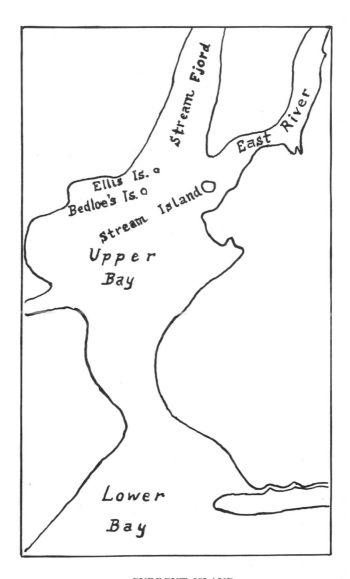

CURRENT ISLAND

higher hill. This hill was 260 feet in altitude, and was seven miles south of them. It is the hill occupied by the Suffolk Sanatorium, less than a mile north of Farmingville. Because of intervening hills, Karlsefni on Belle Terre could not see the ocean about eighteen miles to the south. Had he been able to see it, he would probably not have considered it worthwhile to scout out the land.

When Leif had visited King Olaf Tryggvason, the king had given him two Gaels (Irish), advising him to make use of them if speed were ever required, for they could run faster than deer. Of these two, the man's name was Haki and the woman's Haekia. Leif had loaned this couple to Karlsefni, who now had use for them. He set the Gaels on shore and ordered them to run southward to   **K 12** scout out the nature of the land, and to return before the end of the third day. The Gaels, when set ashore, were each attired in a garment called *biafal (kiafal)* open at the sides and sleeveless, with a hood at the top, and held between the legs with buttons and loops. Except for this they were naked. The ships lay at anchor while they were gone.

Karlsefni allowed the Gaels forty-eight hours for their scouting because he estimated that as a reasonable time for the slaves to reach the top of the highest hill and return. That hill, with nothing over 120 feet high to the south of it, is about seven miles from Great South Bay and about ten miles from the ocean, and so from the Gaels Karlsefni learned the width of that section of Long Island.

When the Gaels came running back down to the ships, one of them had a bunch of grapes, and the other an ear of a new kind of cultivated wheat. Karlsefni said he thought they had found land with good qualities. He then took them on board his ship, and the expedition sailed along where the coast (all along the western half   **K 13** of the north shore of Long Island) was indented with bays.

They sailed to a fjord (the Hudson River). There (at the   **K 14** mouth of the fjord) lay an island around which flowed very strong currents, and so they called this island *Straumsey*—"Current Island" (modern Governors Island). There were so many birds on it that one could scarcely set foot between the eggs.

They sailed in through the fjord, and called it Stream Fjord.   **K 15**

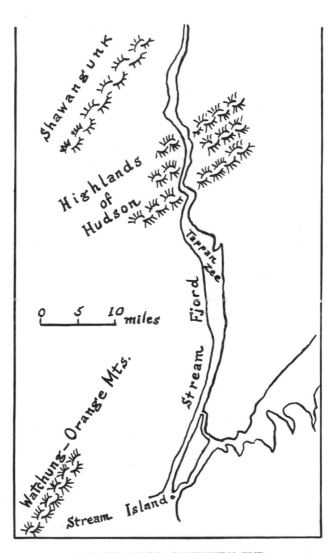

STREAM FJORD—SOUTHERN END

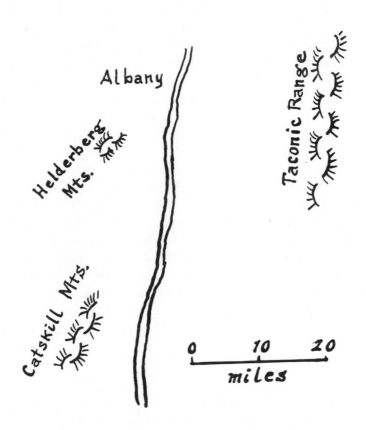

Albany

Helderberg Mts.

Taconic Range

Catskill Mts.

0   10   20
miles

STREAM FJORD–NORTHERN SECTION

It was the invariable custom of the Norsemen to sail as far as possible into a fjord, to the head of navigable waters, for experience in Norway, in Iceland, and in Greenland had taught them that the farther in from the ocean, the more sheltered and hospitable the land and the weather would be. We may be sure that Karlsefni sailed into the Hudson as far as it was navigable—to the site of Waterford about fifteen miles north of modern Albany.

There they carried their cargoes from the ships and established themselves. They had with them all kinds of livestock. They searched the land to find out its products. There were mountains thereabouts, and the country was beautiful to behold.

K 16

Anyone who has seen the Hudson River knows the applicability of their description. From the hill on Current Island the men of Karlsefni's Expedition got their first view of mountains thereabouts, for they saw the long ridge of the Watchung and Orange mountains of New Jersey running from the southwest toward the northeast. A half-day's sail up the Hudson, at the north end of Tappan Zee, and from Haverstraw Bay they saw more of the same range. When they passed through the deep gorge that cuts this range at what are called the Highlands of the Hudson, they saw some of the finest scenery in North America. When they looked back, they saw a range running off to the northeast. To the west of them they saw the high and continuous ridge of the Shawangunk Mountains also running in the same direction. Farther up the Hudson, they saw the Catskill Mountains, with peaks of 3,000 to 3,900 feet. From near the site of Albany, when they went out exploring, they may have seen the Helderberg Mountains to the southwest and the Taconic Range, with peaks up to 2,800 feet in altitude a few miles to the east.

Everyone today should envy the vikings for their having seen the Hudson River in its pristine loveliness—its shores unmarred by crowded housing, highrise apartments, industrial plants belching smoke, refuse dumps, and rotting docks; its mountains unscarred by quarries; its long vistas uncut by bridges. It was a privilege to be the first visitors in wilderness days and to appreciate, as the folk of the Karlsefni Expedition did, that the country was beautiful to behold. The modern voyager up the noble river, who observes with dismay how man has defaced it, may feel vicarious pleasure in the knowledge that human beings nearly a thousand years ago enjoyed its umblemished beauty.

Established as they thought comfortably, they did nothing except explore. There was tall grass. They remained there during the winter.

Back in Greenland, these people had accepted as true Leif Erickson's observation that in Vinland "there came no frost." The testimony of Thorvald Erickson's men had substantiated it. Karlsefni's followers believed—wanted to believe—that winters in Vinland were exceedingly mild. They themselves probably, and Karlsefni certainly, had found the winter at Leif's Shelters just as they expected. There had been no lack of cattle fodder, and the cattle had grazed out all winter because the tall marsh grass scarcely withered. The great areas of "tall grass" which the folk now saw on islands in the upper reaches of the Hudson and along its banks seemed to promise a duplication of the same condition. The would-be settlers were dairymen even more than fishermen and hunters.

In sailing up "through" the Hudson they had failed to take into account that this fjord ran to the north. They did not dream that 150 miles in from the ocean the winter could be much colder than at the mouth of the fjord. They soon were disillusioned. They had a severe winter, but had taken no thought for this during the summer, and they suffered a lack of provisions, and the hunting failed.

Stream Fjord was for them almost a death trap. Deep snows that did not melt away made hunting impossible, and the freezing of the river made fishing almost as difficult and prevented escape until spring.[7]

---

[7] Weather Bureau records (*U.S. Weather Bureau Records, Local Climatological Data. Annual Summary with Comparative Data*, 1966, for New York City and Albany, N.Y.) reveal what happened to the Karlsefni Expedition. In thirty-seven winters beginning with 1930, in the months of December, January, and February, the snowfall at Albany has averaged more than twice that at New York City. In

Karlsefni, it seems, was not with the expedition during that winter. It is a safe assumption that immediately after sailing in through the fjord, he returned to Leif's Shelters and to the house Leif had loaned him, where his wife Gudrid that autumn gave birth to their son Snorri. If anyone thinks it incredible that he, the leader, with his own ship would have separated himself by hundreds of miles from the people of the other ships, let it be noted that there are two occasions in which the saga specifically tells of such separation when Karlsefni sailed away from the others "with one ship." The distance between New York Harbor and the mouth of the Bass River is 225 miles, all by inland waterway, except for one short exposed passage off Point Judith east of Newport, where ocean swells may be encountered. The vikings would think nothing of sailing from Stream Fjord to Leif's Shelters, and would do it easily by daylight in four days. By sailing all of one night through the middle of Long Island Sound they could do it in three.

Karlsefni was not pressured by any sighting of Skraelings at Current Island or in Stream Fjord. It is quite possible and very likely that news of the massacre in Somes Sound by white strangers who came in such a ship as his had been passed from tribe to tribe, and in consequence Manhattan and Hudson tribes of Indians prudently stayed out of sight of such dangerous visitors.

As soon as the ice in the river broke up, the folk moved out of the fjord to the island and expected at the same time to get provisions from hunting, but there was a shortage of food, though their livestock there (on the island) fared well. They had already prayed to God to send them some food, but it did not come as promptly as they hoped.

------

these three months, in nearly half of those thirty-seven winters, Albany has had more than four feet of snow; and in thirty-two of those winters, more than three feet. This fact alone does not tell the fearful story of what the vikings barely survived. While New York City has had an average mean temperature above freezing in the three months, at Albany the mean temperatures have averaged well below: December, 27.8°; January, 23.2°; February, 23.8°.

THORHALL'S
DEPARTURE

After the main party of the expedition fled out of the fjord to the
island at its mouth, Thorhall the Huntsman disappeared. Karlsefni by that time had returned from Leif's Shelters and rejoined
the others on Current Island. He and Bjarni Grimolfsson led the
searchers who found Thorhall. This is the first mention of Karlsefni since the preceding autumn. They found Thorhall on the
top of a cliff where he was lying on his back with eyes and mouth
and nostrils agape, scratching and pinching himself and talking to
himself. They asked him what had brought him there. He replied
that he was old enough not to need them to look after him. Thorhall's experience as an out-of-doors man does not explain his being

found on a cliff on his back. Whether or not his scratching was caused by a case of poison ivy, his "talking to himself" suggests that he may have been composing verses. As a poet he sought privacy.

When those who found him asked him to travel "home" with them, they meant to the camp on Current Island. He went there with them. Soon after this a whale was washed up, and they rushed to cut it up. No one knew what kind of whale it was, not even Karlsefni, who had great knowledge of whales. When the cooks (the women) had boiled the meat, they ate it, and all were made ill by it.

The whale had not been washed ashore in the river, or in the inner harbor, but somewhere in the Lower Bay or along the ocean shore. It is not likely that a diseased condition of the cooked whale meat made the people ill. Eating a large quantity of rich oily meat when they had not had a full meal in weeks undoubtedly caused them painful indigestion. Thorhall, with his experience in uninhabited places, often on long solitary treks, had known extreme hunger before, and had learned that one who has been starving must eat only a very small quantity at his first meal. Either he was careful to eat only a very little of the whale meat and so was the only one who did not get food poisoning, or his "approaching" the others may mean that he had not participated in the whale feast. In any case, he cited his freedom from illness as proof of the special protection of the red-bearded god Thor, in return for verses which he had composed to Thor—verses which were not preserved in the saga because of Christian prejudices. Thorhall got in a word of anti-Christian propaganda that caused the Christians to pray all the more fervently to their god Christ.

Some lines by Rudyard Kipling may have been inspired by the incident of the whale-meat feasting. They constitute a stanza called "Primitive" in a poem entitled "Natural Theology":

> I ate my fill of a whale that died
>   And stranded after a month at sea . . .
> There is a pain in my inside
>   Why have the gods afflicted me?

Ow! I am purged till I am a wraith!
Wow! I am sick till I cannot see!
What is the sense of Religion and Faith?
Look how the gods have afflicted me!

The people of the Karlsefni Expedition believed their prayers to God had been speedily answered because the weather immediately improved. With the return of warm weather, there were no snows to prevent their hunting, and they could row out to fish. From the ocean sands where the dead whale had been stranded, they returned to Stream Fjord, that is, to the island in the bay at the mouth of the river, where they could hunt for game on the mainland, and in the late spring could gather birds' eggs on the island.

The members of the expedition now held a discussion as to their future moves. It is said that Thorhall wished to sail beyond the Astonishing Strands and Keel Cape to explore Vinland northward. Karlsefni, however, wanted to proceed southward along the coast, for he thought that the conditions in the land would be better the farther south they went. Karlsefni decided it would be advisable to explore both possibilities. **K 17**

Thorhall prepared for his voyage. He planned to sail out below the island. No more than nine men sailed with him. The remainder of the company chose to go with Karlsefni.

The words "out below" are geographically significant. In relation to Current Island at the mouth of the Hudson, "out below" meant to the south, out through the Narrows and Lower New York Bay to the open ocean.

The saga would not say "no more than nine men" decided to accompany Thorhall on his voyage if he were sailing in an after-boat. Nine men were a reasonable and an ideal number for a voyage in an after-boat. Indeed, the words "no more than nine" are clear evidence that he sailed away in a ship. For a ship, nine were an adequate though scanty crew.

Thorhall did not intend to withdraw from the Karlsefni Expedition. He proposed to continue the exploration of Vinland in two important particulars. He would first explore the south shore

of Long Island and thence sail around Keel Cape. Then north of
Keel Cape he intended to cruise to the westward from the tip of
that cape to the mainland coast. It is twenty miles across. Thence
he intended a complete exploration of the great bend of coast to
the north and east, which Thorvald Erikson's death had left un-
completed.

The day of their departure, as Thorhall carried water on
board, he recited this ditty:

> When I came, these brave men told me,
>   Here the best of drinks I'd get.
> Now with water pail behold me;
>   Wine and I are strangers yet.
> Stooping at the spring I've tasted
>   All the wine this land affords;
> Of its vaunted charms divested,
>   Poor indeed are its rewards.

This humorous ditty caused much laughter. So also did his
second ditty, which he recited from on board while they were raising sail, a ditty those on shore memorized and remembered. But
while his hearers understood the second ditty well enough to roar
at the vulgar reference to their rectal blasts, and at the same time
wince at his slur at Christian ideas of Paradise and Providence, the
reader will better appreciate this ditty with the aid of the full explanation to be found with it in the translation on page 299.

Thorhall's sarcasm was not, however, intended as a final farewell. His departure was a gesture of cooperation in exploring
Vinland, even though the overenthusiastic claims for Vinland
heard back home had been in large part discredited. At the same
time, Thorhall was out to prove something to himself and to the
Christians, whom he despised. He was showing off, putting on a
performance of toughness, playing it with lightness and humor.
He was demonstrating his reliance on Thor. He left no doubt in
his hearers' minds as to what drink a Thor worshipper deserved.
The Christians who stayed at Stream Fjord would have only water
to drink and were welcome to it. Let Karlsefni look for a warmer
region. For himself, Thorhall sought interior warmth.

And so he sailed northward past Astonishing Strands and Keel Cape, intending to cruise westward around this cape. But they encountered westerly gales, and were driven ashore in Ireland, where they were grievously maltreated and thrown into slavery. There Thorhall lost his life, according to the reports of traders.

After his departure with the nine men, there remained 150 men at the mouth of Stream Fjord, plus whatever women there were, except, we assume, for the normal depletion by deaths through the years. Most of the folk in the expedition, however, were young and healthy.

It is possible that the ship Thorhall had was Leif Erikson's loaned to him by Leif. If so, Leif's historic ship ended her days as a wreck on the western coast of Ireland.

THE LOCATION
OF HÓP

When Karlsefni arrived at Current Island from Leif's Shelters, he found that the people who had come down out of Stream Fjord as soon as the breakup of the river ice permitted were thoroughly disgruntled. They had counted on there being "no frost." They had believed that the grass in the inner reaches of the fjord would remain green and their cattle could graze all winter. They had been bitterly disillusioned. They had suffered a "severe winter," and both hunting and fishing had failed. The unexpected severity of the winter far inside the fjord had brought them close to complete disaster. This fact is the key to what followed.

Karlsefni faced divided counsels. Thorhall and nine men decided they would have no more of that part of Vinland, but since the winters at Leif's Shelters were mild, such as the one Karlsefni himself had just experienced there, they chose to explore to the north around Keel Cape. Judging from the slurs in Thorhall's ditties, many of the men and women of the expedition were disposed to remain on Current Island, where food was now abundant. But Karlsefni said "he thought conditions in the land would be better the farther south they went," and so he proposed to sail southward to seek a warmer region for permanent settlement. This met with general approval. Some of the expedition remained on Current Island, which was such a strong defensive position that Karlsefni left Gudrid and his son there.

K 18   And so Karlsefni sailed out of New York Harbor south along the coast with Snorri Thorbrandsson and Bjarni Grimolfsson and Thorhall Gamlason and their people. At least one other ship, Thorvard's, with Freydis aboard, sailed south with them.

Putting ourselves in Karlsefni's situation, we see what happened. He had proposed to sail southward "off the coast, on the east side of it." He would be sailing along a shoreline that was completely unknown to him. He was aware that no sailing could be more dangerous. It was far more perilous than to sail into the ocean away from land, for the chances of being cast ashore were great. With ships that could not beat into strong head winds, any onshore storm could mean shipwreck or a broken keel, as had happened to Thorvald's ship on Keel Cape. The ships of Karlsefni's party were merchant ships, heavily loaded and with no more than twelve oars each. Twelve oars were enough for maneuvering inside a harbor, but inadequate to proceed against or hold position against any wind of storm velocity. But Karlsefni wanted to keep the coast in sight to explore.

He would, therefore, hope to find each day before dark some inlet into sheltered water where the ships could ride safely through the night. Not knowing the coast he would not dare sail after dark, for fear of running into an offshore reef. Conscious of the peril, he would start each day at dawn. Luckily for him, there was an inlet (Manasquan) only forty miles, or seven or eight hours of sailing, from New York Harbor, so that he would have

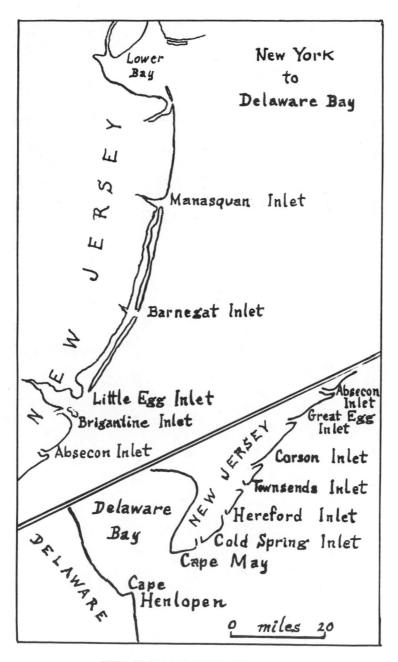

New York
to
Delaware Bay

NEW YORK TO DELAWARE BAY

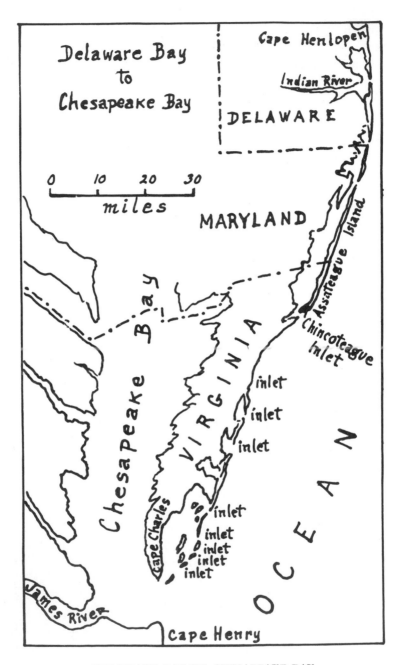

DELAWARE BAY TO CHESAPEAKE BAY

reached it by midafternoon. There can be little doubt that he put in there for the night. There was another inlet (Barnegat) twenty-four miles farther south.

South of Barnegat was Long Beach Island, which took him three hours to sail by, since it was seventeen miles long. This was the first of the large *eyrar*. An *eyrr* (singular) is defined as "a sand or gravel bank," "a spit," "a small tongue of land running into the sea." It was a geographical feature of supreme importance to mariners on a coastal voyage because behind such a tongue of land they could have safe night anchorage. Karlsefni and his men called Long Beach and other similar islands by the seemingly contradictory expression—*miklar eyrar*—"large small sandbanks." They meant long narrow sandbanks. The length was beyond all viking experience with *eyrar* in Iceland and Greenland.

From the southern end of Long Beach Island, it was only sixty-five miles to Cape May and so into Delaware Bay. From Delaware Bay it was only about twenty-five miles to an inlet at the north end of Assateague Island. This island was the longest of the *eyrar*, thirty miles long. From the south end of it Karlsefni had only sixty-five miles, much of it through inland waterways, to go to Cape Charles and the inland water entrance to Chesapeake Bay. In all probability he sailed through Smith Island Bay to Cape Charles, and thus from the shelter of that inland waterway found himself in the broad Chesapeake. In telling the story years later he   **K 19** naturally thought of the inland waterway traversed on the last day of sailing southward as essentially part of the region of the bay.

Karlsefni found large sandbanks where one could enter only at   **K 20** flood tide.   **K 21**

In sailing down the coasts of New Jersey, Delaware, Maryland, and Virginia, Karlsefni found plenty of inlets. After Barnegat, there was one for every two or three hours of sailing, except for the length of the longest island. Most of the inlets were, as the saga describes, so shallow—one or two feet at mean tide—that viking ships with a three-and-a-half-foot draft, could enter only at flood tide. Even with the ocean level two-and-a-half feet higher in Karlsefni's time, the tidal flow into and out of an inlet would tend to create shallows of approximately the same depth of water as now.

An ocean storm might change the depth of the entrance to an inlet, but there would be a tendency for silting and tides to bring a return to the normal condition. The sand had been there for thousands of years. The flow of a river would force a channel. Today of course there are dredged channels.

K 22   He entered a river there and called it *Hóp*. A *hóp* is a tidal inlet, and the word was applicable to a river as far in as the tide reached.

What river did Karlsefni ascend? The question does not remain long unanswered.

The mouth of the James River is invitingly opposite the entrance to the Chesapeake. Karlsefni ascended that river, for the one and only site which meets all the geographical requirements for his Hóp is up the James.

The Geological Survey map called the Westover quadrangle of Virginia shows the site—the shores of Tar Bay and Coggins Point eastward to Powell Creek—on the south side of a broad east-west reach of the James River.

An interesting notation on the Westover quadrangle is that directly across the river from the postulated Karlsefni area is "Berkeley," birthplace of William Henry Harrison, a man who rose to the Presidency of the United States by being more successful than Karlsefni in fighting Indians.

On the land at Hóp they found fields of self-sown wheat in
K 23   the lowlands and vines on the hills. Every brook was full of fish.
K 24   The brook that flows into Tar Bay on the Coggins Point side of the bay is a mile long. The principal dwellings of Karlsefni's followers were near the mouth of that brook.

Coggins Point is sixty-five miles from the ocean as the crow flies, and fifty miles from the mouth of the James River. By the winding turns of the river it is ten miles farther. The range of tide now in the Westover reach of the river is two and four-tenths feet. The water there is now fresh. The James is brackish only up to about fifteen miles downstream from Coggins Point. In Karlsefni's day, when the ocean level was about two and one-half feet higher, the water at Coggins Point may have been brackish, or it may have been salt at flood tide and fresh at ebb.

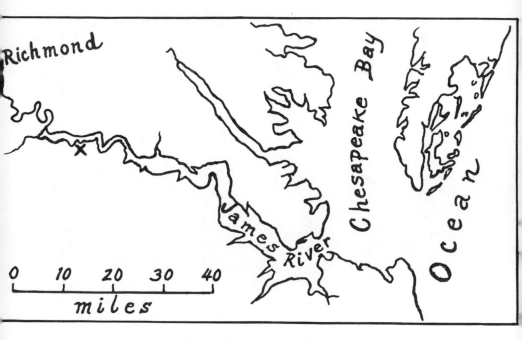

**X—SITE THAT MEETS ALL REQUIREMENTS
FOR KARLSEFNI'S HÓP**

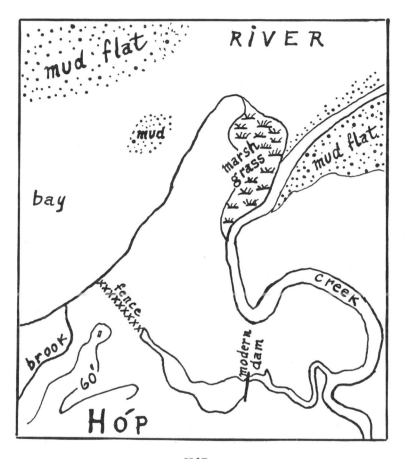

HÓP

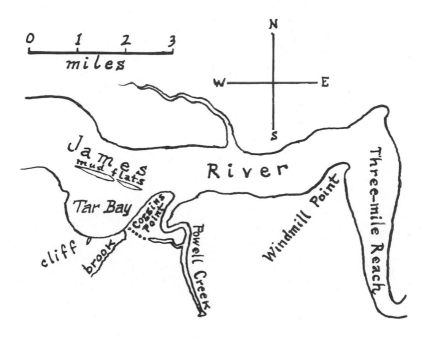

KARLSEFNI'S WINTER CAMPSITE AT HÓP

Near the campsite were extensive mud flats at the mouth of Powell Creek and flanking the river channel out beyond Tar Bay. A flatfish like the summer flounder, by vibrating its fins, digs a hollow in a muddy bottom, wherein it lies at rest. Mud settles on top of it and covers most of its body. The vikings knew of this flatfish habit, and they would dig pits in the mud which would remain as pools when the tide fell; thus they accommodated and caught the fish.

They caught "holy fish" *(helgir fiskar)*. Holy fish were so called because they were supposed to be the proper fish to be eaten on holy days. We might call them Friday fish.

Karlsefni and his men found many animals of all sorts in the woods. They remained there half a month and enjoyed themselves, without keeping watch, for there seemed to be no necessity for posting guards. They had their livestock with them.

Early one morning when they looked out they saw a great many skin boats, with staves being swung about on the boats with a noise like flails.

The downstream current at ebb tide in the midchannel of the James off Coggins Point flows at four or five knots. One can barely row against it. Indians paddling up river would hug the riverbank to take advantage of upstream eddies, and this is why the boats of the savages advancing up river were near enough to Coggins Point for the vikings to hear the sounds of the "staves."

The staves, or whatever they were, were being revolved in the direction in which the sun moves, clockwise. And so when Karlsefni asked, "What is the meaning of this?" Snorri, his partner, guessed it was a peace signal. Any Norseman who had observed the summer sun knew in what direction the sun appears to move—in a circle not far off the horizontal from north to east to south to west. A familiar order often given to a sailor is to coil a rope "with the sun." A man with a stave or any object in his right hand which he revolves horizontally in this clockwise direction could not project that object forward as a weapon except by an awkward overhead backhanded stroke. Clockwise motion was not a threatening or inimical gesture. A counterclockwise horizontal swinging of any object with the right hand moving forward would appear hostile.

K 25
K 26

K 27

K 28

Interpreting the "with-the-sun" movement correctly, Snorri Thorbrandsson said, "Let us show them a white shield." This they did, and the strangers rowed toward them and stared with wonderment at those they saw before them, and then came up on the land. They were swarthy and ill-looking men, and had ugly hair on their heads. They had large eyes and broad cheeks.

The Skraelings seemed to the vikings to be "swarthy" with "ugly hair." This is the first description of American Indians by Europeans. Racial revulsion was in it. The vikings liked yellow or red hair. They were realistically observant in noting "broad cheeks," but less realistic in noting "large eyes." The Skraelings "stared with wonderment," that is, with eyes wide open with astonishment. Surely at that time the eyes of the vikings were as wide open, but the vikings were not observing their own eyes.

The Skraelings stayed there for a while staring at those they saw before them, and then they rowed away southward beyond the point.   K 29

From Coggins Point, Karlsefni's men could see Windmill Point, around which the Skraelings paddled out of sight "southward" into "Three Mile Reach." Windmill Point is only four miles to the east, near enough for canoes to be seen when rounding it.

At the Karlsefni campsite there had to be a place where viking ships could be brought ashore. There were two such places: one at the shore of Tar Bay near the mouth of the brook, the other on the banks of the branch of Powell Creek which came in almost to Tar Bay. That branch was fifty to a hundred feet wide.[8]

Karlsefni's party had built their shelters above the water, some near it and some farther off, and there they spent that winter. There came no snow at all.   K 30

[8] Mr. William Lee Broaddus, a resident on Coggins Point, kindly guided my companion, Rick Mearns, and me to the dam which now makes that branch a lake. Mr. Walter Mooers, one of two men who built the dam to make a fishing lake, told us the area of the lake had been a rice field in 1943, with a spillway. They built the present dam to raise the water level in the lake four feet. The lake is now normally six feet above the creek. It has an eight-foot depth in the former channel, no doubt much silted in from what it was originally, when tidal.

The emphasis on "no snow" was a conscious contrast with the terrible experience of the preceding winter. So also was the statement that their livestock lived by grazing.

K 31

With domestic animals on the ships, there was a most pressing need to get the livestock on land as soon as possible. Karlsefni sought a place where in a few hours his men could erect a short fence which would confine the livestock within a sizable area containing suitable grass for grazing. A remarkable feature of the Coggins Point terrain is that a fence only seven hundred fifty feet long from the west end of the branch of Powell Creek, which is now a lake, to the shore of Tar Bay would enclose the entire area bounded by Tar Bay, the river, Powell Creek, and the branch of the creek. That area is over three hundred fifty acres. For each acre Karlsefni's men had to build only about two feet of fence! That was better than at Leif's Shelters where they had to build a fence a thousand feet long to enclose two hundred fifty acres—four feet of fence for each acre. History tends to repeat. During the siege of Petersburg, the Union army enclosed cattle in the Coggins Point–Tar Bay area with a fence along the same line where Karlsefni's men built one.

K 32

Early one morning in the spring they again saw a great many skin boats rowing around the point. From near the mouth of the mile-long brook on the shore of Tar Bay, Karlsefni's men saw the boats rounding Coggins Point. They were mistaken in thinking the boats of the savages in the James River were skin boats. They were dugouts. But Karlsefni and his men never had an opportunity to examine them.

K 33

The boats rowing around the point looked like coals flung out beyond the bay, and staves were being swung about on every boat. The map shows how Tar Bay fits into the story.

The staves were again being revolved clockwise, and this second time Karlsefni's men again showed white shields, and the Skraelings and they met and began to trade. Those people especially wished red cloth, for which they exchanged fur skins and all-gray skins. They wished also to purchase swords and spears, but Karlsefni and Snorri refused them. In return for unblemished skins, the Skraelings would accept a span length of red cloth and bind it around their heads. When Karlsefni's people began to run short of cloth, they ripped it into pieces so narrow that none were broader than a finger, but the Skraelings even then gave as much for it as before, or more. This continued until Karlsefni's bull ran out of the woods bellowing loudly. This terrified the Skraelings so that they ran out to their boats and rowed away southward along the shore.

Nothing was seen of them for three weeks, but at the end of that time, such a great number of Skraeling boats appeared that they looked like a floating stream, and their staves were all revolving in a direction opposite to the course of the sun, and they were all whooping with great outcries. Then Karlsefni's men took red shields and held them up to view. The Skraelings leaped from their boats, and they met and fought. There was a heavy shower of missiles, for the Skraelings had war slings. Karlsefni observed that the Skraelings had on the end of a pole a great ball-shaped object **K 34** almost the size of a sheep's belly, and nearly as black in color, and this they flung from the pole up on the land above Karlsefni's men. It made such a terrifying noise where it struck the ground that great fear seized Karlsefni and all with him, so that they thought only of flight and of making their escape up along the riverbank. It seemed to them that the Skraelings were driving at them from all sides, and so they fled toward a most advantageous high ground. **K 35**

The first positioning in the battle between the vikings and the Skraelings who landed on the shore of Tar Bay was near the mouth of the brook. That was the only landing place, for only there was land that did not rise sharply from the water. Fighting there, Karlsefni's men had a sixty-foot bluff in back of them. When a noise from the bluff above and behind them caused them to believe that they were surrounded, they panicked. We know with practical certainty the nature of the "ball-shaped object almost the size of a sheep's belly, and nearly as black" which the Skraelings flung from the end of a pole to the ground above the vikings. It was a hornet's nest, which Indians used as an effective weapon. They would obtain a hornet's nest by tying an animal skin around it at night. To use it in battle they had only to loose the tie and fling it from the end of a flexible pole. When the hornet's nest was flung over the heads of Karlsefni's men, none of the vikings was near enough to learn what it was by being stung, forty feet being a safe distance. But it was the noise when the insect bomb struck the ground which caused panic. The high-pitched shrill made by four thousand enraged hornets sounded like more of the Skraelings' war cries. The increasing volume of the sound as more hornets flew out of the broken nest made Karlsefni's men think Skraelings were closing in upon them from above and behind them. It was easy for them to imagine that canoes of other Skraelings had come up the river from the east and into the creek and its western branch and so to the rear of them.

A local echo was also a factor in the vikings' panic and flight. Mr. Augustus Robbins, Jr., of Hopewell wrote me on July 6, 1967: "Bill Broaddus and I went down to Coggins Point yesterday afternoon and there is definitely an echo at the point below Tom McGonicle's house, where you think the Indians landed in their canoes to attack the vikings. We tried our best war whoops along that sandy shore, from the mouth of the little brook, southward for 100 feet, with one of us back 40, 60, and 100 feet up the bluff, and the vikings could easily have thought the Indians were behind them to the north. All the echoes seemed to come down the ravine from the northeast—which would be to the left of the Indians on the shore and to the right of the vikings, no matter where they stood on the bank."

The sensible line of retreat for Karlsefni and his men was close along the riverbank up the slope toward the top of the bluffs to the west. Those bluffs are at the middle of the Tar Bay shore, about two-thirds of a mile upriver from the mouth of the brook. Karlsefni's men ran toward them up the long slope, with the pursuers at their heels. The top of the highest of the bluffs toward which they fled is 120 feet above the water, and is the highest ground for miles around. Its summit is a rectangle with the small end toward the shore. There is a steep drop to the shore at its northern end, and it is flanked on both of its long sides by ravines 100 feet deep. Only at its southern and somewhat narrower end could attackers come to it on the level. It was an admirable defensive position where Karlsefni and his men could hope to hold their own even if attacked from all sides.

At the critical moment of panic, Freydis, doughty daughter of Erik, "came out," presumably from a house near the battle site. Seeing that Karlsefni and his men were retreating, she tried to shame them, and called out, "Why run from these wretched creatures, such worthy men as you are? It looks to me as though you might slaughter them like cattle. If I had a weapon, I believe I would fight better than any of you!" She failed to halt their precipitate flight, for they heeded her not. However, she saved the day. She wanted to join the men, but fell behind, for she was pregnant. Nevertheless, she followed them into the woods, the Skraelings pursuing her. In front of her she found a dead man, Thorbrand Snorrason, whose skull had been split by a flat stone. His drawn sword lay beside him. Freydis took it up and prepared to wield it in self-defense. Then the Skraelings came at her, and she uncovered her breast and slapped it with the naked sword.

By baring her breast, she made an appeal to male gallantry, to which American Indians were not immune. The slapping of her breast with the sword, a gesture of defiance sometimes used by Scandinavians before battle, was unfamiliar to the Indians of the Chesapeake country; it appeared to them irrational, and Indians had immense veneration for the mentally ill. Also, they had a profound religious respect for women.[8] Thinking the gesture of Freydis a potent magic, the Skraelings fled. They ran back down to their boats and paddled away. Karlsefni and his men joined Freydis and praised her courage.

They could do no less. But being men who had been put to shame by a woman, Karlsefni and his ship soldiers were unwilling

[9] Thomas Hariot, Oxford tutor to Sir Walter Raleigh and geographer to the second expedition to Virginia, in *A Brief and True Report of the New Found Land of Virginia,* published in 1588, wrote of the religious belief of the Indians in Virginia: "For mankind they say a woman was made first, which by the working of one of the gods, conceived and brought forth children: And in such sort they say they had their beginning."

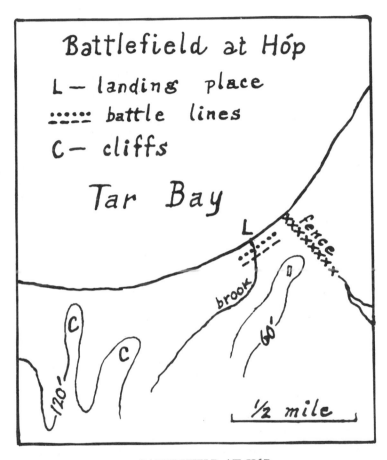

BATTLEFIELD AT HÓP

L—Landing place
Battle line
C—Cliffs toward which vikings fled

to admit that their participation in the battle had ended in igno-
minious panic. Masculine ego required a prideful boast, and so, in
their later telling they said inaccurately that "they came to certain
cliffs where they resisted fiercely." The Skraelings never reached
the highest of the bluffs, and neither did Karlsefni and his men,
unless they continued to panic after the Skraelings had fled to
their boats. It was just after the vikings began retreating up the
slope toward the bluffs that the heroism or good luck of Freydis
ended the battle.

Although Karlsefni's men had been outnumbered, only two
were slain, while many of the Skraelings were. They now returned
to their shelters, bound up their wounds, and discussed what sort
of men that great host had been that seemed to swoop down upon
them from the land side. They realized that there could have been
but one host, the one which came from the boats, and that the
other had been an illusion.

The sound of the hornets created the "illusion" of more savages. In the after-battle discussion as to the nature of whatever it
was that had caused Karlsefni and his men to imagine that they
were about to be set upon by another band of savages from the
rear, masculine conceit impelled them to try to find a good reason
to justify their panic. Unable to find a good reason, they were content to call it an "illusion," which term came close to implying
something supernatural, beyond their power to overcome. There
were those, however, who labeled it a "self-deception." This was
the more imperative in that they had been saved by a woman. But
while they went only so far as masculine ego would let them go in
self-appraisal, they were generous in their praise of Freydis.

During the battle the Skraelings had found a dead man, and
his ax lying beside him. They had taken up the ax and had struck
at a tree, all and sundry trying it, and it seemed to them a treasure,
for it bit well. Later on, one of them had taken it and had struck
at a slab of rock so that the ax broke; then they thought it useless,
since it would not split stone, and threw it away.

The breaking of the viking ax when a Skraeling used it to
strike a slab of rock fits in with the fact that the only place in the
region where rocks are to be found is along the shore of Tar Bay.

There, where the river cut into the bluffs, it exposed marl that lay deep under sandstone. Since there are so few rocks in the area, those which may have been used to mark the grave of Thorbrand Snorrason were probably carried away to be used in building foundations in colonial times.

If firearms had been invented and in the hands of the vikings, it is probable that Karlsefni's attempted settlement on the James River would have accomplished what the Jamestown Colony did. The battle at Hóp, though not fought to a conclusion, was decisive, for it led Karlsefni to abandon his attempt to establish a permanent colony in the great land called Vinland—a decision that discouraged the Norsemen generally.

THORFINN KARLSEFNI COMPLETES HIS EXPLORATIONS

It was obvious to Karlsefni and his companions that they were not invulnerable against the Skraelings. They would have liked to remain at Hóp, but realized they could do so only with fear and warfare. Their decision not to continue to attempt a permanent settlement in Vinland was compelled not only by the nature of the Skraelings but fully as much by their own character.

They sailed out of the river and back northward along the ocean shore, and when they put in at one of the inlets they found five Skraelings clad in skins, asleep. Beside them were containers of animal-marrow mixed with blood. Assuming that these five were exiled from their tribe, Karlsefni's men slew them. It was a lame excuse for the killing.

Later they came to a headland (the Atlantic Highlands of New Jersey) where there were many animals. They found an area that looked like a huge cake of dung, and took it as evidence that animals wintered there. Very likely it was a sea gulls' nesting area. Soon afterward—a short distance farther—they came to the expedition's headquarters at Stream Fjord, where they had everything they needed.

Next in the telling is an admitted uncertainty: "According to the telling of some, Bjarni [Grimolfsson] and Gudrid had remained behind there [at Current Island] with ten times ten men and had not gone farther, while Karlsefni and Snorri [Thorbrandsson] had sailed south with forty men, tarrying at Hóp no longer than two months and returning that same summer."

The past perfect tense of "had not gone" and "had sailed" indicates that "that same summer" was the sailing season that preceded the winter at Hóp. It is inconceivable that Karlsefni and Snorri would have returned with only one ship to spend two months at Hóp after they had previously panicked in battle there.

An interesting probability is opened by the words "according to the telling of some." We know that Karlsefni was determined to extend the exploration of Vinland as far as he could. The saga's words, "tarrying at Hóp no longer than two months," seem to be an interpolation to explain how Karlsefni and Snorri spent part of their time during that preceding sailing season, in the year 1012. In the first two months of that season Thorfinn had time to establish the settlement at Hóp and explore the upper reaches of the James River to the point where he saw mountains (about which the reader will learn later in this section). Satisfied that the settlement was in good working order, it could be that he and Snorri did not tarry at Hóp "that same summer" but with their one ship "sailed south," and returned to Hóp "that same summer." This further sailing would have been down the coast and no doubt

K 36

around the tip of Florida into the Gulf of Mexico. Allowing for three months in that exploration, they could have returned to Hóp well before the end of the sailing season and spent the winter there.

That third winter in Vinland, some members of the expedition had remained on Current Island, a safe place for Gudrid and her child. Those at Current Island kept the camp as a base to which Thorhall and his nine men were expected to return, and to which Thorfinn and others who had gone to Hóp would report back. The folk on Current Island no doubt busied themselves with harvesting the crops they had planted there. Seeds for crops which the expedition had brought for a permanent colony and seeds from the resulting crops had to be planted each growing season. The food supply for the expedition was a major problem to which some members of the expedition necessarily devoted themselves, while others went exploring.

After the people who had wintered at Hóp came back to Current Island (to Stream Fjord because the island was at the mouth of the fjord), which they reached early in the sailing season—only a few days of sailing from Hóp—Karlsefni did essentially the same thing he was said to have done the preceding sailing season—he went exploring "with one ship." This time his exploring was with a special urgency. As responsible leader he was concerned over Thorhall the Huntsman's failure to return, and of course he did not yet know what had happened to Thorhall, who had gone to explore the coast of Vinland beyond Keel Cape. Karlsefni had seen with his own eyes that Markland was an immense land, and he had seen that Vinland was also immense. Leif Erikson had a fixed idea that there were three new lands which he had named, one of them a large island. But Karlsefni was now asking himself: Are there three? Or only two? There is the great island, which Leif named Helluland and Karlsefni's men called Biarney. How about the others? Were they two separate lands, or were they all one? Was Markland a part of Vinland? Karlsefni would now find out.

While most of the men remained behind, Karlsefni sailed

northward around Keel Cape and then bore off westward with
land on the port side. It was all one wilderness there with almost
no clearing anywhere. When they had traveled a long way they
came to a river which flowed out of the land from east to west.

K 37

K 38

There are only two west-flowing rivers in all the Atlantic sea-
board of North America. Both of them are on the west side of
Nova Scotia. One is Annapolis River with its outlet at Digby Gut.
The other is Apple River north of Cape Chignecto.

K 39

They steered into the mouth of the river and lay to by its
southern bank.

·If they entered Annapolis River, they would have chosen the
safe anchorage off the south shore at the site of the present town of
Digby. If they entered the mouth of Apple River, they had no
choice but to lay to by the southern bank, for only on that side is
there high ground and depth of water at ebb for them to have anchored there.

Whichever of the two west-flowing rivers it was, Karlsefni had
crossed the Bay of Fundy. This was a fifty-mile crossing, though
only half of it was out of sight of land. It was, however, a gap between the coast of Vinland and what Karlsefni knew was part of
Markland. That gap would have to be explored before he could
know positively whether Markland and Vinland were joined together and were both parts of one great land. To complete his exploration he had to investigate that gap.

While his ship lay to by the southern bank of the river, some
of the crew told a garbled story of the death of Thorvald Erikson
six years before. It went thus: One morning Karlsefni saw on the
far side of the clearing a glittering speck, and he and his men
shouted at it. It stirred. It was a one-footed creature. It came
bounding down toward where the ship lay.

Thorvald, the son of Erik the Red, sat at the helm. The one-
footed creature shot an arrow into his intestines. Thorvald pulled
out the arrow and said, "We have found here a rich country, for
there is much fat around my paunch." Thorvald died of this
wound soon afterward.

Then the one-footed creature ran off to the north, and Karlsefni's men raced after it and saw it from time to time, until it

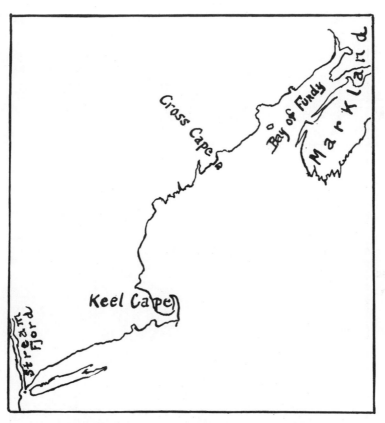

**KARLSEFNI "WITH ONE SHIP" SAILED TO EXPLORE
THE GAP BETWEEN CROSS CAPE AND MARKLAND**

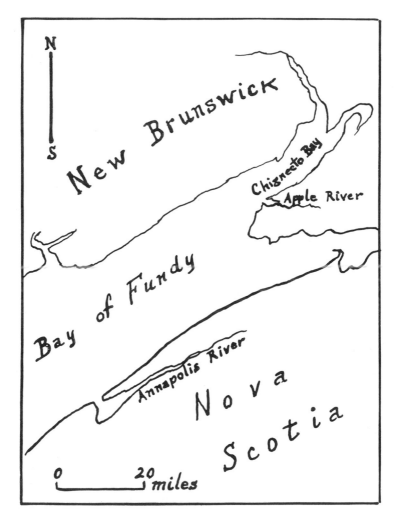

TWO WEST-FLOWING RIVERS

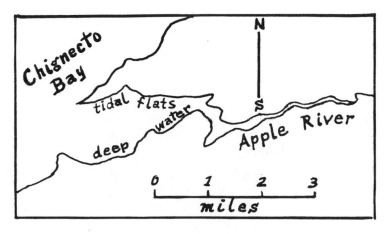

APPLE RIVER

hopped into a bay. Then Karlsefni and his followers turned back. One of the men recited this ditty:

> They say they chased   a creature resembling
> A one-footed man,   down to the shore;
> A fantastic freak,   it had strength to course
> Beyond a peak—   Hear it, Karlsefni![10]

K 40   With thoughts of the death of Thorvald Erikson, they sailed away to the north.

From whichever river, Karlsefni sailed north into Chignecto Bay and far enough into Cumberland Basin and also into Shepody Bay and into the Petitcodiac River to make certain that the land of Markland was continuous with Vinland.

On their return toward Stream Fjord, they thought they
K 41   could see Uniped Land, the Land of the One-Footers. In other words, they believed they had caught sight of the mountains of Mt. Desert Island in the distance, where one Skraeling had fled to the shore and "beyond a peak" and Thorvald Erikson had been killed. They recalled that Thorstein Erikson had wanted to recover the body of his brother Thorvald, and now they might do so, but they decided not to risk their lives any longer.

Following the coast westward and southward on his final re-
K 42   turn to Stream Fjord, Karlsefni saw mountains which he and his men now discovered. These were distinct from the mountains of Mt. Desert, which had been discovered by Thorvald Erikson years before. The mountains now discovered were the Presidential Range of the White Mountains of New Hampshire.

Karlsefni concluded that these mountains and the mountains
K 43   of Hóp formed one mountain chain.
K 44   The distance from the Watchung Mountains of New Jersey

[10] This ditty shows that the vikings associated the day Thorvald died with the idea of a man who fled from them on one foot. The words "they say" and "hear it" suggest that the ditty had been composed years before and was now being recited to Karlsefni. "They chased . . . a one-footed man down to the shore" does not apply to the situation in which Karlsefni and his men found themselves down at the shore of the south bank of the west-flowing river, whence obviously they could not chase a creature that "ran off to the north."

(visible from Current Island in New York Harbor) to the mountains seen from far off the Maine Coast is a geographical observation of great importance. That distance laid off to the southwest from New York Harbor shows what Karlsefni and his men believed to be the approximate position of the mountains of Hóp. That distance extends to the mouth of the James River and in an arc to Scottsville on the James. The vikings did not have latitude and longitude. They did have dead reckoning, which on voyages in sight of land, along coasts, and in rivers, could be surprisingly accurate. Young George Washington, canoeing down a portion of the Ohio River from Fort Pitt, estimated 113 miles, where the modern pilot chart makes it 112 miles. In a distance of about three hundred miles, the dead reckoning by Karlsefni and his men would most certainly be within twenty miles of correct.

The evidence is firm that the mountains of Hóp were the mountains of the Blue Ridge seen from up the James River near the site of Scottsville or beyond. They could not have been the mountains that could be sighted from up the Rappahannock sixty-five miles to the north of Scottsville, or up the Potomac 115 miles to the north, or those in the Carolinas more than a hundred miles to the south.

Karlsefni concluded correctly that the mountains of Hóp, those around Stream Fjord, and the newly discovered mountains seen from off the coast as they were returning to Keel Cape formed "one mountain chain." In the course of completing the explorations he thus discovered the Appalachian mountain chain.

He and his men returned to Stream Fjord, and spent a third winter there—their fourth winter in Vinland.

The men quarreled frequently because of the women. Those without wives sought to possess the married women and this caused the greatest trouble.

The quarreling over wives suggests a considerable number of women. Our assumption of about five to each ship is probably fairly close. Karlsefni's son was by no means the only child born in the expedition. The pregnant and breast-slapping Freydis no doubt gave birth to a child in Vinland. During the four years in

Vinland, there were probably as many as a dozen children born there, though Karlsefni's son Snorri is the only one named in the telling.

Snorri was three winters old when in the next sailing season all the ships at Stream Fjord set sail for Greenland. The ships did not sail in consort, perhaps because of ill feeling engendered by squabbles between the bachelors and the married men.

The expedition had been reduced by the departure of Thorhall's ship and by two deaths at Hóp, so there remained 148 men. Births no doubt more than made up for any other deaths there may have been among the men and women; and so in addition to 148 men, there could have been twenty-five or thirty women, and ten or more children—a total of approximately 185 persons to be crowded into five ships. If Karlsefni's and Bjarni Grimolfsson's ships each carried forty men and five women, and Thorvard's small ship at a squeeze carried thirty-five, then sixty persons may have been carried by the other two ships, Thorvald's and the one that had been Thorbjorn Vifilsson's.

There is no mention of the homeward voyages of the two last-named ships. Thorvard's ship made the voyage safely, for a year later in Greenland he and Freydis were preparing their ship for another voyage to Vinland. Let us note what the saga said of them and their marriage: "Freydis . . . was very proud, but Thorvard was a little man. She had been given to him principally for the sake of his wealth. The people in Greenland were heathen at that time." The teller obviously sought to persuade his listeners that Christianity had forever saved people from ill-suited and mercenary marriages. By inference, Christian marriages were ideally happy.

One of the ships that sailed from New York Harbor for Greenland met with disaster. What happened is a story of the extraordinary heroism of its master Bjarni Grimolfsson.

Bjarni Grimolfsson's ship was blown off course into the Greenland Sea (Irish Sea, in one variant). They found themselves in waters infested with maggots, and before they knew it the ship was riddled beneath them and began to sink. They discussed what they should do. They had an after-boat which had been covered with seal-tar. Men say that the worms will not pierce timber that has been so covered. Most of the crew said that as many of them should get into this boat as it could hold. But they found that the boat would hold no more than half the crew. Bjarni then said, "The men who are to go into the boat should be chosen by lot, not by rank." But all the men tried to get into the boat. The boat, however, would not hold them all, and so they adopted Bjarni's plan of drawing lots. Bjarni drew a lot to go into the boat with nearly half of the men. But when they were settled in the boat and about to cast off, a young Icelander who had remained in the ship and who had come out from Iceland with Bjarni, said, "Bjarni, are you going to leave me here?" "It must be," Bjarni replied. "That is not what you promised my father when I left Iceland with you. You told him that we should share the same fate." "So be it," said Bjarni. "We will exchange places. You come into the boat and I will get back into the ship; for I perceive you are eager to live."

Bjarni then boarded the ship and the boy took his place in the boat. And the boat sailed away until it came to Dublin in Ireland and there they told this tale. It is generally believed that Bjarni and the men with him were drowned in the worm-infested sea, for they were never heard of again.

We wonder what the crew thought of the youth who got Bjarni to choose to die to save him. Nowadays, the captain of a ship would not participate in a live-or-die drawing of lots. He would insist upon being the last to leave a sinking vessel. But Bjarni was an honorable viking and as such his word was sacred. He was caught by his promise to the boy's father, by his own sense of responsibility thus awakened, and by the Norse tradition of generosity and the noble gesture. However belated, his heroism is one of the greatest stories of the sea.

When Thorfinn Karlsefni and Snorri Thorbrandsson sailed safely into Eriksfjord, they had in Leif Erikson an eager listener to what they had to tell of their experiences at Leif's Shelters. But a description of the terrible winter in Stream Fjord, which Thorfinn and Snorri had at second hand from the folk of the other ships, was something that Leif would not be happy to hear. Leif probably closed his ears to it or showed that he would prefer to have it hushed up. It was a story that almost seemed to give the lie to what he had told of his own winter in Vinland, and what his brother Thorvald's men had corroborated. Leif so obviously did not want to hear of anything that so flatly contradicted what he believed to be the nature of Vinland that Thorfinn no doubt felt it would be tactless to press the telling upon his host. Thorfinn probably did not tell Leif why he had sailed much farther south in Vinland, and may not even have told him that he had done so.

Later, when Thorfinn got to his own home in Iceland, he told of his return voyage from Stream Fjord to Greenland, in the course of which he and his men seized two Skraeling boys in Markland, who "said there was a land over against their land, the inhabitants of which went about in white garments and uttered loud cries and carried sticks with patches of cloth attached. People believed this must be White Men's Land [*hvitra manna land*]."

All references to White Men's Land in Norse literature may have stemmed from this sentence. Sparse as it is, Thorfinn's telling of his seizing two Skraelings boys in Markland reveals the route by which he sailed to Greenland. He was obviously following the sailing direction of Bjarni Herjulfsson. It was somewhere inside the Gulf of St. Lawrence on the northwestern side of the gulf or of the Strait of Belle Isle that he seized the boys, for when the boys had been taught the Norse language, they told of the land that "lay over against their land." The geography that fits here is that the land "over against" theirs was Newfoundland. Several evidences point to Newfoundland as the land the vikings thought of as White Men's Land or "Great Ireland." In all probability, the white garments were priests' robes, the loud cries were chants, and the sticks with cloth attached were banners in a religious procession.

Karlsefni was later misquoted as having said he spent his last winter in Greenland with Erik the Red. Erik the Red had been dead nine years. What Karlsefni actually said was no doubt that he spent the winter at Erik the Red's, that is, at Erik's family home.

THE TELLING
OF FREYDIS

Freydis and Thorvard sailed their ship into Einarsfjord to their home at Gardar, perhaps at the same time that Thorfinn and Snorri sailed into Eriksfjord to Brattahlid. They had much to tell to Leif Erikson, and during the telling, folk in the fjords watched anxiously for Bjarni Grimolfsson's ship. But days went by, weeks went by, and Bjarni's ship did not come. Everyone feared it had been lost.

Thorfinn expected to spend only one winter at Brattahlid, and to leave Greenland in the spring. Circumstances changed his plans. For that same summer a ship arrived from Norway under the command of two Icelandic brothers, Helgi and Finnboge.

129

Their coming caused much new talk about voyaging to Vinland, not to establish a settlement, but to procure timber, fur skins, and other products. Men said such an enterprise would bring profit and esteem. Indeed it would, for a single shipload from Vinland could make one wealthy in Greenland, where no trees grew large enough to supply wood for furniture, to say nothing of shipbuilding and ship repairs. Now Freydis in Gardar had heard of the brothers' arrival, and she came to Brattahlid to have a talk with Helgi and Finnboge. Both Leif and Thorfinn welcomed her gladly, for Leif was proud of his sister, and Thorfinn felt grateful to her for the part she had played in the battle at Hóp.

Freydis invited the brothers to voyage in their ship to Vinland in consort with her husband's ship, each ship to carry the same number of men, and the brothers to go halves with her on all the profits that might be obtained. They agreed to this.

Since the ship of Thorvard and Freydis and the larger ship of the brothers would be going to Vinland the following spring to get timber and furs, Thorfinn foresaw very profitable trading when they returned the year after. He probably still had some goods in Leif's warehouse with which he could take part advantageously in that trading. There was also the question of handling goods belonging to his fellow Icelanders, Bjarni Grimolfsson and Thorhall Gamlason, who it was feared had been lost at sea. And so Thorfinn asked Leif if he might remain for another winter, which would be his third winter at Brattahlid. Leif was delighted, for he was glad to have company. He had been used to a large family, but now he had with him only his widowed mother and perhaps his thirteen-year-old son.

The understanding between Freydis and the Icelandic brothers that their ships would sail in consort seemed to Thorfinn very wise, and he may have himself suggested it, because of the disappearance of Bjarni's ship, which had not been in consort. And so the two ships of Thorvard and Freydis and of Helgi and Finnboge together put to sea bound for Vinland.

Immediately after they sailed, word got around that Freydis had violated her agreement with the brothers. She had taken into her husband's ship not thirty, but thirty-five men. She had the extra men smuggled aboard dressed as women, and she had concealed them, so that the brothers were not aware of the deception. Thorfinn wondered why she had done this. Freydis was a large woman—like a man in strength. Why should she have chosen to be the only woman in her husband's ship? Was she that jealous of her husband? But no! That little man Thorvard could not be the reason. If Thorfinn wondered whether Leif knew why she had not taken any women with her, he probably felt that if he asked he would embarrass Leif.

The winter passed. Then word was brought to Brattahlid that the ship of Helgi and Finnboge had been sighted. Observers said the ship was loaded to capacity. But there was only one ship. The ship of Thorvard and Freydis was not with it. Deeply concerned for his sister, Leif feared that she had been lost. Then word came that folk on shore had seen Freydis on board the ship of the brothers. And so when their ship came to land, Leif and Thorfinn went to meet it. They were surprised to find that Helgi and Finnboge were not on board, and that Freydis and Thorvard were in possession of the brothers' ship and had with them only Thorvard's men. Leif and Thorfinn had great curiosity to hear Freydis narrate what had happened, and so she said that when she had told the brothers that Leif had loaned his house in Vinland to her, not to them, in spite of the share-and-share-alike agreement, the brothers built for themselves a hall "farther from the sea on the bank of a lake." **F 1** Early one morning when there was a heavy dew she had walked **F 2** alone to the Icelanders' hall and Finnboge had come out and he **F 3** and she had held a discussion seated on a log that lay against the outside wall of the hall. She had told Finnboge that she desired to trade ships with the brothers, because theirs was a larger ship, and she wanted to get away from Vinland, and Finnboge had agreed to the trade. When Leif and Thorfinn asked her about Helgi and Finnboge, Freydis said, "They stayed behind while we left."

All who heard that Helgi and Finnboge had agreed to trade their larger ship for Thorvard's smaller ship were astonished. How could the brothers let themselves be persuaded to accept such an unfair exchange? Karlsefni knew that his fellow Icelanders Helgi and Finnboge were shrewd merchants who would not lightly have entered into such an uneven trade. It was incredible. There must have been more to it. What could Freydis have given the brothers to compensate them for the difference in size and value between the ships? Karlsefni looked at Freydis. Something he saw in her eyes made him wonder. He looked at her little husband, and wondered not so much, but believed he could guess. In her meeting with Finnboge what did she give or promise to give him? And it seemed even more strange to Karlsefni that Helgi and Finnboge would have chosen to remain in Vinland after they had been warned about the many Skraelings in Vinland and the unwisdom of attempting a permanent settlement in that country. Nevertheless, according to Freydis, Helgi and Finnboge had stayed there, against all the advice everyone had given them.

But the trading at Brattahlid was good, and it took Karlsefni's mind away from his wondering, and the time came for him to say good-bye to Leif.

Leif later said of him, "Now Karlsefni was still there, and had his ship ready for departure, and was waiting for a fair wind. It was said by many that never richer ship sailed from Greenland than the one he steered."

Karlsefni departed from Greenland before anyone there heard what actually had happened in Vinland between Freydis and the brothers. Freydis's story did not ring true but nobody questioned it at first in the excitement of her arrival and the trading that followed. After Karlsefni sailed away, Freydis and Thorvard went back to their home at Gardar, which was in the fjord just to the south of Eriksfjord. Their house had not been molested during all the time they had been in Vinland. They still had the respect of their neighbors. Freydis now resumed her life at home. She and her husband gave great gifts to all the men who had been in their ship. This, as was later learned, was to persuade them to keep their mouths shut. But all the men did not keep silent about what had happened, and after a time the truth began to leak out. The ugliest rumors arose and were so persistent that Leif had to take public cognizance of them. As the leader of the Christians he was compelled to act. He forced a confession out of one of Thorvard's men by torture. The man told of something so dreadful as to seem incredible. And so Leif took another of Thorvard's men and tortured him also into a confession; his account tallied in all points with the first. Leif had two eyewitnesses against his sister. To satisfy himself that there was no mistake, he forced still a third confession, and it was again the same terrible tale. This was the story the men told:

"When Freydis came back to Leif's house, and got into bed, she awakened her husband Thorvard with her cold feet. He asked why she was so chill and wet. She spoke with great rage, 'I have been,' said she, 'to the brothers, to ask to purchase their ship, for I wish to buy the larger ship, and they took it so ill that they struck me and handled me roughly. But you, spineless man that you are, will not avenge my shame or your own! And this I have to learn while I am no longer in Greenland! I shall separate from you unless you avenge this!'

"Unable to endure her upbraidings any longer, he ordered us to get up at once and take our weapons, and this we did. Then we went straightway to the hall of the brothers, and inside, and seized them sleeping and tied them up tightly, and led each one out when he was bound. As he came out, Freydis had each one put to death. Now all the men were slain, and only the women remained, whom no man among us would kill. Then Freydis spoke up, 'Hand me an ax!' And when she had it, she went at the five women, and left them dead.

"After this damnable deed we returned to our own house, and it appeared that Freydis believed everything had worked out well. She spoke as follows to us: 'If it be our lot to return to Greenland, I will take the life of any man who talks about what has happened. What we shall say is that they stayed on here when we left.' "

Leif felt intense moral revulsion. His only consolation was that his houseguest Thorfinn Karlsefni had left before the horrible fact became known.

The crime of Freydis put him in a most embarrassing position. He would have to pass judgment publicly against his sister. What Freydis had done in her wholesale slaying of the Icelanders could cause irreparable damage to the family policy initiated by

Erik the Red and carried out by Leif, of attracting shipmasters from Iceland and abroad so as to ensure adequate trade to supply Greenland with necessities. But with the fear and enmity which the abominable deed of Freydis would arouse among Icelanders, what hope could there be that other great vikings like Karlsefni would bring trading ships into Greenland fjords? After what she had done, what Icelander would trust himself among Greenlanders?

What punishment should he mete out to Freydis and Thorvard? If he should exile them or execute them, folk might think he did it to get possession of their wealth, and their punishment would be quickly heard of abroad and would bring wider attention to their crime. What punishment would cause the least unfavorable talk abroad? What punishment would cause a desirable sort of talk?

Leif no doubt received advice from the priest not to take physical action against Freydis and Thorvard, but to make a moral example of them so that they would be scorned by everyone. It was to let their wrongdoing be their undoing—to use them as a means of showing all Christians how wrongdoing can impoverish. It would be a punishment that would demonstrate that all Greenlanders disapproved of what those two had done.

This was the punishment Leif decreed:

" 'I am not minded,' he said, 'to do that to my sister Freydis which she deserves. But I foretell of her and her husband, that their offspring will thrive but little.' From this it followed that no one thereafter thought them capable of anything but evil."

Their punishment, seemingly soft, placed a moral and economic curse upon them, a boycott against anyone's having any dealings with them and their children. Leif's decree had the effective force of a "door-doom," a primitive form of justice whereby relatives and neighbors gathered in front of a wrongdoer's door, and having questioned witnesses, decided on a penalty which would be enforced by the community. No doubt Freydis and Thorvard died poor.

Leif surely had a glimmering of insight into Freydis's inner motives. He knew she despised the little man her father had made her marry. Leif may have realized that she envied his own luck in bringing home a large shipload of withies and timber and in getting possession also of the timber which Thorer's wrecked ship had left on the skerry. He may have sensed in her an envy of Gudrid who had married a wealthy and handsome Icelander, and he may have suspected that to compensate she may have had lustful feelings toward the Icelander Finnboge. Going to the house of the Icelanders without her husband's knowledge and alone was a questionable thing; asking Finnboge to get up and meet her outside was another questionable thing. Afterward she must have realized that the Icelanders listening inside the door of the house had heard her conversation with Finnboge on the log outside the house. When her husband was awakened by her chilled body and wet feet, she had to give him a report that he would believe. She could not get the larger ship by telling her husband that Finnboge had agreed to trade ships, because it was not the truth, and not only Finnboge but Helgi and all their party would deny it and make her out a liar. And she had reason to fear that to discredit her the Icelanders would say she had tempted Finnboge to make love to her. Adultery was punished by the death of the guilty woman. And so she had to tell her husband that she had been roughly handled. All her frustration in being married to a little man boiled up into rage, and she made her outrageous demand that he avenge her by slaying all the Icelanders.

She did not dare leave any of the Icelanders to testify against her, and she was the only surviving witness to what had happened between her and Finnboge. What she publicly told in Greenland became part of the saga, the substance of her conversation with Finnboge as she stated it, but this is in flat contradiction with what she told her husband as to that conversation, as reported by her husband's men after the crime became known. No one can ever know what was actually said when she sat on the log with Finnboge, or went off with Finnboge into the woods.

With heavy heart Leif Erikson recognized what might be the common fate of all Greenlanders if there were a ban against trade with Greenland. Who could thrive in a country that tolerated a violation of a pledge and the committing of wholesale murder? In deciding that Freydis and Thorvard could not be allowed to thrive, Leif was in part motivated by fear of threatened decline and poverty of everyone in the Greenland Settlements.

Leif had been struck heavy blows in the deaths of his father and both of his brothers, and now his sister was revealed as a woman who had savagely and with intention slaughtered thirty-five people. Leif was the sole surviving male of his father's family. He had little comfort in the son called Thorgils, who would inherit after he was gone. This boy was brought from the Hebrides via Iceland to Greenland, and "there seemed to be something not altogether natural about him before the end came." With a sister capable of naught but evil, and with a misfit son, Leif faced a bleak future. It is supposed that he died about the year 1025, for in that year Thorgils was in charge at Brattahlid.

THORFINN RETURNS
TO ICELAND

Thorfinn was said to have sailed with the most valuable cargo any ship ever carried away from Greenland. The pride of the Greenlanders may have entered into that statement, for they wanted great vikings in Iceland, Norway, the Hebrides, and Ireland to know that trading voyages to Greenland could be very profitable. The statement, however, may have emanated from Icelanders with a condescending attitude toward Greenland.

One saga says Thorfinn sailed to Iceland, and went to his home at Reyniness, but there Gudrid met with mother-in-law trouble, for Thorfinn's mother had a low opinion of her, and "Gudrid was not at their home the first winter." But when Thorfinn's mother perceived that Gudrid was "a very estimable woman [*kvennskorungr mikill,* "great lady"], Gudrid went to his house and they got along kindly together." One variant closes with a brief but boastful naming of three descendants of Karlsefni who were bishops. The ending of the other variant is different, its transcriber having added the genealogy of Karlsefni's descendants down to himself.

The Greenlander's saga tells of a voyage Karlsefni made after the winter at home with his mother in Iceland. He sailed to Norway, and arrived "hale and well-fleshed." There he sold his cargo (*varningr,* "wares"). The next spring when his ship lay waiting at the wharf for a fair wind to return to Iceland, a Southerner, a native of Bremen in Saxonland, bought from Karlsefni his ship's beakhead (*husa snotru*). Karlsefni did not know what wood it was, but it was *mausur,* which came from Vinland.

The full meaning of *husa snotru,* literally "house nose" or "house neat's wood," is not certain. It is generally accepted as meaning the carved figurehead at the prow of his ship that the master of the ship would display above the door or roof of his house when he was not on the ship. The word "neat" implies a cleaner, and Finn Magnusson suggests a broom. Could it be a cleaner in the sense of something that frightened off evil spirits, or a broom that swept away enemies?

The most widely accepted view of *mausur (mösur)* wood is boll maple, the very resistant hard diseased lumps and protrusions on American maple trees, which come in fantastic shapes, some looking like animal heads.

The *Greenlanders' Saga* says Karlsefni sailed back to Skaga Fjord and shored his ship there. He bought Glaumbeiarland, set up his house, and dwelt there the rest of his life. The statement that he "bought Glaumbeiarland" has been challenged by Icelanders, who insist that he lived at Reyniness until his death. He may have bought land at Glaumboer, a few miles from his mother's house at Reyniness; for his son, Snorri Thorfinnson, built the first church at Glaumboer. Halldór Hermannsson said, "All this about Glaumboer being the family home is wrong; in any case it is mentioned nowhere else. As the saga tells us, their home was Reyniness which remained in the possession of the family down to the middle of the thirteenth century."[11]

After Thorfinn died, and his son Snorri married, Gudrid went "abroad" and to the South (pilgrimage to Rome), returned to Iceland, and became a nun. Gudrid was the most widely traveled woman of the eleventh century.

Hermannsson thought Gudrid's trip to Rome apocryphal and her becoming an anchorite an anachronism. Nobody knows. But the sagas have now been proved accurate in respect to the geography of far-off Vinland, and there seems to be no reason for doubting a statement concerning the activities of Gudrid in Iceland and her journeying from Iceland.

In the final words of the Greenlanders' account of the Vinland voyages, the fourteenth-century scribe names Karlsefni as the original teller of the tales. No doubt he was, in Iceland. It is understandable that the saga that originated in Greenland is the one which tells of the Freydis murders, for those murders did not become known even to Leif Erikson until after Karlsefni had left Greenland. But the statement that Karlsefni was the teller of most of the Greenlanders' saga (in Iceland) seems to be corroborated by the fact that it, and not the saga that originated in Iceland, gives in detail what happened to Karlsefni after he went home to Iceland and later journeyed to Norway and back.

We simply do not know what may have been omitted or added from other tales in any of the sagas, except for the revelation of the Freydis murders. The only valid questions therefore are: Who must have been the original teller at any point in a saga? Where was that person when he first told? Anything beyond this, as to which saga or variant is more trustworthy, is supposition that should appeal only to those who enjoy supposition as a form of entertainment.

The *Greenlanders' Saga* says that this saga was told "most exactly of all" by Karlsefni. From this it appears that what we have

---

[11] Hermannsson, *The Problem of Wineland*, p. 45.

in it, except for what Thorvard's men told of Freydis, is what Karl-sefni heard told or himself told in Greenland. What he had to tell of his experiences at Leif's Shelters was of major interest to Leif Erikson, who had intense pride of ownership in his Vinland house, as we know from his always volunteering to "loan" it. As for Karl-sefni's extensive explorations in Vinland beyond Leif's Shelters, these necessarily included the bitter suffering of his followers in Stream Fjord during a severe winter, and would have scored Leif as having given an unreliable description of conditions in Vinland. Thorfinn's kindliness of nature, revealed by his having sensed Leif's sadness at the prospect of a meager Yule feast, no doubt im-pelled him to withhold those larger experiences out of deference to Leif's feelings. Out of courtesy he refrained from telling in the presence of Leif's neighbors what would have discredited and hurt Leif. When he later was at home in Iceland, he told his friends and neighbors of his explorations in Vinland beyond Leif's Shel-ters. Karlsefni's great explorations are given only in the variants of *Eirik's Saga*—tales that must have had their inception in Iceland, in part at least from Karlsefni's own lips.

Hermannsson said perceptively of Thorfinn and of Leif, "The Tale of the Greenlanders explicitly states that its presenta-tion of those events rested upon what Karlsefni told about them. . . . The most appropriate title of it would be *Thorfinns saga karlsefnis*. . . . Few men are more deserving of having a saga bear their names than Karlsefni. He is one of the most engaging characters in the saga literature, and can certainly be counted among the world's great explorers. He was an excellent example of those men who furthered trade and navigation and settled new lands during the Viking Age. He was a man of good stock, en-dowed with an enterprising and adventurous spirit, of peaceful disposition in turbulent times, yet courageous, wise, and judicious, generous with his wealth, and firm in friendship and in love. His wife is no less remarkable. . . . Beside these two, Leif is a shad-owy figure. He doubtless was an intrepid sailor and a brave man, lucky as his nickname indicates, and one who attained fame among the Christians for having brought the faith to the land of his domicile. But otherwise we get no impression of his personality or of his qualities. He is little more than a name to us."[12]

This sounds unfair to Leif Erikson. Was Hermannsson motivated by partiality to Icelanders?

The memory of Vinland was shared by both Leif Erikson and Thorfinn Karlsefni. But Thorfinn knew much more about it. He had the larger memories. Instead of some thirty miles of its coast which were all that Leif had seen,[13] Karlsefni had seen about three thousand miles of it.

[12] Ibid., p. 29.

[13] Sixty miles including what Leif saw in Markland, which was part of Vinland.

KARLSEFNI AND THE
VINLAND MAP OF 1440

In 1965 Yale University Library sponsored and published a Map of 1440 that showed Vinland. This pre-Columbian map[14] corroborates the evidence in the sagas. We do not need the map to verify the sagas; however, it is a welcome addition to our knowledge.

As background for appreciation of the 1440 Map, consider the

---

[14] The Yale Map of Vinland is proved pre-Columbian by many internal evidences of its genuineness, and not only by every test known to experts but also by the discovery in the Latin legend in its upper left corner of medieval cryptography—double acrostics.

records through the centuries from Karlsefni's day. These have been compiled from Gams's *Series Episcoporum Ecclesiae Catholicae,* Ratisbon, 1873; and *Diplomatarium Norvegicaum,* vol. 17B, Christiania, 1913.

1010	The Karlsefni Expedition sails to Vinland and in four summers Karlsefni explores three thousand miles of the coast and rivers of North America.
1014	Karlsefni returns to Greenland.
1015	Freydis, Helgi, and Finnboge sail to Vinland.
1016	Freydis returns home. Karlsefni, with Gudrid and his son Snorri, sails to Iceland.
1017	Karlsefni sails to Norway.
1018	Karlsefni returns to Iceland.
c.1025	Leif Erikson dies, at about the age of forty-five. He is buried in the churchyard of his mother's church at Brattahlid. Of 144 persons whose skeletons have been exhumed there, the average age of nearly half has been determined as about thirty-five.
1029	Gudleif Gudlaugson sails from Dublin to the west and southwest to a "great land," where he meets Bjorn Asbrandson, who had sailed from Iceland in 999. A land called "Great Ireland" had been said to lie "VI days' sailing west of Ireland." The transcriber probably had erred by omission of one stroke from VII. The actual distance out of sight of land from Ireland to Newfoundland is 1,050 miles—seven days' sailing distance. (See Pohl, *The Viking Explorers,* pp. 187–89.)
1047	Trond Halfdanson flees from Norway, visits Vinland. On return is shipwrecked and dies in Greenland. His body is taken back to Norway.
c.1075	End of viking period.
1112–13	Erik Gnupson is consecrated first bishop of Greenland. He was probably the builder of the cathedral at Gardar, a structure 74 feet long and 26 feet wide. There were twelve parish churches in the Eastern Settlement of Greenland, and four in the Western Settlement. The Eastern Settlement also had a convent ded-

icated to St. Benedict and a monastery dedicated to St. Olaf and St. Augustine.

1117   Bishop Erik sails to get acquainted with Vinland, which was part of his diocese. From Vinland he returns to Greenland. The legend on the Vinland Map of 1440 says this voyage occurred "in the last year of our most blessed father Pascal."

1121   The Icelandic Annals give this as the date of Bishop Erik's voyage to Vinland. He may have made two voyages to Vinland.

1122   The cathedral at Gardar is dedicated.

c.1123–25   Erik's successor Arnold is consecrated as bishop of Greenland.

1150   Joannes Kukus is consecrated as bishop of Greenland. He dies in 1187.

1170   The *Historia Norvegiae,* anonymously written about 1170, says: "On the north side of the Greenlanders [north of the Eastern Settlement] hunters have found some very small people whom they call Skraelings. . . . They have no iron at all, and use walrus tusks for arrowheads and sharp stones for knives."

1188   Joannes II, Smiril, is consecrated bishop of Greenland. He dies in 1209. A skeleton holding the bishop's crozier has been fairly well identified as his.

1200   The climate of Greenland becomes a little colder, and continues so for about 150 years. At about this time it is believed the *Graenlendinga Saga* was first written down.

1206   On the Ides of February, a letter of Pope Innocent III mentions the bishopric of Greenland.

1212–30   Helgius Augmundi is bishop of Greenland.

1234   Nicolaus is consecrated bishop of Greenland.

1237   Bishop Nicolaus requests permission to substitute beer for Sacramental wine, since wine was practically unobtainable in Greenland. The request is later denied.

1239   Bishop Nicolaus sets sail for Greenland.

1246   Olav, consecrated bishop of Greenland, sent to persuade Greenlanders to submit to Norwegian Crown.

1247	Bishop Olav arrives in Greenland.
1261	Greenland surrenders its independence to Norway, which later led to its rule by Denmark.
1262–64	Bishop Olav is in Iceland.
1266 (7?)	A voyage is made to the Arctic under the auspices of Bishop Olav.
1270	A priest retiring from Greenland brings home a description of Eskimos.
1271	Bishop Olav is in Norway. He later returns to Greenland.
1276	A letter written on December 4 by Pope John XXI says, "The diocese of Gardar is so far distant that one can scarcely make the voyage thither and return in less than five years. . . . You have informed Us of the exceeding territorial extent of the bishoprics of the Kingdom of Norway. . . . Furthermore, that in certain parts of said Kingdom coined money is not in use, nor does corn [wheat] grow, nor are other kinds of staple food produced, but human life is sustained almost entirely on milkfood and fish."
1279	On January 31, Pope Nicholas III, in a letter to the Archbishop of Nidaros, writes, "We gather that the island on which stands the City of Gardar [the word "city" was used for the site of a cathedral] is seldom visited by ships, because of the ocean surrounding it." On June 9, the Pope in a letter took cognizance of the fact that "year after year, wine and hosts [wheaten bread] have to be supplied to the priests in those regions where wheat and grapes do not grow."
1280	Bishop Olav dies. Theodorus (Thord) Bokki is elected bishop of Greenland.
1282	Pope Martin IV writes on March 4, "The tithe of Greenland is received entirely in cattle-skins, the skins and tusks of seals, and whale-bone."
1285	Icelanders find land "to the westward off Iceland."
1289	King Eric of Norway sends Rolf to Iceland to seek the "New-land." Bishop Theodorus arrives in Greenland.

1290	"Rolf travels around in Iceland and summons men for a new-land voyage."
1314	Bishop Theodorus, who was in Norway in 1309, dies. Arnius is consecrated bishop of Greenland.
1315	Bishop Arnius sets sail for Greenland.
1334	It is believed that by this date *Eirik's Saga* had been written down.
1343	Bishop Arnius dies. Joannes III, Skalle Eriksson, is consecrated bishop of Greenland.
1347	A Greenland ship arrives in Iceland with seventeen men. It had been to Markland (part of Vinland).
1355	The Paul Knutson Expedition sails to investigate conditions in Greenland, to exterminate Eskimos, and to rescue the lost colonists of the Western Settlement of Greenland.
1362	After having been to Vinland, and after leaving ten men with their ship in Hudson Bay, a party of Norsemen ascends the Nelson River and by way of Lake Winnipeg and the Red River reaches the site of Kensington, Minnesota.
1363	Seven survivors leave Hudson Bay and sail to Greenland.
1364	They pick up Ivar Bardson in Greenland and return to Europe.
1365	Alfus is consecrated bishop of Greenland.
1368	Bishop Alfus sets sail for Greenland.
1371	Orkney fishermen arrive in "Estotiland" (Newfoundland).
1376	One of the fishermen goes southwest to Drogio (Nova Scotia?) and spends thirteen years among Indian tribes along the coast beyond Drogio.
1876–78?	Bishop Alfus dies. The Greenland See is vacant until 1386.
1379	Icelandic Annals say, "The Skraelings raided the Greenlanders, killing eighteen men and carrying off two boys as slaves."
1380	Four ships reach Greenland at the same time.

1385	Henricus is appointed bishop of Greenland.
1386	Bishop Henricus arrives at Gardar.
1388	Georgius is appointed (by rival Pope) to be the bishop of Greenland. The Orkney fisherman returns to Drogio.
1392	The fisherman reaches Newfoundland.
1394	Bishop Henricus in Greenland is ordered to be exchanged with Bishop John of Orkney.
1397	The Orkney fisherman returns to Orkney.
1398	Impelled by the fisherman's description of forested land to the west, Henry Sinclair, earl of Orkney, sails to Nova Scotia. Antonio Zeno, his admiral and secretary, returns from Nova Scotia to Orkney.
1399	Earl Henry returns to Orkney.
1401–6	During these years the names of three bishops of Greenland are Bertold, Peter II, and Andus I.
1408	September 16, Thorstein Olafson and Sigrid Bjornsdatter are married in Hvalsey Church (in a small fjord between Eriksfjord and Einarsfjord in Greenland).
1409	A letter written by two Greenland priests says many people attended the wedding ceremony.
1410	The Icelanders who attended the wedding sail to Iceland. This is the last written record of happenings in the Eastern Settlement of Greenland.
1411	Jakob Peterson Teppe (or Treppe) is appointed bishop of Greenland. He dies in 1425. Thereafter no bishop or priests are resident in Greenland, though appointments of bishops of Greenland continue (the names of ten of them are in Vatican records) until the last one dies in 1537.
1424	Claudius Clavus Swart, a Dane, visits Greenland.
1474	Pining and Pothorst sail to Greenland for the king of Denmark.
1477	A young Italian sailor, Cristoforo Colombo, visits Iceland and picks up waterfront gossip of land to the west.

It is obvious from these listed records of eleventh- to thirteenth-century voyages to the west of Iceland that during the 250 years after Karlsefni's time, direct contact with Vinland dropped off and knowledge of Vinland faded until there was uncertainty as to what land lay to the southwest of Greenland. A manuscript from about 1300, but based on a twelfth-century source, mentions the location of Vinland, and naming Karlsefni, brings into question the Karlsefnian concept that Markland and Vinland were connected and therefore parts of one great land:

"South of Greenland is Helluland; next lies Markland; thence it is not far to Vinland the Good, which some think goes out from Africa; and if it be so, the ocean must run between Vinland and Markland. It is related that Thorfinn Karlsefni got wood for his ship's beakhead, and went afterwards to explore Vinland. . . ."[15]

Another pre-Columbian manuscript, Codex No. 115, also expresses the same geographical notion as to the southern end of Vinland: "Vinland, which some think goes out from Africa. . . ."

It may seem utterly fantastic that some Icelanders thought of Vinland as connected with or as part of Africa, but what we have in the two quotations is evidence that the vikings (in all probability Karlsefni—who else?) sailed as far south as the Gulf of Mexico and saw the north shore of Cuba or Yucatan, and assumed that what they saw was a western extension of the north coast of Africa.

Records of fourteenth-century voyages to the west are more definite than any in the twelfth or thirteenth centuries. King Magnus of Norway and Sweden authorized the Paul Knutson Expedition which sailed in 1355 to Greenland to look into conditions there and to find, if possible, the colonists of the Western Settlement who had abandoned their farms and gone west or southwest. For those who accept the Kensington Inscription, the Paul Knutson Expedition sailed from Greenland to Vinland, and "from Vinland" (the east coast of the continent) went around into Hudson

---

[15] From a manuscript written between 1400 and 1450 in the Arna-Magnean Collection and translated in Reeves, Beamish, and Anderson, *The Norse Discovery of Vinland*, pp. 12–13.

Bay, and there left men to take care of their ship, while the others journeyed inland as far as to the site of Kensington, Minnesota, in 1362. But whether or not one accepts the Kensington Inscription, the Paul Knutson Expedition was a fact.

Toward the end of the fourteenth century, an Orkney fisherman spent twenty-six years along the east coast of North America. When he returned to the Orkneys in 1397, he gave a circumstantial account of his experiences. He said he first reached an island where there was one man who "spoke Latin." From his description, this island was unquestionably Newfoundland: "It is a little smaller than Iceland." Newfoundland is actually slightly larger, but the approximation in size is definite identification. The fisherman further told of spending years in a much larger land beyond the island: "Towards the south is a great country, . . . with woods of immense extent. . . . It is a very great country, and, as it were, a new world. The people . . . live by hunting. . . . Far to the southwest are cities and temples dedicated to their idols, in which they sacrifice men and afterwards eat them. . . . In those parts they have some knowledge of gold and silver."[16] It appears that the fisherman had heard of Mexico, and of cannibals in the Caribbean.

For anyone acquainted with the records from the eleventh to the fourteenth century there could be no particular surprise when the Vinland Map of 1440 was presented to the world. There were of course some skeptics as to its genuineness, but they showed themselves to be uninformed. In addition to the affirmative findings of thorough technical studies of every kind (age of paper, ink, association with other documents, etc.) , an absolute proof of genuineness is in the revelation of the medieval cryptograph in the legend on the Vinland Map: HENRICUS ET SPE ERO. (See Alf Mongé and O. G. Landsverk, *Norse Medieval Cryptography in Runic Carvings,* pp. 119–120.)

More than half of the comments in the study of the Vinland Map published by Yale University Press, *The Vinland Map and the Tartar Relation,* were by Mr. R. A. Skelton, Superintendent of the Map Room of the British Museum. What motivated Skelton

---

[16] From Major, ed., *The Voyages of the Venetian brothers Nicolò and Antonio Zeno.*

was, as he says, "trying to recapture the processes of thought and synthesis which went into the construction of these maps."[17]

Scholars think of evidence in several different forms. Cartographers demand maps as evidence; some other scholars demand manuscript texts; some demand artifacts, etc. Skelton is not limited to cartography, and his judgments and conclusions are frequently tempered with awareness of the contrary point of view, and he allows for opposites.

The Vinland Map of 1440 illustrates four Karlsefnian geographical concepts. First is the size of Vinland, which on the map is called "Vinland Island." But what an island! Consider its immensity.

Skelton says in comment on the map of Greenland on the Vinland Map, "There is not much difficulty in supposing the drawing of the coasts south of about 75°N (i.e., south of King William Land on the east, and of Melville Bay and perhaps Cape York on the west) with their relatively correct orientation and location of main features, to be the product of experience."[18]

What Skelton is saying is that without adding in the northernmost quarter of Greenland, the north-south length of the southern three-quarters of Greenland on the 1440 Map represents fifteen degrees of latitude from 75°N to the southern tip at Cape Farvel (Farewell) at 60°N. If he is correct, that entire map of Greenland represents the twenty degrees of Greenland's actual north-south length. When we observe that the north-south length of Vinland on the Map of 1440 is twice that of the map of Greenland, it seems fair to say that Vinland on the 1440 Map represents forty degrees of north-south distance. From the northern tip of Labrador (at 60°N) such extension reaches to 20°N, which is south of the Gulf of Mexico. The conclusion seems inescapable that the Vinland Map of 1440 is corroborative of Karlsefni's discovery that Markland—the whole of the wooded region both north and south of the mouth of the St. Lawrence—was part of Vinland, and that the whole of Vinland was a land of tremendous size.

[17] Skelton, Marston, and Painter, *The Vinland Map and the Tartar Relation,* p. 206.

[18] Ibid., p. 195.

Skelton warns against making a comparison of a kind which we do not here attempt. He says it is "hazardous and may be extremely deceptive to construct a latitude scale for lands represented in the west of the Atlantic from that of lands in the east" (of the Atlantic).[19] In the face of this, however, he goes on to suggest that the northern of the two inlets in the map of Vinland may be Hudson Strait, although this suggestion ignores the direction of Hudson Strait. From Baffin Bay through Hudson Strait to Hudson Bay is a five-hundred-mile-long waterway running from the southeast to the northwest. It is difficult to see how the northern of the two inlets in Vinland on the Map of 1440 can be a representation of anything other than the St. Lawrence River flowing from a great lake from the southwest to the northeast.

There is nothing in the Map of Vinland to suggest that its maker had heard of the Paul Knutson Expedition, or of Hudson Strait, or of Hudson Bay.

The second Karlsefnian concept in the 1440 Map is in the relative positioning of Iceland, Greenland, and Vinland. The map maker turned the Scandinavian Peninsula by nearly ninety degrees in order to squeeze it down into his map. To do this, he gave it a west-east direction. He conceived of a rondure of the limits of the known lands of the earth. He showed the three continents—Asia, Africa, and Europe—bounded with a great curve outside of which was nothing but ocean. To incorporate Iceland and Greenland into his concept, the map maker drew those two islands far to the south of what he probably knew or had heard was their actual position in relation to the west coast of Norway. No matter. He was not primarily concerned with showing either of them, but with showing Vinland. This seems to be the only valid reason why he pictured Iceland only half its own width from the southwest tip of Norway. It was the general practice to have a legend in an upper corner of a map. In his desire to have room for the Latin lines in the upper left corner, we find another reason why the map maker put Greenland much too far south. But with all the distor-

---

[19] Ibid., p. 221.

tions of the positioning of Iceland and Greenland in relation to Europe, the map points to a Karlsefnian concept in the positioning of the northern tip of Vinland in relation to the southern coast of Iceland. Karlsefni did not know latitude in degreees, but he knew something of angle distance from the sun in the use of sun shadows. He and other vikings often did what is called "latitude sailing." In an east-west voyage they would keep at the same shadow distance from the sun, with some refinement in compensating for the advance of the sailing season. They observed sun shadows around midday. Karlsefni as a mariner in all probability observed the sun shadows when he arrived at the northern tip of Labrador and learned that he was there only a little south of the south coast of his native Iceland. The difference in sun-shadow angles was most important information. It was something he could have known, something he certainly wanted to know, and something he would have preserved in some rough-drawn chart. The Vinland Map of 1440 suggests a persistence in Iceland of knowledge of the proper placement of the northern tip of Labrador in relation to Iceland. It shows the northern tip of Vinland only a little farther south than the southern coast of Iceland, as it actually is by only three degrees. The northern tip of Labrador, which is the northern tip of the eastern seaboard of North America, is at 60° 25′ North.

A third Karlsefnian concept in the 1440 Map of Vinland is that its maker showed Markland and Vinland as *all one land,* and ignored the twelfth-century geographical concept: "South of Greenland is Helluland; next lies Markland; thence it is not far to Vinland." So far as records go, the concept that Labrador and all of Markland were part of Vinland was Karlsefni's.

The Latin legend at the upper left corner of the Vinland Map is translated by R. A. Skelton as: "Eric [Henricus], legate of the Apostolic See and Bishop of Greenland and the neighboring regions, arrived in this truly vast and very rich land [Vinland], in the name of Almighty God, in the last year of our most blessed father Pascal, remained a long time in both summer and winter, and later returned northeastward [? — *ad orientem hiemalé*] to-

SUN-SHADOW DEVICE FOR LATITUDE SAILING

It floated in a basin held by a sailor.
The vertical stick was set to various
scheduled heights during the season.
The end of the shadow in relation to the
circles revealed the ship's position
in relation to the desired latitude.

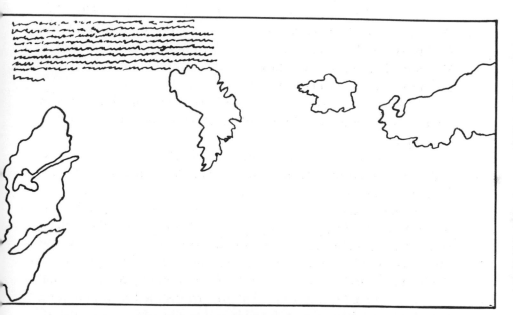

FROM VINLAND MAP OF 1440, SHOWING RELATIVE PLACEMENT
OF NORWAY, ICELAND, GREENLAND, AND VINLAND

ward Greenland, and then proceeded in most humble obedience to the will of his superiors."[20]

The word *hiemalé* does not mean "north," but "winterish" or "cold and stormy." If the Latin words which mean "east winterish" justify Skelton's "northeastward," then my comment would be that with the wrong placement of Greenland on the 1440 Map, the top third of Vinland does not lie to the southwest of the Greenland Settlements, and it was only from the middle portion of Vinland pictured on the Map that the bishop could have sailed northeastward toward Greenland.

The phrase "this truly vast land" suggests that Vinland was larger than an island, and was indeed twice as long north-south as Greenland.

The words quoted from the legend, "bishop of Greenland and the neighboring regions" imply that the bishop's diocese included Vinland.

A fourth Karlsefnian concept in the Vinland Map of 1440 is in the fact that the turns of direction and contours of the eastern coast of the middle section of Vinland are remarkably similar to the actual coastline from the southern end of Labrador (mouth of the St. Lawrence) to the rounding of the southern tip of Florida.

The similarity is so close that we are justified in repudiating the idea of accidental swiggles. There are obvious swiggles on all the western side of the map of Vinland and on its southern end. Remembering, however, that Skelton accepted the contour of the southern three-quarters of Greenland on the 1440 Map as "the result of experience," we can with greater assurance accept the much closer similarity of middle Vinland to the actual coastline as the result of experience. It is possible but unlikely that the knowledge of that middle section of Vinland came from the Orkney fisherman who spent thirteen years (1376 to 1388) as a captive among coastal Indians, being passed from tribe to tribe because he could teach them how to fish with nets. Henry Sinclair, earl of Orkney, could not have been the source of the map maker's knowledge of that

[20] Ibid., p. 140.

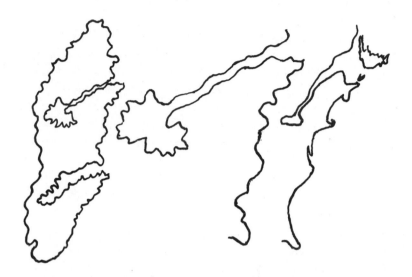

MIDDLE SECTION OF VINLAND COMPARED WITH MODERN MAP

VINLAND	MIDDLE VINLAND	LABRADOR to FLORIDA
Map of 1440	in larger scale	from modern map

middle section; for Earl Henry explored only Nova Scotia, and when departing crossed the Bay of Fundy to the Massachusetts coast from which he sailed home in 1399.[21]

The southern of the two estuaries in the 1440 Map of Vinland patently represents waters south and west of Florida—the Gulf of Mexico.

If Karlsefni, with Snorri and forty men, in the early summer of 1012 sailed farther south than the entrance to the Chesapeake, being the persistent explorer that he was, he no doubt reached the tip of Florida and sailed into the Gulf of Mexico. If he found there evidence of the existence of an immense river like the Mississippi, as he may readily have done from the color of the water outside its mouth, he may have sent some men in the after-boat to explore that river. He would have dared do this since he had seen that the shores of the gulf and of the ocean between the tip of Florida and the entrance to Hóp consisted of sand beaches. An after-boat party returning along such a shore would sail close to shore, and whenever a strong onshore breeze arose, would quickly land and beach the boat above the reach of waves and tide. An after-boat sailing close to beaches was safer than a ship, because the men in her could choose the weather conditions for all the hours of their sailing.

Skelton says that the idea of Vinland as connected with Africa (a westward extension of the north coast of Africa) came from a geographical notion of the twelfth century.[22] If Skelton's dating of the notion is correct, then the concept of the Caribbean, etc., could not have stemmed from explorations by Orkneymen in the fourteenth century. The twelfth-century notion may well have been Karlsefnian in origin.

In the legend at the top of the Vinland Map, Bjarni, meaning Bjarni Herjulfsson, is named before Leif Erikson. This shows acquaintance with the viking saga which ascribes its telling to Karlsefni. The legend calls Bjarni and Leif *socij* (the *j* being medieval usage). Skelton translates *socij* as "companions." Bjarni

---

[21] See Pohl, "Prince 'Zichmni' of the Zeno Narrative," *Terrae Incognitae*.
[22] Skelton, Marston, and Painter, op. cit., p. 139.

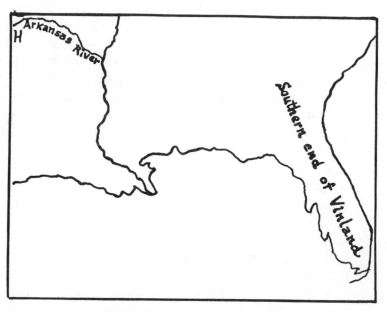

H—SITE OF HEAVENER RUNESTONE

and Leif were not companions. Bjarni's voyage of discovery occurred seventeen years before Leif's, and Bjarni was more than twenty years older than Leif. A proper translation would be "co-operators."

The legend that squeezes Greenland on the Vinland Map says, in Skelton's translation: "From the island of Greenland . . . sailing southward amidst the ice, the companions Bjarni and Leif Eriksson discovered a new land." This mention of ice is instructive. Many writers on the subject of the viking voyages have been saying in a chorus, repeating it after each other, that in Erik the Red's day there was no mention of ice in the waters around Greenland. Skelton says positively, "The narratives of the Greenland voyages in this period contain no mention of ice as a hazard to navigation.[23] This assertion is contrary to fact. In viking times the Icelander Rafn, who was known as the "Limerick Merchant" because he traded with Ireland, said that "south from inhabited Greenland are deserts, uninhabited places, and icebergs." In *The Viking Explorers*, pp. 43, 44, will be found quotations from the *Floammana Saga* which tell how Thorgils Orrabeinsstjup, a personal friend of Erik the Red, was held on the coast of Greenland for all of a year by ice, and eventually was able to reach Eriksfjord in Greenland only by "sailing between the land and the ice." This is as it is today. Where do the members of the negative chorus think the ten thousand or more icebergs each year were to be found in Erik the Red's time? The ice of glaciers flowing down from the Greenland icecap had to go somewhere. In the waters around Greenland, the icebergs have been swept along by the shore currents for thousands of years.

The reiterated error denying that there was dangerous ice in the waters near Greenland does not invalidate Skelton's sketch map of sailing routes to Greenland in the eleventh to the fourteenth centuries to avoid the worst of the ice,[24] but it does compel this comment: Sailing directions improved with the experience of mariners throughout the years, but that does not mean that the icebergs shifted their course or originated from a different source.

[23] Ibid., p. 185.
[24] Ibid., p. 170.

Skelton says, "The technique of Norse navigation occasioned neither the use nor the making of charts, to which none of the medieval records makes any reference in this connection; and it appears the more unlikely that any map of the American discoveries was drawn before 'the age of written history.' The narratives or logs of the expeditions, handed down with remarkable particularity in the stories of the saga tellers, conveyed sufficient precision to satisfy their audience and to make a map even more supererogatory, and indeed inconsistent with this mode of transmission, than a written transcript. . . . If (as we think possible) no map illustrating the American landfalls of the Norsemen was drawn before the twelfth century at earliest—that is, long after the death of the adventurers who made them—its chain of transmission must have been verbal, not graphic."[25]

In this skillfully argued passage Skelton almost persuades us that the vikings drew no charts. But the vikings were not peculiarly backward as compared with other sailors before their time and since. Of course mariners who wanted to come through alive made some charts. A mariner did not have to be literate to draw a chart. It would seem incredible if an experienced mariner like Karlsefni, sailing with the purpose of exploring, made no sort of chart. It seems also that the eastern coast of the middle section of Vinland on the Map of 1440 is very convincing evidence that Karlsefni drew a chart. Those who refuse to accept it as evidence must show us how a twelfth- or thirteenth-century explorer acquired such a correct knowledge of that coast.

[25] Ibid., p. 209.

PART TWO

Identifications and
Archaeological Discoveries

IDENTIFICATIONS AND ARCHAEOLOGICAL DISCOVERIES

"mountainless and wooded, with low hillocks."   **B 1**

This was Bjarni's first geographical observation about the land he first sighted, the one farthest from Greenland. This description is applicable to hundreds of areas along the Atlantic coast of North America. It will however be abundantly demonstrated that the land Bjarni first sighted was Cape Cod.

But would Bjarni, starting from Iceland for Greenland, have got so far off course as the latitude of Cape Cod? The out-of-course voyage becomes less questionable when it is remembered that vi-

king ships sailed efficiently only with following winds. They often
were driven in the direction Aeolus willed. While it is likely that
no one storm would have carried Bjarni more than a quarter of
the distance from Iceland to Cape Cod, his telling said he had encountered "north winds," plural. He was driven by several northern blows. In the fog he drifted much of the way, carried by the
Arctic Current (the Labrador Current) and eddies on the northern side of the Gulf Stream.

In this connection a specific contribution was made by the
yachting editor of the *Manchester Guardian*, Mr. J. R. L. Anderson. As skipper of the forty-five-foot British cutter *Griffin*, he sailed
in April of 1966 with a five-man crew from Scarborough, York-
shire, England, in search of Vinland. From the waters between Iceland and Newfoundland, Anderson allowed winds and currents to
carry the *Griffin* with the announced purpose of following the
course over which Bjarni Herjulfsson had drifted in fogs with
north winds. The *Griffin* met the same hazards, the same currents,
and the same sort of weather. Her crew had many adventures and
some real hardships. The crew of a small boat propelled by sail can
discover much that motorboat sailors, these days, would not notice.
The men on the *Griffin* were able to make deductions somewhat as
the vikings did. The *Griffin* found herself on June 27 in the
neighborhood of Cape Cod, Massachusetts. In her skipper's opinion, this was the latitude of the first land sighted by Bjarni Herjulfsson. Anderson came to the conclusion that Nova Scotia and
Maine would be too far north for Bjarni's first landfall, and Long
Island and New Jersey too far south.

B 2   Bjarni "sailed for two days before they sighted another land."

Here is the key that unlocked the Vinland puzzle.

For a hundred years scholars in the viking field have taken as
a geographical measuring rod the number of days' sailing Bjarni
reported. It was generally accepted that in inland waters, as in the
fjords of Norway, a day's sail, which necessarily had to be re-
stricted to daylight hours since there were no lighthouses, was
about seventy-five miles. This was the distance a viking ship with
its one square sail under favorable conditions with a following

wind would sail in twelve hours. Across open ocean, when the ship was sailed throughout the night as well as in the daytime, a "day's sailing" in twenty-four hours was about 150 miles.[1]

The number of days of sailing reported by Bjarni from the land he first sighted all the way to the southern tip of Greenland are "two" plus "three" plus "four"—a total of nine days. Nine at 150 miles each make a total of 1,350 miles. This would seem to have been the greatest possible distance that the land he first sighted could have been from the southern tip of Greenland. This limit would seem to preclude Cape Cod, since Cape Cod is 1,700 miles from the nearest point of Greenland. The total of 1,350 miles from Greenland would reach only to somewhere in Nova Scotia. For a long time the scholars who belonged to what I called "the Northern School of Theorists" because they refused to allow that Bjarni and Leif ever got south of the Canadian border, seemed to have the support of an unanswerable argument. Nine days of sailing simply would not stretch to the New England coast. Nine days of sailing would extend to only two lands southwest of Greenland, to Newfoundland and Nova Scotia; yet the saga which told of Bjarni's and of Leif's voyages speaks of three lands. Was the saga in error? I did not believe so. And yet for some years I faced the seemingly insoluble puzzle. Finally I turned to men of practical experience with ships of sail. I laid the problem before fellow members of the Ship Lore Club in New York City. They quickly solved it.

One of them said, "You have been figuring from shore to shore. But a sailor makes his landfall when he first sights land. He can see mountaintops long before he sees the shore."

"That does it!" I exclaimed. "And a lookout at the masthead would add additional mileage!"

Thus I began to understand what kind of information eleventh-century viking mariners would desire. The time a crew of a ship spent coasting along any shore would be their own business. They would not speak of it because it would be of no value as guidance to other mariners. What other mariners would want to

---

[1] Precise data will be found in Pohl, *The Viking Explorers*, chapter 6.

hear would be the direction and the approximate distance from one land to another out of sight of land. Such information was all that Leif Erikson needed when he set out to sail in reverse of Bjarni's directions. All that was important to Karlsefni, who wanted to know where Bjarni and Leif had been, was to learn how many days' sailing out of sight of land lay between the four lands, Greenland and the three lands to the southwest.

The *Flateyjarbók* said that from the first land he sighted, Bjarni "sailed two days before he sighted another land." The words "before he sighted" definitely tell us that the two days of sailing had been out of sight of land. When he sighted that second land, how many miles was he from it? The answer would depend upon the height of the land he sighted, and also upon the height of the ship's mast or the height of the eyes of a lookout from far up the mast. How tall was the mast of a viking trading ship? The mast had to carry a single square sail of sufficient size to propel the ship at a speed of about six knots. Ship architects gave the answer: "Not more than thirty-five feet, or about half the length of the ship."

From the masthead, thirty feet above water, an observer had a visible horizon of seven miles. This distance to the horizon was determined by an easy formula. The square root of the number of feet of altitude above sea level of the eye of an observer (or observed object), multiplied by 1.3226 gives the number of statute miles of horizon visibility. This is simple enough. The only time it ruffled me was when I heard the asinine assertion by a Ph.D. who was without horse sense ("no farm sense," the Swedes say), that this formula for horizon visibility applies over land but never over water!

Add to seven the number of miles a height of land can be seen at sea level, and the total is the distance from which that high land could have been sighted from Bjarni's ship. If what was first seen was a mountain or hill lying inland, its distance from the shore must be subtracted.

The dunes along the ocean side of Cape Cod are only an eighth of a mile from shore. They are 150 feet in height, and would be visible for twelve miles from sea level. Add to those twelve miles the seven for the masthead horizon, and we see that Bjarni's ship may have had Cape Cod visible to the stern of her for nineteen miles as she departed.

From those high dunes of Cape Cod to Cape Sable at the western end of Nova Scotia, the distance is 213 nautical miles, or 245 statute miles. In two days Bjarni may have sailed three hundred miles, so that he may have first sighted the coast of Nova Scotia sixty or more miles east of Cape Sable. Sixty miles east of Cape Sable is a hill of 370-foot altitude. That hill, visible at the horizon for twenty-nine miles, is south of Liverpool, about three miles north of White Point Beach, or about seven miles from the outermost points of land in that section of the coast. Subtracting seven for the distance inland, and adding seven for the masthead horizon, we have the distance from shore of twenty-nine miles from which Bjarni may have sighted Nova Scotia. The telling in the saga is that it was while they were as yet far from shore that his shipmates asked him whether this was Greenland. Bjarni replied that it was not, because he saw no mountains or glaciers. It was sometime after that question had been asked and answered that "they drew near this land" and lowered the sail, keeping the ship temporarily under the control of oars.

"extensively forested and appeared level"   **B 3**

Bjarni and his men made this observation when they drew close to the shore of this second land. This observation enables us to tell approximately where their ship was when they made that observation. For fourteen years it had been my privilege to make frequent visits to Nova Scotia. Sometimes I arrived by steamer at Yarmouth or Digby, but more often I entered by auto from New Brunswick. *The Sinclair Expedition to Nova Scotia in 1398* had been privately printed in Nova Scotia. My placing the book in forty stores scattered throughout the province brought me an intimate familiarity with every section of the country. I also autoed into infrequently touristed areas while on the trail of Glooscap, the visiting Prince of the Micmac legend whom I equated with Prince Henry Sinclair, earl of Orkney. For two summers I was engaged in archaeological work in Nova Scotia in connection with the Sinclair-Glooscap identification. Everywhere in all parts of Nova Scotia I had found hills and valleys. It was a country no part of which, it seemed, could be described as "level." Yet I had accepted Bjarni's reported observation as an accurate description. Such had been my trust in the accuracy of the saga that I had in three published books presented Bjarni's observation as perfectly applicable to Nova Scotia. I had done this, I confess, without investigation of the south coast from offshore. However, in August of 1964 I took ship from Halifax to New York. When the ship cleared Halifax Harbor I was on the top deck at the stern looking back. For as long as we remained in sight of land, the coast of Nova Scotia as seen from the ship presented the appearance of a forested land, its edge against the sky looking as level as the top of a billiard table. Captain Raymond G. Wilkie of Nova Scotia, who has sailed along the entire coast of the province many times, says that the only stretch that looks level begins at Halifax and extends eastward for thirty miles.

This identification of Bjarni's observation warrants emphasis. My acceptance of the word "level" as accurately descriptive of part of the coast of Nova Scotia, before I had checked on it, showed faith in the saga but was an unintentional breach of my readers' confidence, since it was a stating of an assumption as a fact. What I had done was not so reprehensible as something that was done later by an author who published a theory that Bjarni's first and third lands were both in Newfoundland. That author's theory is in trouble since the coast of Newfoundland lying between what he pointed to as Bjarni's first and third lands has hills 150 to over 400 feet, and one of over 500 feet, all close to the sea. Because this area could not appear level when seen from the sea, he could not ask his readers to accept it as Bjarni's second land. How could he conceal this failure of the pattern in his theory? You may guess what he did. He deliberately omitted the second land. He dared to omit it because he knew that most of his readers would not be informed and alert enough to note the omission. That fictionizing author's theory cannot stand up under investigation.

B 4   "After three days' sailing"

Without letting his shipmates go ashore on Nova Scotia, Bjarni hoisted sail and "sailed out upon the high seas," with gales from the southwest, and "after three days' sailing they sighted a third land which was high and mountainous." With gales blowing, it was of course safer for him out of sight of land than near land.

Three days' sailing was 450 miles. From Halifax eastward, the length of the Atlantic seacoast of Nova Scotia including Cape Breton, is about 220 miles. The distance from Cape Breton to Cape Ray, the nearest point of Newfoundland, is 125 miles. From whatever portion of the coast of Nova Scotia Bjarni sailed away on a swing out and around out of sight of land, it was somewhat less than three days' sailing to Cape Ray at the southwestern corner of Newfoundland. In all probability he first sighted the coast of Newfoundland about a hundred miles north of Cape Ray.

At what distance from its shore could Bjarni have been when he first "saw" Newfoundland? Table Mountain, 1,700 feet in altitude, is eight miles from Cape Ray. Extending to the northward ten to fifteen miles inland from the western coast is the Long Range. This rises in places to over 2,000 feet. These mountains of Newfoundland can be sighted from the west at sea level for at least thirty miles from shore. Add seven for the mast-height horizon, and we see that Bjarni could have sighted Newfoundland from thirty-seven miles away.

"high and mountainous"   B 5

These areas mentioned in the saga are along Newfoundland's western side, not its eastern. There is another fact which tells us along which side of Newfoundland Bjarni sailed. Since at first sight for all he knew this land might be Greenland, and since he was seeking to rejoin his father, who he had been told back in Iceland would be in the new settlement on the west coast of Greenland, it is quite certain that he chose to coast along the western side of Newfoundland. His impression of it was that it was "mountainous with glaciers." In Newfoundland, near the shore of the Strait of Belle Isle, are Gros Morne, elevation 2,651 feet; Mt. St. Gregory, elevation 2,235 feet; and a mountain near Bonne Bay, elevation 2,625 feet. Great snowfields are seen on the northern slopes of these mountains until late summer, and sometimes throughout the late summer. Fresh snow usually occurs early in the autumn. A heavy snowfall is possible during any month in that region, and has in fact been known to occur in August.

B 6   Bjarni and his men "coasted along" the third land and "perceived that it was an island."

We are not told for how long a time they "coasted along" this land. They would have used this expression "coasted" only in reference to a land long enough to require a considerable number of hours of coasting, surely more than one day, and perhaps two or three days. The third land was certainly not a small island which they could see was surrounded by water as they approached it and left it astern. Since it was a land of considerable size, the coasting would not have made it possible for them to "perceive" that it was an island until they were brought to realize that they had actually circumnavigated it. It is obvious that they could perceive that a large land was an island only after they had coasted the western side of it, and only if it lay between them and the ocean. When they had been carried by north winds in fogs, they had got to the south of this land without having seen its eastern side, and only after they had coasted its western side and only after they came to its northern end and were free of it and found themselves once more in the open ocean and thus had been brought to realize that they had actually circumnavigated it, and not before then, could they perceive that the third land was an island.

In view of the sailing directions of Bjarni's entire voyage from Iceland to Greenland, it is certain that the third land perceived to be an island was Newfoundland.

The western coast of Newfoundland from Cape Ray to Cape Norman extends for about 360 miles.

B 7   "They now sailed for four days."

"They left this land astern, and sailed on with the same fair wind [wind from the southwest]. The wind rose mightily and

Bjarni commanded them to reef. . . They now sailed for four days. Then they sighted a fourth land. . . . and came to land in the evening."

An almost excessively strong fair wind with a reefed sail drove the ship at the speed which viking mariners had in mind when they used the expression "a day's sail." The four days of sailing to the northeast brought Bjarni to within sight of the southern tip of Greenland. The distance from Newfoundland to Greenland, however, nearest point to nearest point, Cape Norman to very close to Bjarni's landing at Herjulfsness, is about 730 miles. This is too much for four days' sailing. But the distance out of sight of land is corroborative of the saga.

With the strong wind from the southwest it is likely there was no fog to prevent Bjarni's seeing Belle Isle with its 660-foot elevation thirty-two miles to the east of north from Cape Norman. A 660-foot elevation is visible for thirty-three miles at sea level. Adding seven miles for the mast-height horizon, we find that Bjarni may have been forty miles from Belle Isle, or seventy-two miles from Cape Norman, before he sailed out of sight of land.

In approaching Herjulfsness in Greenland, Bjarni could have seen the highest mountain along the west coast of the southern end of Greenland, a mountain which has an elevation of 4,900 feet. Applying the formula, the square root of 4,900 is 70, which multiplied by 1.3226 gives us 92 miles. Adding 7 for the mast-height horizon, and subtracting 9 for the mountain's distance inland, we have 90 miles as the distance from Herjulfsness at which Bjarni could have first sighted Greenland. From the 730 miles distance from Newfoundland to Greenland, we therefore subtract 72 and 90, leaving 568, or less than the 600 miles which would have been an estimated four days' sailing distance. The saga tells us that it was after four days' sailing that Bjarni sighted Greenland. It was presumably in the morning. It was that evening when they came to land.

"sailed to the land and anchored"   L 1

In approaching Bjarni's third land, the land which Bjarni saw last and had perceived to be an island, Leif "sailed to the land and anchored." The word "anchored" tells us he had entered some sheltered cove or harbor where the ship could rest.

The harbor which gives access to a lookout area where there is no grass is described in *The Viking Explorers,* pages 88, 89. Those pages show Canada Bay on the eastern coast of the northern peninsula of Newfoundland as the most likely and almost certain landing place of Leif Erikson, and they show why Hooping Harbor, Fourche Harbor, and Orange Bay are much less likely. Leif's landing place inside Canada Bay could have been Torrent Cove or Otter Cove. Either would have afforded an easy climb up a brook to an altitude of a thousand feet. In a forested region where trees naturally preclude meadow grass, it would not have occurred to Leif to make a critical comment on the absence of grass. His disapproval was expressed when after the climb he found himself in a large treeless area which was not a meadow suitable for grazing cattle, but was to his surprise infertile. The infertile area at 1,000 feet above and to the west of Canada Bay is five miles wide, north-south, and it extends for more than ten miles in a direction to the south of west.

L 2   "ice mountains"

From the lookout area, ice mountains were visible far away. Blue Mountain, which has an elevation of 2,128 feet, was perhaps the farthest away of the mountains Leif saw to the southwest. Its distance from the Canada Bay lookout area is forty-seven miles. The map shows several mountains which Leif unquestionably could have seen, with altitudes between 1,500 and 2,000 feet. These are at distances of twenty-one to thirty miles from Canada Bay.

The Long Range Mountains of Newfoundland have snow-fields in summer on their shaded northern slopes. From Canada Bay one looks toward their northern sides. In the distance the snow gleams white like ice fields or glaciers.

L 3   *"Helluland"*

From the sea to the mountains Leif saw what appeared to be a level land of rocks. To the southwest of him, and thus between him and the mountains, he saw ten miles of tableland of rocks. In

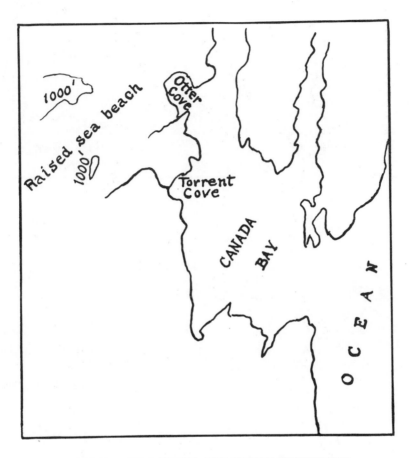

WHERE LEIF LANDED AND NAMED HELLULAND

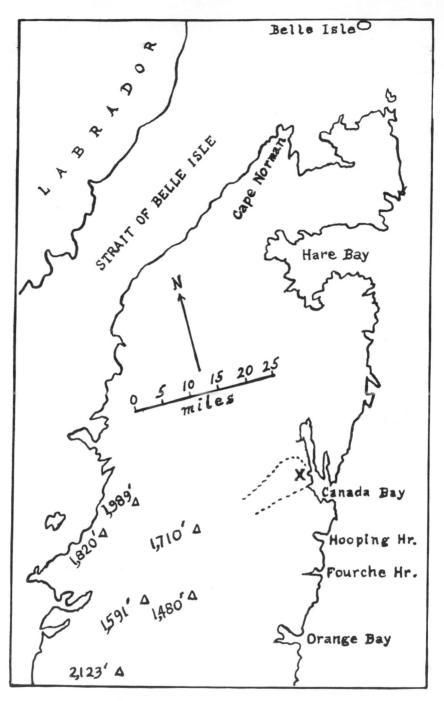

WHERE LEIF STOOD IN A STONE FIELD

X—open area of ledges five miles wide and more than ten miles long, whence one can see snowfields on northern slopes of far-distant mountains

that distance the tableland rises only ten feet a mile. It looked level indeed. So far as he could tell, it extended all the way to the mountains.

Helluland means "Land of Flat Rocks" or "Flagstone Land." The geological map of Newfoundland issued by the Department of Mines of Canada marks everything from Canada Bay west for more than thirty miles and to the southwest for over a hundred miles as "Diabase Dike Swarms." A dike is a tabular body of igneous rock. In many places in that immense area the rocks are flat and break out in flaggy or fieldstone style.

The identifications of Leif's three observations on the great island which he named Helluland leave no doubt that he landed on its east coast. In addition, we know his landing was on that coast because the *Flateyjarbók* specifically says that when he and his men departed from the great island they went out on the open ocean—*(efter thetta sigle their j haf)*. *Haf* means "ocean," "high seas." *Haf* tells us that when Leif got outside the harbor where he had landed he was not in the Gulf of St. Lawrence, but out in the Atlantic.

"level and completely wooded"   **L 4**

Leif found the second land to be as Bjarni had reported it. He found also that it had "broad stretches of white sand" and "the   **L 5** shore region did not slant steeply."

This observation of wide sands is a feature of Nova Scotia in the region where its immediate wooded hinterground looks level when seen from the ocean. In the first thirty miles of coast to the east of Halifax are these beaches of sand: Cove Bay, one mile long; Lawrencetown Beach, more than one mile long; a beach at Graham Head, one and one-half miles long; one near Meisener Head, more than two miles long; in Clam Bay, two beaches each more than one mile long; Martinique Beach, two miles long. Leif's observation that the shore region did not slant steeply is a description applicable throughout the thirty miles.

"an island . . . to the north of the land."   **L 6**

The most elusive of the more than eighty geographical obser-

vations in the Vinland sagas was this one. Since the Atlantic seacoast of continental North America extends from northeast to
southwest, any island near it would literally be to the south of it,
or could be said to be to the east of it, but could not be said to be
to the north of it or west of it. Several theorists, beginning with
W. A. Munn in 1914, found an island, or several islands, lying to
the north of the northern tip of Newfoundland, and thus "north
of the land," interpreting "land" to mean a large island. Their
finding also of a "cape that extended to the north" (see L 8) from
the northern tip of Newfoundland, plus two or three other geographical facts, gave them complete confidence that they had lo-
cated the region of Leif's landing in Bjarni's first land. With four
or five or six details in their favor, they ignored at least a dozen
other geographical observations in Bjarni's and Leif's tellings.

Careful perusal of the text with consideration for all the details in Leif's telling brought realization that Leif's statement that
he landed on an island that lay to the north of the land was a statement based upon a very brief, almost momentary observation. One
or two hours after he made it he sailed away to the *northward*
from that island. He thus lost sight of "the land" to the south of
that island, and presumably never visited the land to the south of
that island. He never verified whether it was, as he assumed, part
of the land connected with the land where he spent the winter, or
whether it was itself merely an island so large that its shore disappeared over the horizon from where he saw it, as though it were
part of a coast extensive enough to be called "the land."

This realization led to the finding of Great Point of Nantucket as an island that lay about five miles to the north of Nantucket Island. Great Point was an island when Leif arrived; for the
combination of high tide (see L 9) and the raising of local ocean
level by a two or three days' northeaster had covered the ten-foot-
high sandspit which connects Great Point with Nantucket Island
and is at other times exposed. Great Point is frequently an island.
There is no reason to suppose conditions were essentially different
in Leif's day. One thousand years is a short time geologically. The
quantity of ocean water that occasionally pours across the sandspit
cuts down its height, whereas the winds tend to build it up.

The highest dune of Great Point has an elevation of forty feet. The lee of Great Point would have afforded an anchorage for Leif's ship, such as he and his men would have been lucky to find. In such an anchorage they rode out the storm until the dawn of the day the wind veered. On Great Point, which is about three-quarters of a mile long and a third of a mile wide, the only trees are stunted cedars, six feet high at most. Bushes and beach grass give stability to most of the dunes.

"dew on (or "in") the grass" **L 7**

On Great Point there is a grass-covered hollow, well below high-tide level, surrounded by dunes. In that grass is a natural well of rainwater. This water was formerly pumped into the Great Point Lighthouse for the use of the keeper and his family, but the lighthouse has now been completely mechanized.

It is unprovable, of course, but it is possible and very probable that Leif and his men dipped their fingers into that water in the grass, and associated it with the drops of water from days of rain during the northeaster—drops which they saw clinging to blades of grass and which in the early morning light looked to them like dew. It was remarkable to find sweet water in the midst of sand dunes, and Leif's wonder at it may have been why he spoke of it a year later when he first told of his voyage.

"that cape which extended to the north from the land." **L 8**

This observation enters into the telling of directions as Leif sailed from the island into a sound. It thus appears to have been part of the experiences of that first day in the new land. However, it was not until some days later, after they had decided where they would spend the winter, that an exploring party discovered the fact that there was a cape which extended to the north from the land where they had built their house. That information, not available to them during their first day, came when they ascended to the top of a hill less than a mile and a half from their house. From that hill, Black Ball Hill, which has an elevation of 159 feet, they saw to the northwest the eastern shore of the land almost as far as to the site of Plymouth, and to the east of them, the narrow and lower portion of Cape Cod extending for twenty miles to the north from the land upon which they were. They saw the high ground near the northern end of the cape, and its northern end curved toward the west.

L 9   "sailed into a sound. . . . They steered in to the west of the cape."

The sound lay between the island and the cape. The island was south of or toward the south side of the sound, and the cape was to the north of the sound. The sound is identified in several ways. The wind on the fair day was from the south or southwest and was blowing Leif's ship northward. Leif's telling shows that he and his men modified the ship's direction, for they "steered in" to the west. Thus their course from the island was to the northwest. In his telling a year later, Leif showed that he and his men thought of "that cape which extended to the north from the land" as that narrow portion of Cape Cod from the site of Orleans to the tip beyond the site of Provincetown. He did not think of the Barnstable Peninsula (from Sandwich to Chatham) as part of the cape. In saying that he "steered in to the west of the cape" he meant that he sailed toward and along the south shore of the Barnstable Peninsula beyond the base of what he later recognized as the cape, that is, to the west of the site of Harwich Port. Leif said the inland waterway across which he sailed was a "sound." He thought of Nantucket Sound as a passage "between the island and . . . the land."[2]

The distance from Great Point of Nantucket to the Bass River is about nineteen nautical miles. With currents taken into account, and the probable force of the wind, the crossing of the sound by Leif's ship took about five hours. Leif's arrival was not late in September, as was erroneously stated in *Atlantic Crossings Before Columbus*, page 81. The mention of salmon "in the lake

[2] When I first identified Leif's "sound" as Nantucket Sound, shown on every map of New England as a sound, no wildest imagining could have prepared me for the blast that came from faraway Texas, from a university professor who wrote me that I was in error because Nantucket Sound is not a sound. If we must be pedestrian, let us look at the dictionary definition of a sound: "A long broad inlet generally parallel to a coast, or a passage between a mainland and an island."

and in the river" is very important because it shows that Leif arrived several days before the salmon ceased running. He arrived about the end of August, or the first of September. At that season on their first day Leif and his men had about fourteen hours of daylight.

Here is an approximate schedule of how they spent that day:

On Great Point after dawn	— about 2 hours
Crossing Nantucket Sound	— about 5 hours
The ship grounded about two hours before low tide, and rowing in the Bass River to the lake and back against the tide in both directions	— about 4 hours
Sailing the ship up the river to the lake	— about 1½ hours
Daylight remaining in which they built shelters	— about 1½ hours
	Total 14 hours

Since ebb tide occurred about halfway through the period during which the ship was grounded, and since ebb tide at the mouth of the Bass River occurs six hours and forty-three minutes after flood at Great Point of Nantucket, it is certain Leif and his men left Great Point about one hour before high tide there.

"a long distance to look to the ocean from the ship."   **L 10**

The Bass River has already been named as the river Leif ascended. But how can we know it was the Bass River? Several rivers flow into Nantucket Sound from the Barnstable Peninsula. It would not be enough to say that the Bass River is the largest of these and hence the most likely one. What, if anything, in Leif's telling identifies the Bass River?

The saga says of the water in the sound where the ship was grounded that "it was very shallow there at ebb tide." There are shallows off the mouth of the Bass River, but there are shallows also all along the south shore of the Barnstable Peninsula, in some places extending out for two miles. We know the ship was grounded near the mouth of the river for they "ran the boat to the land, into a river." The mention of shallows does not indicate the location. Note, however, that "at ebb tide" it was still shallow. At ebb there was some water under and around the hull of the ship, enough to keep it upright. The ship "stood." It had not heeled over high and dry on a mud flat. Leif's ship, a trading ship, had a draft of at least three and one-half feet. Since there are three and one-half to four feet of normal tide in Nantucket Sound, and the ship's keel touched bottom about two hours before ebb tide, there must have been at least two feet of water at ebb remaining under her and on all sides of her—"very shallow," as Leif said. Formerly, careless translators and those who based their theories upon their translation were led astray. Benjamin Franklin DeCosta's translation published in 1899 was quite misleading, for it brought up a picture of broad exposed mud flats: "a long distance between their ship and the water."

Let us look at the Icelandic text to see precisely what it says:

uar	tha	langt	til	siofar	at sia	fra	skipinu.
was	there	a long distance	to	look	to the ocean	from	the ship.

The word *sia* can mean merely "salt water," but not so here. The ship had entered a "sound" (Icelandic word *sund*), and in the context, *sia* in contradistinction to "sound" means "sea" or "ocean."

A year later when Leif had returned to his home in Greenland, his listeners wanted to know how they could find the river he ascended. His telling indicated to them precisely which river it was. He was speaking of a wilderness, with no hill or headland close to the mouth of the river, no large rock of unusual shape, no means therefore of giving the position of the mouth of the river in relation to any nearby feature. Whenever I am asked where the Bass River is, I reply, "About five miles east of Hyannis." There was no such identifying place-name for Leif to use. He could refer only to the "sound" and to the "ocean." But limited to these, he was nevertheless able to give his listeners precise geographical information, in the Icelandic words that have been quoted. From where the ship was grounded in shallow water at ebb tide near the mouth of the river, Leif said that the ocean was so distant that it was barely visible. How could this be?

Directly to the east of the stranded ship and miles away was the narrow sandbar which we call Monomoy. That sandspit is sometimes attached to Cape Cod as an extension southward, and sometimes it is an island. It makes no difference which it was in Leif's day. Leif had no doubt seen Monomoy before he landed on Great Point. He had certainly seen it from the top of the highest dune on Great Point where he probably stood on the shoulders of some of his men, with his eyes raised about ten feet above that highest dune, and thus at about fifty feet above sea level. Applying the formula for horizon visibility, the square root of 50 (say of 49) is 7, and 7 multiplied by 1.3226 gives $9\frac{1}{4}$ miles as the distance of Leif's visible horizon when he looked around from Great Point. Most of the dunes on Monomoy are twenty feet in height and some rise to thirty feet above sea level. To an eye at sea level they would be visible for about six miles.

But was Monomoy where it is now a thousand years ago? The answer is indicated in the fact that according to the maps and sailing directions of the earliest post-Columbian visitors, that is, since the days of Champlain, Gosnold, and the arrival of the *Mayflower,* Monomoy has not changed its position in relation to Cape Cod. "All of the earliest maps which are worth considering at all, including the rare manuscript map of 1606–07 by Champlain, clearly show that the representation of what we know as Monomoy Point or Island stretched from the very earliest times relatively as it is shown on the very latest chart of the United States Coast and Geodetic Survey."[3] Since Monomoy has been where it now is for more than 350 years, there is no good reason to assume that it was somewhere else one thousand years ago.[4]

---

[3] Warren Sears Nickerson, *Land Ho! 1620* (Boston: Houghton Mifflin, 1931), p. 79.

[4] The sands of Monomoy are presumably positioned by the line of the eastern shore of Cape Cod, which shore is said to be wearing away at the rate of three feet a year. Monomoy may have been three thousand feet farther east years ago.

From Great Point Leif could have seen dunes on Monomoy which were within fifteen miles of him. The southern end of Monomoy is only about eight miles from Great Point. From Great Point he saw Monomoy for about half its length. He knew it was a narrow sandspit on the east side of which was the open ocean, and on the west side the "sound."

From the masthead of Leif's grounded ship, the dunes of Monomoy off to the east gleaming in the sun of the late afternoon of a "fine day" were barely visible. The six miles of dune visibility plus the seven miles of masthead visibility meant that the man at the masthead could have seen the dunes if they were thirteen miles away. From the mouth of the Bass River to Monomoy is twelve miles. In Leif's day it could have been twelve and a half miles. To those dunes at the ocean edge it did indeed seem "a long distance to look." This was Leif's skillful and efficient way of telling seafaring Greenlanders how far they must sail into the "sound" from the open ocean to find the mouth of the river he ascended. This was a feature of his telling which his listeners, with appreciation of such practical information, vividly remembered and which thus became fixed in oral transmission.

L 11   "conveyed the ship up the river and to the lake."

The mouth of the Bass River is five hundred yards wide. To Leif and his men this was a sizable stream that invited investigation. No doubt they were steering toward it when the keel touched bottom. The river mouth was undoubtedly visible to them from their grounded ship. This is why, as the saga says, "they were so eager to go ashore that they could not wait for the tide to rise under the ship, but ran the boat to the land, into a river." From the ship to the lake from which the river flowed was about five and a half miles. Their rowing this distance and back against tidal flow in both directions could not have been accomplished in less than three hours. Undoubtedly they spent about an hour inspecting the shores of the lake for its available fresh water and camping site. They knew the duration of tides well enough to time their return to the ship close to the moment when it refloated.

With incoming tide and wind from the southwest they conveyed the ship up the river to the lake which they had found satisfactory for temporary shelter.

Two skeptics who at first opposed this identification of the river asserted that in Leif's day there was insufficient depth of channel in the Bass River for a viking ship with its draft of at least three and a half feet. They believed they had an absolutely unanswerable argument. They based their skepticism upon several incontrovertible facts: (1) The ocean level since about 1880 had been observed to be rising at the rate of about one foot in a century. (2) At Saugus, Massachusetts, archaeological investigation had revealed that the ocean level was three feet lower three hundred years ago. (3) On the Virginia coast submerged pine trees with Carbon 14 (C^{14}) dating of eight hundred years showed that the ocean level was eight feet lower eight hundred years ago. What could be more logical than the obvious arithmetic? From the observed one foot in one hundred years, three feet in three hundred years, and eight feet in eight hundred years, it seemed safe to conclude that the ocean level was ten feet lower a thousand years ago than at present. The Bass River, now with five or six feet of depth of channel, the skeptics said, "in Leif's day could have been no more than a brook."

This apparently inescapable judgment, since it was quite erroneous, should be a classic example against jumping to a conclusion.

In the days of Leif Erikson and Thorfinn Karlsefni, the earth's atmosphere was somewhat warmer than now. With some of the ice melted from Antarctica and Greenland, the sea level was correspondingly higher. Dr. Rhodes W. Fairbridge of the Department of Geology, Columbia University, in his "Report of Sea Level Changes" to the International Oceanographic Congress, on September 7, 1959, showed the considerable oscillations which are known by the dating of fossil mangrove and barnacles which can grow only between high- and low-tide levels, and of coral which grows only up to the low-tide level. The ocean level a thousand years ago was from $\frac{1}{2}$ meter to 1 meter, or about $2\frac{1}{2}$ feet higher than at present. But by A.D. 1200 extreme cold weather came in

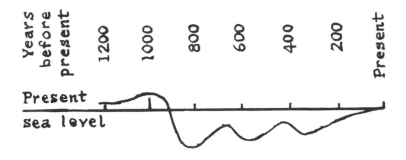

CURVE OF CHANGES OF SEA LEVEL

what is called the "Little Ice Age." Meadows in Greenland that had grown vegetables and some grain suffered permafrost. The ocean level dropped 10 feet rather suddenly, so that eight hundred years ago it was about 8 feet lower than now.[5]

L 12   "they decided to remain there that winter."

We do not know whether Leif had intended to winter in the new land or return home that summer. He may have decided to remain when he realized that he had luckily found a place that was perfectly suited for wintering. There were several factors in his decision. First, and of primary importance, was convenient access to a plentiful supply of good drinking water. About a hundred yards from where he decided to build a house is a spring at the shore of Follins Pond that flows at the rate of ninety gallons an hour—enough for a regiment. A second consideration in selecting a winter campsite in the wilderness was an area that offered promise of security against savages. The first settlers in a new country invariably chose a location with an eye to defense, often an island or easily defended elevation. The Dutch at the site of Albany, New York, settled on an island in the Hudson. The English

[5] R. W. Fairbridge, "Recent World-Wide Sea Level Changes and Their Possible Significance to New England Archaeology," *Bulletin, Massachusetts Archaeological Society.*

at Jamestown, the Walloons at Nova Belgica, the English at Boston, settled on islands. The map of the Bass River region shows that the south shore of Follins Pond, while not an island, was almost one. Overland access to it was possible by a narrow approach in only 10 degrees out of the 360. Leif's house, within a short distance, was more than three-quarters surrounded by water. In Leif's day a canoe could have crossed the Barnstable Peninsula without portage or, at most, with one portage of not more than a hundred yards. There is a modern proposal to cut a ship canal from Nantucket Sound to Cape Cod Bay via the Bass River waterway. Indian tribes on the peninsula were well aware of the streams and lakes and marshes, and to avoid having to cross them, their trail from west to east passed the portage site and followed high ground to the north of and out of sight of Follins Pond. Leif's caution in keeping half of his men always in the camp, and ordering the other half to go no farther away than would permit their return before nightfall, suggests that he and his men had seen the Indian trail and knew there were inhabitants in the region who might be hostile. As it happened, his winter campsite was not visited by savages during his occupancy or during the following three years, or so we assume from the saga.

"they built a large house."   **L 13**

The discovery of the site of Leif's house in Vinland had for two centuries been the principal goal of searching theorists. The intensity of the desire to find his house site had made it appear that little else mattered. At a time when I still shared the feeling that his house site was the all-important thing to find, I saw its half-cellar hollow. But because all cellar holes I had seen had stone walls or foundations, and it did not, I ignored it. This is, of all the mistakes I have made, the one I most deeply regret. Before evidence was found which established that hollow as the site of Leif's house in Vinland (see K 1), a roadway belonging to a housing development was bulldozed across it.

"ship shed."   **L 14**

The remains of that other building, the ship shed, were seen

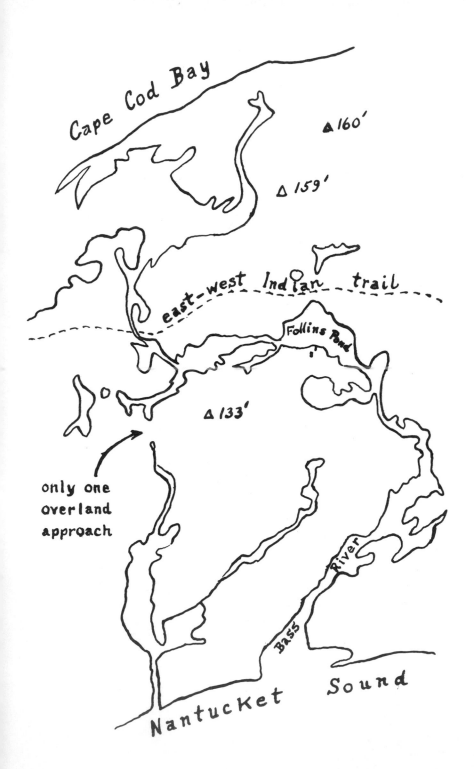

in May of 1952 by Howard C. Mandell, president of the Massachusetts Archaeological Society, by Dr. Maurice Robbins, and by me. They were only 250 feet from the site of the house. Illustrations are given to show how Leif and his men got the ship up from the shore of the lake where its keel was at least 3½ feet under, to the floor of the shed where it was 2 feet above high-tide level. In the operation of raising the ship 5½ feet up the shore incline, they moved it overland for a distance of 140 feet, until its stern was about 80 feet from the water.

Leif's ship, stripped of mast and gear, weighed about fourteen tons. The force needed to move this weight on rollers up an incline of one foot in seven was two tons. How much force could an average man in Leif's crew have applied with his back under the side of the hull? Two moving-van men showed the answer when they were trying to get their long vehicle around a corner of a narrow street, but could not clear the turn because an automobile parked at the corner was several feet out from the curb. The two men quickly solved their problem. They put their backs to the rear bumper of the automobile and lifted its rear end over to the curb. In doing this, each man lifted about five hundred pounds, and seemed to think nothing of it. Less than half of Leif's crew could readily have shored his ship. His entire crew would have made light work of it, and would not have needed the help of a windlass.

Here is the process by which they got the ship out of the lake and up into the shed:

First, they cut long lengths of tree trunks and stripped them of bark. They laid these parallel, perhaps three feet apart, from the water's edge to the inner end of the shed. These constituted a slideway or railway. The men prepared about forty logs of four or

**THE ONLY OVERLAND
APPROACH TO LEIF'S
SHELTERS**

WEIGHT OF MEN AT STERN RAISING THE PROW TO
START IT ON ROLLERS

five-foot lengths stripped of bark to serve as rollers, perhaps a roller for every eighteen or twenty inches of the length of the keel. Then about two-thirds of the crew bunched together in the ship at the stern to lower the stern in the water and lift her prow to get it started on the rollers. Then some of the men put their backs against the hull and pushed the ship up the incline, with other men placing rollers under the advancing prow until the entire length of keel as it came out of the water was on rollers. The pressure of the men's backs obviated any need for bilge blocks. When the ship was in position in the shed, extra rollers were probably placed under the keel. Where the keel pressed down unduly on any one of the rollers, that roller would bend down slightly to compensate. Props to keep the ship on even keel were placed slantingly to abut against the strakes a little below the gunwale. Two or three bilge blocks may have been used amidships on each side. Since the floor of the shed was level, the ship would not of itself start to roll out, and therefore it could be left all winter on the many rollers. As we shall see, however, there was one winter later on when the ship was lowered from the rollers to keel bearings that held the keel only one or two inches above the ground.

A shoring for a viking ship.   L 15

Publicity in the *Saturday Evening Post,* June 9, 1951, and in the *Reader's Digest* in September of that year, was pleasant and welcome. It appeared that smooth waters lay ahead for acceptance of my theory. This seemed the more certain when I first heard that some of the leaders of the Massachusetts Archaeological Society had decided to undertake a digging project in the area to which my theory pointed. My immediate reaction was that it would be perfectly splendid. With sober reflection a few minutes later, I felt consternation. They were asking me to show them precisely where they should sink their spades into the soil. They wanted me to tell them what they might expect to uncover. Out of the hundreds of thousands of square miles along the eastern portion of North America, I had dared to select a strip of land only a few acres in extent along one shore of a backwoods lake as the spot where Leif Erikson had spent a winter on our continent more than 950 years

**MEN AT SIDES
WHILE MOVING SHIP**

SHIP SHORED IN SHED ON ROLLERS

before. Had I been too rash in such pinpointing? My theory was now facing challenge by fact finders. I must show the members of the Massachusetts Archaeological Society where they would find positive evidence of viking occupancy, or my theory would be discredited. Could I tell them where there was such evidence when I myself did not know where it was? The south shore of Follins Pond would be a theater stage for a pitiless demonstration. It would be an arena in which my theory must wrestle with demanding, hardheaded specialists. Believe me, I was close to desperation.

I scrambled after all the possibilities of underground evidence of viking occupancy. I thought first of metal artifacts. Iron objects would probably have rusted away in the sandy and alternately wet and dry soil. As for bronze objects, could one hope that Leif Erikson or one of his men had lost a valued belt buckle on Cape Cod? The surface of the ground gave no hint as to where any lost object might lie. Mine detectors had been carried over every square yard of the area without indicating any buried metal. I decided to say nothing about the possibility of unearthing metal artifacts.

I thought of a kitchen midden, a refuse heap where Leif and his men and subsequent viking occupants of his house had flung out from the doorway the remains of meals, the bones of animals and fish, and the ashes with some charcoal from the fireplace. Some identifiable object from viking times might be found in such a refuse heap, but there was no surface evidence that such a heap had survived.

There was only one thing remaining that I could think of to suggest to the members of the Massachusetts Archaeological Society what they might find underground. That was evidence associated with a viking ship. The lives of Leif and his men in the North American wilderness depended upon their ship. They needed it in good condition to return to their homes in Greenland. Its undecked interior would be damaged by rain or snow that turned to ice. They would not leave their ship exposed in freezing weather. They must have hauled it on shore for the winter in accordance with the custom of all Norse mariners. They must have built a shed to keep it covered. All possibilities were reduced to this one—underground evidence that a viking ship had been shored for the winter. This was my hope. The chances seemed slight indeed, until, with a lift of the heart, I realized that I knew that there was only one place in the mile-long turns of the south shore of Follins Pond where a viking ship could have been brought ashore. That place was a gully, with something like a beach at the lake edge. The floor of the gully rose only slightly above the lake. Everywhere else along the south shore of the lake was a steep bank ten to thirty feet high with large boulders along its base. There was no place where Leif could have brought his ship ashore except in the gully which presented a gentle slope up from under the surface of the lake. The 160-foot length of gully floor rose to only five feet above high tide. That gully floor was thirty-five feet wide, and was enclosed by steep banks twenty to thirty feet in height on both sides and at the inner end.

In preparation for an appointed meeting with the president of the Massachusetts Archaeological Society, I concentrated my attention upon that gully. Something I observed, which I have never before mentioned, was a condition there different from anywhere else along the south shore of Follins Pond. It was a thirty-foot width of access to the gully from under the surface of the lake and at the lake shore. This underwater area was free of boulders. There were at least a half-dozen boulders in a sort of congestion at each side of that free approach. Obviously, the approach to the gully had been cleared by human agency, and I believed, by Leif and his men.

At the inner or southern end of the gully floor I observed a ridge of earth about eighteen inches in height and extending for twenty-three feet transversely across the end of the gully. At its ends and at right angles to it were two other ridges, one six feet long, the other shorter. These ran toward the lake. The ends of these short ridges tapered off to nothing. These three ridges appeared to be the remains of the walls of a rectangular structure that had been twenty-one or twenty-two feet wide inside. Suddenly, with almost a sense of shock, I felt I was seeing visible remains of the ship shed Leif Erikson had built.

On the day before the scheduled dig, Mr. Mandell went with

me to inspect the entire south shore of Follins Pond. We walked along the shore, commenting on what appeared to be possible sites for rewarding investigation, for he said they had planned for several separate groups of diggers. I showed him where a dozen piles of stones in three or four rows of three or four stones each had looked like a cemetery, but where one of the piles had been proved by a distinguished archaeologist to have been the work of nature, though another equally well-known archaeologist had subsequently declared that others of the piles had been assembled by man. There or near there on the next day, diggers uncovered a burial pit, revealed by soil discoloration. Not far from it other diggers uncovered a large Indian hearth, consisting of small stones which the squaws must have carried up the steep bank from the edge of the pond.

A physicist had familiarized me with statistical probabilities and their weight in a reasoned argument. Afterward I calculated the chances of anyone's guessing where in the Bass River waterway an archaeological dig would uncover a shoring for a viking ship, and of telling in advance the approximate size of the ship for which it had been made. This involved taking into account about fifty places along the river and on the north shore of Follins Pond where a ship could have been shored. A guesser would have had only one chance out of 14,000 of foretelling correctly the site and size. But I was not guessing. I was following a theory.

As a climax to the guided tour, I led Mr. Mandell to the gully. I showed him the earth ridges. He helped me measure them. Standing with him above the middle of the transverse ridge I pointed down the middle of the gully.

"Here is the most promising place for the Massachusetts Archaeological Society to dig tomorrow," I said.

"Dig for what?" he asked.

"For evidence that a ship has been kept on shore here for the winter, not built here, but stored." I had no notion as to the form in which that evidence might be. I did not at that time even know the technical word "shored," and so said "stored."

"How large a ship?" Mr. Mandell asked.

I had been told the dimensions of an oceangoing trading ship, a *knorr* such as Leif had. It was a ship of larger carrying capacity than the war vessels of viking times on exhibition in a museum at Oslo. I knew it had a high curved prow and stern, with one mast and a single square sail. It was undecked, with a space amidships for cargo, over which there was a tentlike covering. There were thwarts for rowers only near the ends. Steering was done with an oarlike rudder at the stern on the right side, the steerboard or starboard side. The ship was double-ended, pointed at both ends. In my mind's eye I pictured Leif Erikson's ship in the gully. This therefore was my reply to Mr. Mandell:

"The evidence should indicate a ship 18 feet wide and about 65 feet over-all length."

The shoring uncovered the next day was for a ship 18 feet wide and 69 feet long.

On the morning of Saturday, May 10, 1952, some fifty members of the Massachusetts Archaeological Society met at an appointed junction of two roads near Follins Pond. They were divided into three groups, two of which investigated the high ground nearest to the skerry toward the west end of the south shore of the lake. The largest group, led by the Director of Excavations, Dr. Maurice Robbins, entered the gully. It was with satisfaction that I later observed that the first thing this group had to do before they could begin digging was (with the owner's permission) to cut down the trees growing in the gully floor. Thereafter, what they found was all underground. No one could ever say that Frederick J. Pohl had previously known of what they unearthed and that he had somehow measured it. No one could accuse him of having planted it.

Immediately after the trees had been cleared away, the first trench, which was dug in the median line of the gully floor, exposed a vertical post three inches in diameter and about two feet in length. Its top was thirteen inches underground. Its bottom rested on a flat rock about a foot across. It was held vertical by two flat rocks set slantingly against its sides. Unquestionably it had been set in place to support a weight. In view of the theory upon which the party in the gully was functioning, those who uncovered the post thought it could be a keel bearing. It certainly seemed to be in keeping with what I had hopefully prognosticated. That prognostication now became a practical guide to further digging. Slightly over three feet from the post toward the west side of the gully the first trench had exposed also a slightly inclined stake less than two inches in diameter. This suggested that it could have been a prop used to keep a shored ship on even keel. If so, it seemed likely that a similar prop should be found on the east side at about the same distance from the post. I measured that distance and marked a spot for the diggers to excavate. They uncovered a prop within two inches of the spot I had marked. It seemed obvious that the post and the two props were parts of a ship shoring. They pointed to the whole pattern. All the trenches dug thereafter were directed by that pattern, with no wasted effort. From the more than six feet of distance between the two props, it was apparent that where the post had supported the keel, the ship was fully six feet wide. The end of the keel had not rested on that particular post. Dr. Robbins therefore directed the digging of a trench from the post toward the water. That trench uncovered another planted vertical post eleven feet from the first, down the median line of the gully.

All the keel bearings in line with the two posts were quickly uncovered by a trench dug to the inner end of the gully floor. These were three other planted posts and four stones on a level with the tops of the posts. One stone was accidentally removed in the digging, leaving the hollow where it had lain, so that its position and size were known. The thickest of the keel-bearing posts was five inches in diameter. Farther out from the line of the keel than the first two props were three more shoring props and two soil discolorations showing where props had rotted away. Fortunately there were enough keel bearings and props to reveal the length and shape of the ship that had been shored.

The unanticipated swift unearthing of the ship shoring was sensational. Newspaper men who witnessed it made it headline news not only in America but in Scandinavia. The next morning, however, they got material for a contrary story, from a pronouncement by a member of the Massachusetts Archaeological Society who had not previously entered the gully and did not know, as I

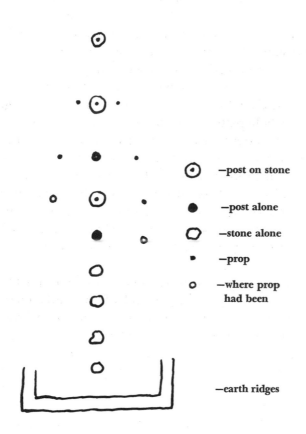

—post on stone

—post alone

—stone alone

—prop

—where prop
had been

—earth ridges

SHIP SHORING AND REMAINS OF SHED

also did not, that during the preceding day's excavation, Dr. Maurice Robbins had been compelled to dig a ditch down to the shore to drain water out of the trenches. The early-morning skeptic gave himself less than three minutes to inspect the excavations, for it seems he already knew what he was going to say. He suddenly and loudly declared: "Those pieces of wood are above the water table. Therefore, they cannot be more than a hundred and fifty years old —two hundred years at most. If older than that, the wood would have completely rotted away. This is where an American ship was concealed from the British in the War of 1812, or possibly during the War of the American Revolution. This is the end of your theory, Mr. Pohl!"

This rush to be quoted was not in the spirit of research. At the moment I found no words to make reply. I did not even have the wit to tell him what I had observed the day before, and ask the newspapermen present to substantiate me, that everything uncovered in the trenches had been very wet, and therefore the wood had probably been wet for centuries.

But these were afterthoughts. A year later I would have called the skeptic's attention to the three-foot canyon of winter erosion down the middle of the gully, since the dig had removed the tree and vine coverage. However, on that morning after the discovery, I was more of a novice than anyone there would have guessed. I had no background of archaeological experience. Instead of protesting as I should have, I was speechless. The newspapermen dashed away with a new story.

As we later unhappily realized, the rainwater drainage for centuries infected the wood of the shoring with new carbon so that accurate carbon dating was impossible.

Dr. Robbins removed the posts of largest diameter. He gave me several pieces of one, including the bottom end of it. That bottom end showed the bites of an ax that had been used to sever it from a tree trunk. The impressions of the ax blade which had cut in and stopped were complete in several instances. They showed the actual size of the ax and the curvature of its edge. The blade of the ax was just under two and three-quarter inches in length. This was a size common among the vikings, but much smaller

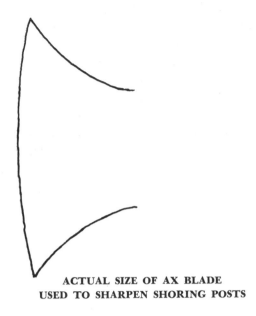

**ACTUAL SIZE OF AX BLADE
USED TO SHARPEN SHORING POSTS**

than the blades used by Colonial New Englanders when they resisted the British.

The shape and dimensions of the ship for which the shoring
had been made were definitely established.

The inclination of the shoring props was less than two inches
to a vertical foot. The props on each side which were farthest out
were about eight and a half feet away from the line of keel bearings. The tops of those props were, we estimate, about sixteen feet
apart. They would have abutted against the under edge of the waterline strakes, strakes which were thicker and stronger than the
other strakes. Each gunwale extended out about one foot beyond
the waterline. The width of the ship for which the shoring in the
Follins Pond gully was made was as nearly as can be estimated
eighteen feet.

We knew that the keel must have been slightly longer than
the distance from the first post to the last stone of the keel bearings. That distance was fifty-eight feet. The length of the keel must
have been at least fifty-nine feet. The curved stempieces at bow

and stern of a viking ship extended beyond the keel for about five feet. The overall length of the ship that had been shored in the Follins Pond gully was believed to have been about sixty-nine feet. The official report of the M.A.S. said "about seventy feet."

I had been told that the official report in the *Bulletin* of the M.A.S. would present a diagram of the shoring which Dr. Robbins had drawn. When the report was published without any diagram, but with a quotation of a prejudgment against the shoring, I felt that the skeptics were having the last word, a word which it would be arrogant of me to challenge. It was then that several men familiar with shipyards and much better acquainted than I with the negative prejudgments to which skeptics are prone, advised me to make an independent study of the shoring to see whether it would tell us for what kind of ship it was set up.

The facts uncovered by the dig were the basis for my study. The tops of nine keel bearings, four of the five posts and the five stones, were at a level, as had been shown by a transit instrument in the hands of Dr. Maurice Robbins. The top of the fifth post was two inches below that level. Those two inches had presumably rotted away. The original inclined surface of the gully floor at the time the shoring had been made had undoubtedly been dug out to a level slightly below the tops of the keel bearings. Soil flow had since then restored the gully floor to an inclined surface. The M.A.S. diggers found the end of the shoring nearest the lake at thirteen inches underground, and the inner end at more than three feet under. The soil levels under the topsoil were sand on top of a peat bog resting on blue clay. The keel bearings showed that the ship had a level, not a curved keel. They also showed that the ship had an equal draft fore and aft, since a ship with a deeper draft aft is shored on inclined bearings to keep its deck level.

A ship is brought ashore bow first. Fortunately, in the Follins Pond gully it was at the end of the shoring nearest the lake that the props which held the ship on even keel had survived. Their positions showed that the ship's stern was pointed. The bow would have been no less sharp. Thus we knew that the ship for which the shoring was made was a double-ender.

Unquestionably the shoring was more primitive in every detail than would be typical in the late eighteenth or early nineteenth century in New England. Of this there was ample evidence,
as shown in my *Atlantic Crossings Before Columbus,* p. 118. One
most revealing fact that stood out from all the above-stated observations was that the keel-bearing stones and planted posts of the
shoring in the Follins Pond gully had upheld the weight of the
ship that had rested upon them, and had kept her keel a few
inches above the prepared level surface of the ground.

My study narrowed down to this question: Do those keel
bearings tell us anything about the weight of the ship that had
rested upon them? In other words, what was the maximum weight
which those keel bearings could have supported? A definite answer
to this question was published with the diagram in the *Bulletin* of
the M.A.S. for April 1955.

The findings were more fully presented on pages 119 to 122
of *Atlantic Crossings Before Columbus.* Since that book is out of
print, I repeat here the essential details:

A "bearing value" of a support is the maximum weight it can
hold without being pushed down until its top is flush with the
ground. The fact that the tops of the planted keel-bearing posts
were on a level with the tops of the keel-bearing stones is evidence
that the keel had indeed been held clear of the ground. Therefore,
the ship for which the shoring was made must have weighed less
than the total bearing values of the keel supports.

The factors which determine the bearing value of a support
are its diameter, the kind of soil in which it is embedded, and to a
slight extent, its length. Bearing values can be ascertained with
close accuracy for the purposes of those who plan foundations and
drive pilings.

The original notes made by Dr. Maurice Robbins in the Follins Pond gully gave the horizontal diameters of the keel-bearing
stones and posts:

Stone under first post	$13'' \times 14''$
Stone under second post	$19'' \times 19''$
Third post	$4\frac{1}{2}''$

Stone under fourth post	7″	× 11″
Fifth post	3″	
Fourth stone	7″	× 9″
Fifth stone	c. 7″	× 9″
Sixth stone	13″	× 10″
Seventh stone	c.13″	× 10″

The seven stones have a total horizontal area of slightly less than seven square feet. The average length of the posts is two feet. Professor Donald M. Burmister, of the Department of Civil Engineering and Soil Mechanics at Columbia University, an authority in his field, made what he called a generous assumption in estimating that the total areas of all the keel bearings are nine square feet. Professor Burmister allows 2 to $2\frac{1}{2}$ tons to the square foot for the bearing values. This gives the total immediate and temporary values as 18 tons, and the total after "settling," which occurred in a few weeks, as $22\frac{1}{2}$ tons.

Thus the bearing values of the shoring in the Follins Pond gully tell us that the ship which was held up on the shoring weighed less than $22\frac{1}{2}$ tons. This means that it was not made for any known type of American ship. Every known type of American ship of the size indicated was two to three and a half times too heavy to have been supported on the keel-bearing posts and stones in the Follins Pond gully. This is not a matter of opinion. It is a fact, as witnessed by all the records as shown in Henry Hall's *Report on the Shipbuilding Industry in the United States,* published by the Department of the Interior, 1884, and in the exhaustive and authoritative studies by Howard I. Chapelle in *The History of American Sailing Ships,* 1935, and *American Sailing Craft,* 1936. Furthermore, of all the ship types known to have been in use in New England waters in post-Columbian times and down to the present, any vessel of the dimensions indicated would weigh from 40 to 70 tons. Any of the types known to have been in use in New England in the late eighteenth or early nineteenth century (sloops, schooners, and late-type, decked chebacco boats) of the size indicated would weigh 60 to 70 tons. Some earlier (seventeenth-century) types of open or half-decked shallops, and some ketches and some later (eighteenth-century) types such as pinkies, of the size indicated, would possibly weigh as little as 40 tons. So would a more recent faster-sailing type of New England fisherman, but her draft would bar the latter from this discussion. A large whaleboat might have been 60 feet long, but certainly not more than 10 feet in beam.

Because Americans in the nineteenth century built clipper ships and racing yachts which outsailed British ships and made world records, there has been a smug assumption that American ships were always superior in construction. This was not so. At first there were no trained boat builders in America. Ships of the early colonies were makeshift vessels from European models, crudely built by trial and error. In planning vessels of oceangoing size, American shipbuilders had three aims: speed, cargo capacity, and seaworthiness. As a generality, speed calls for lightness of hull, lightness of draft, sharp bows, and narrowness of beam. Large carrying capacity requires fuller lines, marked breadth of beam, and rather deep, strong hulls. The demands of seaworthiness tend to tip the scales in favor of construction of somewhat greater weight than would be necessary or desirable where speed alone is the objective.

New England ships of the late eighteenth and early nineteenth centuries, and of the dimensions indicated, were heavy because they were stiffened against longitudinal bending and transverse racking, and because they were decked. The deck of an oceangoing vessel must be strong enough to withstand the crushing weight of waves that may break upon it. A deck adds more than fifty percent to the weight of a ship; for in addition to deck beams and stanchions and heavy knees to hold the beams, and the weight of a hatchway, which requires strong bracing, the hull itself must be built with greater solidity to be rigid enough to support the knees and deck beams. A decked ship is also more heavily masted.

To get a vessel 69 feet overall and 18 feet in beam, of any heavy American type, into position on a shoring, would call for timberwork, such as cross members, and possibly a "marine railway" with some cribwork; in any case, timber in such quantity

KEEL BLOCKING BY WEDGES

that the use of less suitable material like stones would be unlikely to say the least.

In all the history of shipbuilding, is there any ship of the size indicated, which would have been supported on the shoring in the Follins Pond gully? The answer is Yes. There was one such type, and, so far as is known, only one. A vessel of the given dimensions, an open boat of lapstrake or clinker-built construction, of the type used by the vikings, with most of her hull planks only three-quarters of an inch thick, would weigh, without her equipment, as little as 10 to 13 tons. The ninth-century Gokstad ship in the Oslo Museum, 76½ feet overall, 17 feet in beam, fully equipped, weighed, according to Professor A. W. Brøgger's estimate in *The Viking Ships,* 20.2 metric tons, about 22½ short tons. Stripped for hauling up, without ballast, mast, oars, anchor, and gear, the Gokstad ship weighed less than 15 tons.

Open viking ships had wave-riding qualities, since they lacked rigidity and were actually flexible.

It is positively demonstrated and beyond contradiction that the keel-bearing posts and stones in the Follins Pond gully were set up for a ship that weighed as little as a viking ship. We know of no other type of ship in all the history of shipbuilding that could have been supported on that shoring. There is an unanswerable conclusion. That shoring was for a viking ship.

But was it for Leif Erikson's ship? Here follows strong evidence that seems to answer that question:

Let us consider what had happened to Leif's ship. The replacement of substantially more than half the length of the original keel with makeshift devices in the emergency on Keel Cape produced at best an imperfect fitting of the new section of keel to the garboards. When the ship was back on the ocean waves, the working of the ship unavoidably opened some seams and joints between the new timbers. And certainly while the ship was out of the water and shored in the shed the following winter at Leif's Shelters, the drying of the green wood of the new timbers caused shrinking which further opened seams. For more than half the length of the ship, the joints between the new section of keel and the new garboards had to be recalked. But the many rollers on which the keel rested denied access to the garboards, and so Thorvald's men were forced to undertake considerable labor to be able to do the recalking. First, with keel blocking by wedges driven in from each side, they raised the keel enough to release the rollers. Then by gradual knocking out of wedges simultaneously all along the keel they lowered the keel until it rested on a row of stones that held it one or two inches above the ground. Why did they perform the additional labor of digging away the ground under more than half the length of the keel and of planting posts? The easy thing to do with a ship that needed recalking of garboards would have been to lay her on her side, or careen her to expose her bottom. But the ship that had been on the shoring in the Follins Pond gully was not careened. Why not? Men with experience in the handling of ships say that the only logical reason is that her hull at her middle at the gunwale was of insufficient strength to support her weight, as was the case with a viking ship. Access to the garboards was not possible until the ground had been dug away under a keel-bearing stone and a post planted in its place. This was done under each of five keel-bearing stones. Since the posts were only two feet in length, the digging away of earth and their planting provided only two feet of free space under and close to the keel—not enough space to perform effective carpentry work—just enough space to recalk the juncture of keel and garboards. The recalking was no doubt piecemeal at each dug-out area, which was refilled before the next area was dug. For relaunching, there was the labor of jacking up the keel high enough to place the rollers under it.

Leif Erikson's ship was at his campsite in Vinland for four winters, with the need for recalking after that fourth winter. Later, Karlsefni's ship was at Leif's Shelters for two winters, and the small ship of Thorvard and Freydis for one winter, but the bringing of them into the shed and leaving them on rollers would not have disturbed the keel-bearing stones and planted posts. Was the shoring in the Follins Pond gully for Leif Erikson's historic ship? We cannot be sure. It is clear that the ship for which that shoring was made needed the recalking which his ship needed after its keel had been replaced by Thorvald and his men. The evidence does not prove that it was his ship that was supported on that shoring, but the evidence does go far toward convincing us that it was his ship.

"Salmon abounded in the river and in the lake"   L 16

One appeal the new land had for Leif and his men was a plentiful food supply, easily procured.

They found salmon larger than they had ever seen, both in the river and in the lake. Except when the ship was shored in the winter months, the mooring hole in the rock islet or skerry in Follins Pond was probably used to moor the ship, and not for salmon fishing.[6] Leif's men would have done their salmon fishing in the lake from their after-boat, or from the shore. A bright fire at night on the bank five to ten feet above the water would attract the salmon, and the fish would have jammed in so close together that men could scoop them up out of the water by hand. As for catching salmon in the river, the large rock at the narrowest point of the river about a mile and a half from the house was in the ideal position for a mooring hole (which it has) which could be used by a small boat fishing for or spearing salmon. A hearth described in 1861 by the Reverend Abner Morse which would seem to have

---

[6] A ship is said to be moored when fastened at both ends, usually by an anchor at the prow and a line to shore at the stern. A mooring hole is a chisel-driven hole from three to five inches or more in depth, in a rock within a few feet of what had been the water's edge when the hole was made. The hole is usually in a surface slanting away from the water, so that a metal pin or wooden peg resting in the hole will not be pulled out by a strain on the hawser attached to it, but can be brought out by an upward fling of the hawser.

been a viking hearth like those "in Scandinavia . . . near fishing places," was unearthed about 1840 in the low bank directly opposite the mooring-hole rock, locally called the Blue Rock. Presumably, the salmon there taken from the river were smoked or dried for winter consumption less than a hundred feet from where they were caught.

The saga's telling us that Leif and his men fished for salmon is a factor that I failed to take into account when I first supplied data to Professor Melvin Landon for his astronomical computation (see *Atlantic Crossings Before Columbus*, p. 81) by which we sought to establish the date of Leif's arrival upon the coast of the North American continent. From the times of full moon, Professor Landon ascertained that high tide occurred at Great Point of Nantucket at 6 A.M. on September 28 in the year 1003. I had accepted that as the probable date of Leif's landing. But more careful consideration of the time schedule of Leif's first day in the new country points to a high tide on Great Point at about 8 A.M. This occurred on September 30. However, the mention of the salmon fishing requires a further correction. When there were salmon at Cape Cod, the salmon ceased running shortly after the first week in September, according to information supplied by the United States Fish and Wildlife Service. The salmon-fishing evidence thus points to one synodic month earlier. A synodic month is approximately twenty-nine days and twelve hours. Subtracting this from September 30, gives September 1, 1003, as the approximate date of Leif's arrival. Professor Landon says, "This is as close as you can get it."

On my first visit to Follins Pond and the Bass River, my discovery of the two mooring holes seemed to be of greatest significance. I looked upon them as the best corroborating evidence. Later, when a half-dozen evidences had been established by three archaeological digs, the mooring holes seemed of less importance. Because they had been overemphasized, I omitted mention of them in *The Viking Explorers*. The weakness of a mooring hole as evidence, even though it is precisely at the spot to which theory points, is that no one can say with certainty by whom it was made. No one can prove its age. I have this to say, however. The mooring holes made by the Swedes when they landed in 1638 at Fort Christina on the Delaware River look less weathered than those in Minnesota. Mr. H. R. Holand's claim for the mooring holes in Minnesota is that they were made in 1362, the date of the Kensington Runestone Inscription. The mooring holes in Follins Pond and the Bass River look older, more weathered than those I have seen in Minnesota. The same is true of the most weathered of the mooring holes which I have seen along the Atlantic Coast, in Newport Harbor, in Kingston Bay north of Plymouth, Massachusetts, and in Nova Scotia. But such judgment is subjective and cannot establish anything. It merely posits a supposition. It does not take into account the varying hardnesses of rock and conditions of climate.

"cattle fodder" *(fenedr fodr)* . . . "grass" *(graus)*.   **L 17**

An identification of botanical facts cannot be used to pinpoint geography.

Cattle fodder in the open all winter sounded like paradise to Greenlanders.

The grass, which Leif said was "little withered" throughout the winter, was in all probability marsh grass *(Distichlus spicata)*, with some sedges. Marsh grass is variously called "salt grass" and "fresh grass." It covers large swampy areas along the Bass River and the north shore of Follins Pond, and along the waterway to the west of Follins Pond, and along waterways all over Cape Cod. The Plymouth Colony in its early days sent men in boats to Cape Cod to gather the salt grass as hay for their cattle. The marsh grass grows to a height of about three feet. Some which I cut in September 1964 and kept on a shelf at home was still partly green two years later. Seeing it standing uncut on the Cape, and observing how it kept its color through the winter, Leif guessed it had remained edible. His assumption that it "seemed" there "might" be no lack of cattle fodder in the winter was later proved correct when Karlsefni brought cattle to Leif's Shelters.

"Eyktarstad"   **L 18**

A. M. Reeves wrote in *The Finding of Wineland the Good*, p. 181:

We are informed by a treatise, inserted in the printed text of

Rimbegla, written by Bishop John Arnason, that the method adopted by the ancient Icelanders for the determination of the various periods of the day, was to select certain so-called "eykt-marks" *(eyktamörk)* about every dwelling as, peaks, knolls, valleys, gorges, cairns, or the like, and to note the position of, and course of the sun by day, or the moon and stars by night, with relation to these "eykt-marks." The circle of the horizon having been thus artificially divided in the absence of clocks or watches, certain names were assigned to the position which the sun occupied at, as we should say, certain "hours" of the day; "dagmalastadr," literally "day-meal-stead," indicating the position of the sun at the "day-meal," which was the principal morning meal. We have, unfortunately, no accurate data which might enable us to determine the position of the sun at "dag-malastadr"; such information we have, however, concerning "eykt," for it is stated in an ancient Icelandic law code, that "if the southwest octant be divided into thirds, it is "eykt" when the sun has traversed two divisions and one is left untraversed."

There is excellent authority for interpreting "eykt" as a point on the horizon one-third of the way from West to South. In modern compass terms this would be at West 30° South. As stated in *The Viking Explorers,* pp. 107–8, it is now recognized that the vikings had more astronomical knowledge than had formerly been supposed. They had a horizon directional finder, or bearing dial. There had been many commentaries on the meaning of *eykt.* It had been generally accepted that *eykt* nearly coincides with *none,* the ninth hour, about 3:00 P.M., when the chief meal was eaten in Rome. Richard Cleasby and Gudbrand Vigfusson, in their *Icelandic-English Dictionary,* say,

The passage in Edda—that autumn ends and winter begins at sunset at the time of Eykt—confounded the commentators, who believed it to refer to the conventional Icelandic winter, which (in the Old Style) begins with the middle of October and lasts three months. In the latitude of Reykholt—the residence of Snorri—the sun at this time sets at about half-past four. Upon this statement the commentators have based their reasoning both in regard to *dagmál* and *eykt,* placing the eykt at half-past four P.M., and dagmál at half-past seven A.M., although this contradicts the definition of these terms in the law. The passage in Edda probably came from a foreign source, and refers not to the Icelandic winter but to the astronomical winter, viz., the winter solstice or the shortest day; for sunset at half-past three is suited not to Iceland, but to the latitude of Scotland and the southern parts of Scandinavia.

In summary of all the factors, we know within five or ten minutes as to precisely when Leif and his men observed the setting sun at the horizon. The astronomical evidence seems unimpeachable. The evidence of Leif's telling is that he and his men in Vinland on the shortest day (*um skamdegi*) of the year observed that the setting sun touched the horizon in the Eykt direction at about 4:30 P.M. This astronomical observation indicates that Leif's campsite in Vinland was south of the latitude of Boston. The latitude of the south shore of Follins Pond is 41° 42′ 20″. At that latitude the sun on the shortest day in winter sets at 4:31 P.M. local time. The Icelandic text says literally, "The sun had there Eyktarstad [*Sol hafde thar eyktarstad*]."

The descending disk of the sun touching the horizon or being still visible at the horizon while it was disappearing could be an appearance continuing for more than ten minutes. But in the mention of mealtime the saga has a significance which deserves special attention, for it is an untampered-with record of men who followed instinctual guidance to an extent we moderns have forgotten how to do. Leif and his men gave heed to their internal clocks, their built-in time sense. Their appetite-alerted knowledge of mealtime was not a question of as much as ten minutes one way or the other. As a group they knew their mealtime within five minutes of accuracy.

From the top of a hill only a quarter of a mile south of Leif's house, there is to be seen, or was to be seen before the recent growth of trees, what looks like a level land horizon from the northwest to the south and beyond. That land horizon, being higher than a sea horizon, introduces a time error. It makes sunset appear to occur sooner. This, however, tends to offset the fact that actual sunset occurs several minutes before apparent sunset.

"vines [*vin vid*]."

Flexible vines which would make binding material were of great value in a day when metal nails were extremely costly. This is why Leif ordered his men to "cut vines" as well as timber for his ship's cargo. In spite of the apparent association of vines and grapes in his telling, it should be clear that the vines he ordered cut were not grapevines. Grapevines are not sufficiently flexible to serve as withies. He would not have given grapevines cargo space.

No vines of any kind grow north of Nova Scotia. Without any evidence whatsoever, it has been asserted by those who want us to believe that the land where Leif found vines was Newfoundland, that vines grew in Newfoundland when the climate was warmer one thousand years ago. Proof that they did is lacking. It is possible that they did. It is unlikely, however. This is why I have said that botanical evidence cannot pinpoint geography. The present fact is that on Cape Cod flexible vines (*Smilax rotundifolia*) called greenbrier, because of their many long sharp thorns, grow so thick that they often obstruct passage through the woods. They are a notable feature of the terrain. But when cut—that is, stripped of thorns—they make excellent withies. Since *vin vid*, meaning "vine wood" or "vine trees" is the expression Leif used, we can dismiss the argument of those who bring forward one of the primitive meanings of *vin* which is "meadow," and who say it points to grass, not vines. Leif used the word *graus* ("grass") separately from *vin vid*. And for what earthly reason would he have taken grass to Greenland as part of his ship's cargo?

L 20   "wine berries [*vin ber*]."

In the combination *vin ber, vin* means "wine" rather than "vine." In Old Icelandic *vin* had both meanings.

The grapes corroborate the time schedule. Leif and his men arrived in the land of vines about the end of August or the first of September and fished for salmon until the salmon ceased running approximately between the 8th and 10th of September. Then they built a house, in two or three days. After that they started cautious exploring, and then Tyrker found grapes. Wild grapes ripen on Cape Cod in mid-September.

Leif gave the land a name that fitted its products, and called it Vinland.

Thorfinn could not have failed to appreciate Leif's cleverness in inventing a name that brought to mind two products of the land, a name with double meaning, a punning name; for Vinland meant "Vineland" and also "Wineland." It meant both Land of Withies and Land of Grapes.

Leif came of a land-naming family. In coining "Vinland," he may have been thinking of a legend that had existed for centuries, a story of a land beyond the western ocean which had in it many grapevines. Lucian of Samothrace, in the second century B.C., wrote what he called "A True Story":

> I tell all kinds of lies in a plausible and specious way—everything in my story is a more or less comical parody of the poets, historians, and philosophers of old, who have written much that smacks of miracles and fables. I myself, thanks to my vanity, was eager to hand something down to posterity, that I might not be the only one excluded from the privilege of poetic license, and as I had nothing true to tell, I took to lying. I shall at least be truthful in saying that I am a liar. By my own admission I am not telling a word of truth. Once upon a time, setting out from the Pillars of Hercules and heading for the western ocean with a fair wind, I went a-voyaging. My motive was intellectual curiosity and a desire for adventure, and my wish to find out what the end of the ocean was. The second day the wind freshened, and drove my ship for seventy-nine days. I came to a high wooded island, and in it were a number of large grapevines and a river of wine, from which I got drunk.

The legend of a wineland to the west was probably fostered by the bringing into western European ports of wine on ships from the Mediterranean. Northern Europeans associated wine with ships which came to them out of the ocean.

Some of the references to Vinland called it Wineland. It was more generally known as Vinland, which is the precise spelling in the *Graenlendinga Saga,* and is the spelling used in the Map of 1440 at Yale University Library.

"the western part of the land"   T I

From observations easily made by small boat in Nantucket

Sound to the west of the mouth of the Bass River, and by men who climbed to the top of German Hill, Thorvald knew that Nantucket Sound extended westward into another sound. The tidal set indicated an extensive inland waterway.

The sparseness of the report of the men who explored the inland waterway to the west raises a question as to whether the after-boat party did not actually see much more than the saga tells. It seems improbable that no single outstanding geographical feature of the land to the west had impressed them. There is no reason to suppose they stopped exploring when they reached the western end of Long Island Sound. Being such men as they were, who had been sent on purpose to explore, they would most probably have pushed into and through the East River and so into New York Harbor.

It was probably not until after crops had been planted at Leif's Shelters that they started out, and they returned by harvest-time. What with delays in waiting for fair winds, and the exploring of bays and inlets, the small-boat party was kept busy for three months. The distance from the Bass River to the western end of Long Island Sound is two hundred twenty miles as the crow flies. If Thorvald's men followed the turns of bays and inlets and rivers, they explored at least three times that length of coast.

For maximum safety at night, they would drill a hole on the land side of a rock near the water's edge on the sheltered side of an island, into which they would put a peg with line attached, and so moor the boat. The mooring holes in the Follins Pond skerry and in some rocks near the east end of the south shore of the pond, and the hole in the Bass River rock are all more than an inch in diameter. So also are those found in Manitoba and Minnesota between Hudson Bay and Kensington, Minnesota, in what appears to be the pattern of the Kensington Party journey. So also are those which the Swedes made at their first arrival at the site of Wilmington, Delaware, and others along the Atlantic seacoast from New York to Newfoundland. But Mr. Bernard W. Powell found mooring holes very much smaller, only seven-eighths of an inch in diameter near Greenwich, Connecticut. Since these are of a size sufficient for the mooring of an after-boat, a search should be made for holes of that smaller size on all the rocky islets in Buzzards Bay, Narragansett Bay, and off the Connecticut shore, such as the islands at Stonington, and the many islands known as The Thimbles off Stony Creek. If an extensive pattern of weathered seven-eighths-inch mooring holes were established, it might stand as evidence of Thorvald's after-boat exploring party.

It was more desirable to have the mooring line attached to a peg in a hole in a rock rather than tied to a tree, for in an emergency, such as an attack by savages, someone would have to go on shore to untie the line from a tree, but the peg in a hole in a rock could be instantly released by an upward fling of the line by a man on board the vessel. In 1947 when I first explored the Bass River and Follins Pond area, my finding of mooring holes there came as a novelty to most readers, who had never heard of them before. Such a deep impression was made that some readers did not realize that the subsequently discovered archaeological evidences were far more important. In *Atlantic Crossings Before Columbus* (1961), I wrote, pages 99–100, "There is no way of proving that any particular hole in North America was made by the vikings. If any man claims that his grandfather made a particular mooring hole, he can have it, except for one thing, that the unusual height above water of the mooring holes of the Follins Pond skerry and of the Bass River Blue Rock strongly indicate that those two holes were made at a time when the sea level (tidal level in river and lake) was several feet higher than today.

"eastward with the merchant ship"   **T 2**

Note how this matches with the geographical directions indicated in L 8, L 9, and L 10.

"Keel Cape," where Thorvald erected the broken keel as a monu-   **T 3**
ment is adequately identified in Part One.

"eastward along the land [*austr firir landit*]."   **T 4**

In the nineteenth century, Benjamin F. DeCosta mistranslated these Icelandic words as "in a northerly direction on an East Coast," as though they were descriptive of the New England coast from Cape Ann to Portland. This egregious error led many astray. The Cape Ann to Portland coast—"the coast to the northward"— was referred to in the first sentence of the telling of that summer's voyage. The words *austr firir landit* tell us that Thorvald sailed down east.

T 5   "they sailed . . . into the mouths of a fjord that was near there."

By definition a fjord is a long and comparatively narrow arm of the sea indenting a mountainous coast. Its rocky walls descend without interruption to considerable depths, and these walls rise to considerable heights. The *Encyclopedia Americana* says, "The Hudson River from the head of tidal water (near Beacon) down to New York Bay has the characteristics of a fjord." The Highlands of the Hudson from Storm King Mountain past West Point and Bear Mountain to Dunderberg Mountain, and to the south the Palisades, make the lower half of the Hudson a true fjord.

According to the sagas, there were two fjords in Vinland. South of Cape Breton Island, there are only two fjords along the eastern coast of the continent of North America. One is the Hudson. The other is Somes Sound in Mt. Desert Island in Maine. Hollywood used Somes Sound for scenes in *The Viking*, supposed to occur in a fjord in Norway.

Ordinarily one would expect a fjord to have one mouth. The most widely accepted rendering of the Icelandic words *fiardar kiafta* in the nineteenth century had been "the mouth of a fjord." But *kiafta* was plural. I consulted Dr. Halldór Hermannsson, professor of Scandinavian Languages and Literatures at Cornell University, and curator of the Fiske Icelandic Collection at Cornell. Dr. Hermannsson informed me that "fjord mouths" is the correct translation.

Somes Sound has four mouths or entrances: one between Mt. Desert Island and Sutton Island; one between Sutton Island and Little Cranberry Island; one between Little Cranberry Island and Great Cranberry Island; and one by which Thorvald and his men probably entered, the so-called Western Way between Great Cranberry Island and Seawall on Mt. Desert Island.

T 6   "headland which extended out there"

**MT. DESERT ISLAND
SHOWING THE MOUTHS OF A FJORD**

Mr. B. L. Hadley, superintendent of Acadia National Park, wrote me that the headland at the mouth of Somes Sound is a "small isolated mountain which is called the *flying mountain,* the Indian tradition being that this piece flew off from the larger mountain near it, and alighted in the Sound." It is a most apt description.

The mountain scenery and what happened inside the fjord impressed Thorvald's men unforgettably. Their narrative from this point on is so vividly circumstantial that we are able to trace their steps within ten or fifteen feet to at least five places to which they went.

T 7   "There they berthed their ship and put out the gangplank to shore"

There are three ways of holding a ship at rest. When "anchored" it swings on a hawser from the prow. It is said to be "moored" when it is held away from touching land by a hawser at each end, the one from the prow usually to an anchor, and the one from the stern either to a fixed float or to a bollard on a wharf, or to an object on shore such as a tree or a rock. A ship is moored where there are tides or currents or winds that might cause it to be damaged by hitting something if it were allowed to swing at anchor. A ship is said to be "berthed" when it is brought sideways close to a wharf or to the shore. It is there held from drifting away by lines from the ends, but usually some intervening device or soft buffer is used to prevent its side from actually touching and scraping the object to which it is berthed.

The natural berthing site at the eastern side of Flying Mountain is so extraordinary that its existence identifies it with practical certainty as Thorvald's landing place.

There is a twelve-foot tide in Somes Sound. The water level changes two feet an hour. Thorvald and his men left their ship berthed to rocks in such tidal water because they saw there was no danger of its hull touching bottom.

Even with the ocean level about two and one-half feet higher a thousand years ago, and the land of Mt. Desert about two and one-half feet below its present post-glacial uplift, the difference of five feet would in no way change our identification of the berthing site, because the tides in Somes Sound are twelve feet.[7]

"Thorvald and all his companions went up on the land"   **T 8**

All left the ship because nobody could approach it overland behind their backs. Another word besides "all" in the quoted sentence is a geographical pointer. They went "up" on the land. The beach led them to where they scrambled up a fifteen-foot bank which today may be mounted by a stairway.

"Thorvald then remarked, 'Here it is fair' "   **T 9**

The word "fair [*fagurt*]" was an all-inclusive term. It meant "beautiful," a place where there was a convenient meeting of salt water and mountain. More importantly, it meant a place where timber could be cut on slopes above and rolled down to a shore where it would not have to be unhandily transported by a small boat out to an anchored or moored ship and there be lifted over the gunwale, but could be carried on board over a gangplank. To Thorvald personally the word "fair" meant "homelike." Both Brattahlid and this land (to which he had gone up) were on the west side of a north-south fjord. The land which he called fair had all advantages. Between the mountain and the salt water of the fjord was cleared meadowland suitable for grazing cattle, with springs of fresh water for the cattle and the men. Cattle on the moors at Brat-

---

[7] As stated on page 131 of *The Lost Discovery,* I had understood that the state geologist of Maine was of the opinion that there had been no appreciable changes in shoreline in relation to tide levels in Somes Sound in the last thousand years— and this at a time when I believed that there had been a steady rise in ocean level over that period. I later accepted the showing of Dr. Rhodes W. Fairbridge of the Department of Geology of Columbia University that the ocean level in Thorvald Erikson's day had been about two and one-half feet higher than at present. This left a confusion—a way open for my readers to assume that at the Maine coast the land had risen about two and one-half feet, and thus the tide levels in Somes Sound in relation to the land are now precisely the same as in Thorvald's day. This is by no means established, and my failure on page 115 of *The Viking Explorers* to correct the impression that it had been was called to my attention by Mr. Virgil L. Mitchell of San Jose, California, in a letter in October 1967. I am happy to make this correction.

tahlid were enclosed by waterways and high ridges. On the twenty-five acres of cleared land to which Thorvald had come and which he admired, cattle could be enclosed, or prevented from running away into the forest, by the water of the fjord in front, by the unscalable side of the mountain in back, and by a short two hundred feet of fence that could be built from the south end of the mountain to the shore. This feature of readily enclosable land was a primary consideration to any land-seeking man who lived by dairy culture.

T 10   "on the sands . . . three mounds"

Francis Parkman says of the habits of the Indians whose winter homes were up the Penobscot and other rivers of Maine: "Their summer stay at the seashore was perhaps the most pleasant and certainly the most picturesque part of their lives. Bivouacked by some of the innumerable coves and inlets that indent these coasts, they passed their days in that alternation of indolence and action which is a second nature to the Indian. Here in hot weather, while . . . the upturned canoes lay idle on the pebbles, the listless warrior smoked his pipe under his roof of bark."

In Valley Cove between Flying Mountain and St. Sauveur Mountain, the sand area extends for less than fifty feet. This small area is a historic spot, for here, 484 years before Columbus, occurred the first recorded encounter between Europeans and American Indians. It was not to the credit of the Europeans. Who sees himself? The vikings never seemed to realize that they themselves were as much to blame as the natives of North America for the battles that took place between them. Poul Nörlund, in *Viking Settlers in Greenland,* frankly admits that there "can scarcely be any doubt that the old warlike Norsemen, self-assertive and intolerant folk of quality as they were, treated the Skraelings roughly and without pardon whenever they fell in with them." In this respect the vikings of the eleventh century were no worse than the English, Spaniards, and Dutch in the sixteenth century, and the Americans in the eighteenth and nineteenth centuries.

T 11   "they ascended the headland"

The location of the sands in Valley Cove, the Indian trail from those sands up Flying Mountain, and the views from the summit, especially the one toward the north end of Somes Sound —all together show how perfectly the saga is fitted with geographical clothes.

"They saw some hillocks within the fjord"   **T 12**

Visible from lookout ledges near the summit of Flying Mountain, in a line just clear of the slanting side of Acadia Mountain, and three and three-quarter miles away, was the encampment of the Indians who resided in the summers near the head of Somes Sound. The little hillocks were Indian huts or teepees.

"Then came a call above them"   **T 13**

Dr. Hermannsson of Cornell said the call that came from above to Thorvald and his men was a "certain supernatural warning." This quoting him is not to charge him with believing that a supernatural being had awakened the sleepers, but that Thorvald and his men thought one had. The geography of Valley Cove tells us what the voice actually was. It was an echo from the 679-foot wall of St. Sauveur Mountain. Sightseers in yachts cruising into Somes Sound turn into Valley Cove, which is locally known as Echo Cove, and there they shout to awaken the echoes, the reverberating echoes. The wording of the call in the saga suggests reiteration in its repetition of "you and all your men."

"Krossanes [Cross Cape]"   **T 14**

One of the arrows shot at Thorvald's ship during the battle in Valley Cove may have overshot and landed in the sands, for about the year 1930 a perfect arrowhead was found there. The stone head of the arrow that caught Thorvald under the arm as he held the tiller was probably kept by Thorvald's men to show to Leif. Probably this was the arrowhead that fell into the possession of Thorvald's brother Thorstein, and was ultimately dug up in the graveyard of Thorstein Erikson's farm at Sandnes, and is now in the Copenhagen Museum. A comparison should be made to find out whether the arrowhead from Sandnes is of the same material and style as arrowheads from Valley Cove in Somes Sound.

An intensive search of Jesuit Field has been made for Thorvald's grave. I found in the field a large granite boulder which has on its face two crosses six feet apart. My friend Ralph Urban and I dug in front of it, but later, I recognized that natural cracks in granite often form crosses. I wished I could dig at the most likely spot in the field, where a house now stands on the central eminence. Thorvald's grave will probably never be found. But we can be certain that he was buried somewhere in Jesuit Field on that "promontory" to which he gave the name Cross Cape.

K 1   "a strong fence of palings"

Karlsefni's palisade was the largest single construction at Leif's Shelters. Since Leif's house had sleeping space for thirty-five men, it must have been about fifty feet long. A palisade that enclosed it would most likely have been at least twice that length. It seemed reasonable to think that even after a thousand years some surface evidence of the long lines of the palisade must have survived. I envisioned those lines as ridges where Karlsefni's men had banked earth against the palisade posts to strengthen the fence. I remembered the earth ridges of the remains of the ship-shed walls. Surely, I thought, the remains of the fence of palings would have left some visible ridging, even if barely discernible. But in all my traipsing through the woods near Follins Pond I found no such ridging. The search for the palisade seemed hopeless.

In April of 1964, however, I reexamined two aerial photographs which I had looked at in 1958 with unseeing eyes. The photographs had been taken in 1947, the year of my first visit to the area. I knew that at that time there was no house within a quarter of a mile of the Follins Pond gully except the one occupied by Mr. and Mrs. S. A. Canty. The photographs had therefore recorded the terrain as it had existed from earliest colonial times and perhaps before. It was a thrilling moment on the trail of the vikings when I found in the two aerial photographs what seemed certain evidence of Karlsefni's strong fence of palings. The palisade was in the woods in a place to which no road had ever penetrated, up to the time the photographs were taken.

The two photographs showed a dark rectangular spot that represented something approximately fifty feet in length. Since this spot was darker than any tree shadow in the photographs, it presumably was a hollow. This was surrounded by a rectangle which showed something in the order of about 115 feet long and about 85 to 90 feet wide. A circle or oval might be the work of nature—the contour of a hill, for example. But four sides of a rectangle with seemingly perfect right angles could not be the work of nature. They must be the work of man. Furthermore, it seemed obvious that if such a large construction had been made in colonial times, there would have been some roadway approach to it, or at least a path. If such roadway or path had ever existed, traces of

**LEIF'S SHELTERS—MAP DRAWN TO SCALE
OF AERIAL PHOTOGRAPHS
THAT REVEALED PALISADE**

it could not have escaped the recording by an aerial camera. But no such traces of a road or path appeared in the photographs.

In light of the many previously established geographical iden-tifications, it seemed practically certain that the rectangle in the aerial photographs showed the location of Karlsefni's palisade. I immediately went to the area and tried to find the rectangle. The site was patently somewhere on the top of the hill between Follins Pond gully and the shore spring. Even with the most careful exam-ination of the ground, however, one could not tell the precise loca-tion of the rectangle. There was no detectable surface evidence of what the aerial photographs showed.

I consulted with Dr. Junius B. Bird, Curator of Archaeology at the American Museum of Natural History in New York. Surely, I said to him, a fence of palings would have left some visible sur-face evidence? None at all, he said. He told me there would have been no such banking of earth as I had assumed, or not enough to leave any surface ridges after several centuries.

And so it was. This is why it is the more amazing that the eye of a camera hundreds of feet in the air had been able to detect what the eye of a person on the ground could not see.

I wanted to use an aerial photograph as an illustration in my forthcoming book *The Viking Explorers*. But in the aerial photo-graphs, which are overlapping 9″ x 9″ contact prints,[8] the rectan-gle is too small for easy recognition and altogether too small to make an effective illustration. Its actual size is less than $\frac{3}{16}$ of an inch (about 6 mm) in length. With the intention of providing a printer with a satisfactory illustration, I had the company that had taken the photographs make a 24″ x 24″ enlargement of one of them. On the enlargement, however, details were lost.

Since there was no trace left aboveground of what the camera had seen, the only hope was to find evidence underground. The planted ends of the posts which had rotted away in the light-col-ored sandy soil of the Cape would be discernible as dark discolora-tions, called post molds. I was assured of this by Mr. F. Newton

---

[8] The revealing 9″ by 9″ contact prints made by the Aero Service Corporation of Philadelphia are numbered 164 1302 and 164 1303, and are dated September 27, 1947.

Miller, a member of the Metropolitan Chapter of the New York State Archaeological Society. He had assisted Dr. William A. Ritchie in the uncovering of post molds at Wading River on Long Island. He said he had no doubt that a palisade on Cape Cod would have left easily recognizable post molds in the yellow soil.

The photographs called for digging. But where? We could not determine with close precision where the lines of the presumed fence of palings had stood. We of course compared the revealing photographs with other aerial photographs taken after a housing development had brought bulldozers and roads. But those other photographs were in different scales, and there were no permanently fixed points on any of the photographs from which to lay off linear measurements.

We undertook many computations. I made at least twenty, with a different result each time. Various triangulations were applied to the problem, and in these Mr. Owen R. Gunn, an architect, assisted. The nearest we could come to locating the rectangle was our reaching the conclusion that the eastern side of the presumed fence of palings was on Mr. Gunn's property, and the western side on the property of his neighbor, Mr. George M. Paulson. We believed, though we could not feel sure, that the major portion of the palisade area (about ninety feet wide) was on Mr. Gunn's side of the property boundary line. As it happened our best measurements brought us only to within about twenty-five feet of the eastern side of the palisade. This explains the digging of the three squares off to the right in the illustration on page 228.

I organized a dig. Mrs. Robert D. Barnes had been most strongly recommended as the one to conduct the search for the palisade, for her training had been in the uncovering of post molds at Angel Mounds, Indiana. She and her husband had first met and had fallen in love on the day they participated in the Massachusetts Archaeological Society dig in 1952 that uncovered the shoring for a viking ship in the Follins Pond gully. It was romantic justice that they should both be placed in charge of the palisade dig in September 1964. Newton Miller and I agreed to defer to them.

Robert Barnes had available all manner of measuring instruments. He and his wife laid out a professional grid that covered the hilltop. Since the same trees were there as had been standing when the photographs had been taken, it seemed safe to assume that most of the palisade area was, archaeologically speaking, undisturbed.

On September 12 Robert and June Barnes and Newton Miller began by digging the square numbered H–11. They next dug the square G–10 and on the thirteenth dug the square F–9. With corners coinciding, the 3 five-foot squares crossed more than fifteen feet in both the north-south and east-west directions.

The three squares are shown blank in the diagram. They demonstrated, however, that the hill had been formed as a sand dune. They showed that under the layer of topsoil, yellow sand of a consistent color extended down for several feet. While the results of digging these squares were entirely negative, these three squares were important as "controls" in contrast to what we later found. The light yellow sand gave Newton Miller positive certainty that any post molds in the area would be instantly and unmistakably recognizable.

My latest measurements had caused me to believe that the line of dug squares, no matter how far it was continued, would fail to cross the line of the fence of palings. Therefore, on September 14, I dug a narrow and shallow and unconforming trench, which I believed would cross that line. It cut at a diagonal across grid lines in a most unprofessional and inexcusable manner. It was nearly at right angles to the line of coinciding corners of the three squares. Its direction was partly determined by trees. I dug it midway between two large trees, to avoid as far as possible the tree roots. It revealed nothing. Before my next meeting with Robert and June Barnes I repented of having dug the trench, and on September 19, I begged them to forgive my unorthodox activity. In a chastened mood I asked them to put four stakes in the ground to mark the square E–6 on their grid, so that I might extend my heretical trench into an orthodox square.

The square uncovered a post mold. Immediately the adjacent squares F–6 and E–5 were dug. A line of post molds was established, and before nightfall on September 19, we had also dug squares D–5, C–5, G–5, and G–4. The next day we dug K–6 and half of K–5. On September 23 and 24, when Mrs. Pohl came to the Cape and wanted to see some post molds, I dug square H–6 and half of H–5.

The dark post mold discolorations ran to an average depth of nine inches. They were three to five inches in diameter, with occasionally a larger one. Many of the molds were pointed at the bottom, showing that they had been sharpened posts planted by human agency.

The bunching of post molds on a two-foot shift of line to the east in squares G–6 and H–6 suggests that the entrance to the palisade may have been at that spot.

As most clearly appears in K–6, the posts were planted in a zigzag pattern.

I called a halt as soon as we had accomplished our immediate purpose, which was to establish as fact that there was a line of post molds. The uncovering of thirty-five feet of post molds was enough to demonstrate that there had been a fence of palings. My thought was to leave the remainder of the palisade area to some professional. Whoever it is will no doubt uncover the line of post molds to the north and to the south to the corners of the palisade, and thus determine the precise length of the palisade. Half of the north end and more than half of the south end of the fence of palings should be found in ground which bulldozers have not touched. We may hope that the northwest corner of the palisade, presumably on Mr. Paulson's property, may be uncovered. If so, we shall know the width of Karlsefni's palisade. The entire area within the palisade, and especially near the doorway to the house where Gudrid sat with her infant son when the native woman spoke to her, should be dug and the soil sifted for possible artifacts and for datable charcoal flung out whenever the hearth inside the house was cleared. Some evidence of Leif's house may remain along the east side of the road cut, although it is to be feared the bulldozing for the making of the road has displaced most such evidences.

The area of the fence of palings presents opportunity for what may be one of the most important archaeological projects on our continent. Bulldozed material deposited along the west side of the

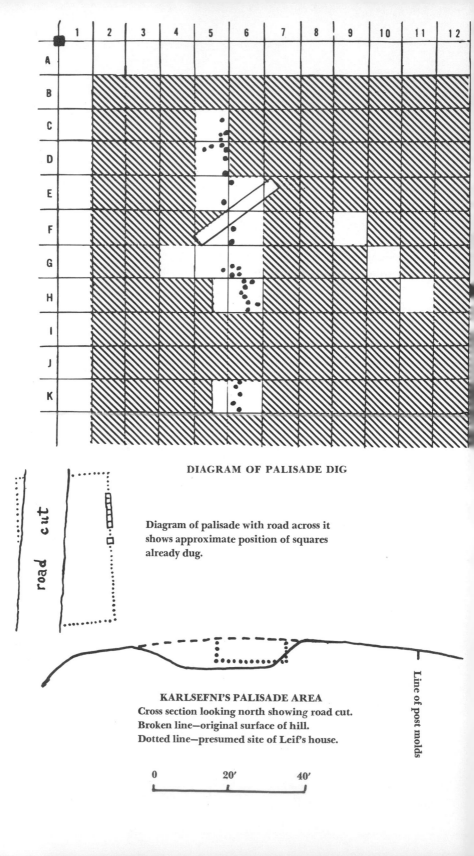

DIAGRAM OF PALISADE DIG

Diagram of palisade with road across it
shows approximate position of squares
already dug.

N
↑

road cut

↓
S

KARLSEFNI'S PALISADE AREA
Cross section looking north showing road cut.
Broken line—original surface of hill.
Dotted line—presumed site of Leif's house.

Line of post molds

0   20′   40′

road cut awaits sifting, and there will be about 275 five-foot squares of undisturbed ground to be investigated. Precise dimensions of the palisade will be revealed. Instrumental measurements of the rectangle in the aerial photographs were made by Richard L. Mearns, and these point to a width of about 87 feet. Numerous measurements I made averaged 86' 10". This is close to 14 Norse *fathmur,* which would be 86' 4". However, the size laid out by Karlsefni may have been in conformity with the ground slopes rather than by Norse linear measure. The position of the palisade fits perfectly with the other evidences of Leif's Shelters. The northeast corner of the palisade was only some 225 feet from the ship shed, and 350 feet from the shore spring. When occupied by the vikings, who no doubt cleared trees from near the palisade on the outside of it, the hilltop commanded a view of the whole of Follins Pond.

Inside the palisade, Snorri, son of Karlsefni and Gudrid, first saw the light of day. He is of record the first child born in America of European parents. The palisade is evidence that Karlsefni made Leif's Shelters his personal headquarters during his first two winters in Vinland. The palisade was built and the boy Snorri was born in the autumn after the second summer the *Graenlendinga Saga* says. *Eirik's Saga* specifically says that Karlsefni's son Snorri was "three winters old" when his parents returned to Greenland, and his parents would certainly have known the age of their son when they left Vinland. Their telling of it later in Iceland is entirely credible and should be accepted as fact. It was in character for Karlsefni to have built the palisade to protect his wife and child when he had the men of only one ship with him, but to have taken his wife and child with him when he rejoined the main party the next sailing season. The number of winters he spent in Vinland was undoubtedly four, the same number that his expedition spent, and not two as the *Graenlendinga Saga* implies. There must be a lacuna in this matter in that saga.[9] This apparent con-

[9] Greenlanders were probably motivated by prejudice in favor of the Erikson family. They were understandably apprehensive lest reports of Karlsefni's explorations that revealed the tremendous size of Vinland with great rivers and forests and untold opportunities, make that country appear so attractive that merchant traders would bypass Greenland.

tradiction between the *Graenlendinga* and *Eirik's Saga* is resolved when we observe that in *Eirik's Saga* we are specifically told where Karlsefni personally spent his last two winters in Vinland, but are left uninformed as to where he spent his first two. The two sagas coalesce perfectly when we accept all that each tells: the *Graenlendinga* account of Karlsefni's experiences at Leif's Shelters during his first two winters in Vinland, and the variants 557 and 544 account of his third and fourth winters elsewhere in that country.

K 2   "Let ten of our men go out upon this cape and show themselves"

Karlsefni's tactics in preparing for the battle with the Skraelings at Leif's Shelters is made crystal clear by the geography. See the map which shows the battlefield.

K 3   The battlefield, including a trail to the shore spring.

The saga says nothing of drinking water at Leif's Shelters. There must have been a plentiful supply, and indeed there was in the copious flow of the shore spring, ninety gallons an hour—enough for hundreds of men. Evidence exists connecting the site of Leif's house and Karlsefni's palisade with that spring. A preface to what is to be said here is a description of a trail west of Diamond Lake near Barryton in Mecosta County, Michigan. To save themselves hundreds of miles of canoeing in dangerous waters of two of the Great Lakes, Indians canoed across the Lower Michigan Peninsula for many centuries. They had only one short carry between lakes from which streams descended to rivers, into Muskegon River to the west into Lake Michigan, and to the east into a river that flows into Lake Huron (Saginaw Bay). The carry on this most important crossover is one of the most deeply marked Indian trails on the continent. That trail is about a mile long. It has packed earth six to eight inches wide, two or three inches deep, for the most part without vegetation since its surface is too hard for seeds to take root. That trail runs directly into the trunk of a tree which is four feet in diameter, a tree four hundred to five hundred years old. The trail continues from the other side of that tree trunk. Here we have positive proof that the trail existed before the tree started its growth.

We find a similar situation at the site of Leif's Shelters. As the illustration shows, a worn trail with very little grass and in places no grass at all in it begins on the steep slope near the palisade. Its upper end points toward the northeast corner of the palisade. Its lower end runs to the retaining wall of the Canty house grounds. That trail existed before the Canty house, the first modern house in the area, was built. The existence of the trail was unknown to Mrs. Canty until I pointed it out to her. Its direction runs not to the back door of the house but toward the middle of a blank wall of the house, as though it wanted to lead one straight through the house to the shore spring. On this trail the feet of Leif Erikson, Thorvald Erikson, Gudrid, Thorfinn Karlsefni, and Freydis passed many times.

"They gave the land a name . . . *Helluland*" **K 4**

The portion of Baffin Island which Karlsefni touched was in all probability the Cumberland Peninsula, where flat rock such as the sagas describe caused Karlsefni to give the country the same descriptive name that Leif had given to Newfoundland.

"with northerly winds two days' sailing distance" **K 5**

From the Cumberland Peninsula of Baffin Island to the northern tip of Labrador (Cape Chidley), out of sight of land, is 300 miles, precisely two days' sailing distance.

"and again saw land. It was well wooded" **K 6**

Karlsefni found woods all along the east coast of Labrador, and around the southern end of Labrador, and west inside the Gulf of St. Lawrence, and south along the coast of New Brunswick and Nova Scotia.

"There was an island off to the southeast of this land" **K 7**

These words show what Karlsefni was doing when he made this observation. He was following the coast on the northwest side of the Strait of Belle Isle. The island to the southeast was of course Newfoundland.

"because they found a bear there they called it Bear Island **K 8**
[*Biarney*]. They called the wooded land *Markland*"

Karlsefni's naming of lands coincided with Leif's in two in-

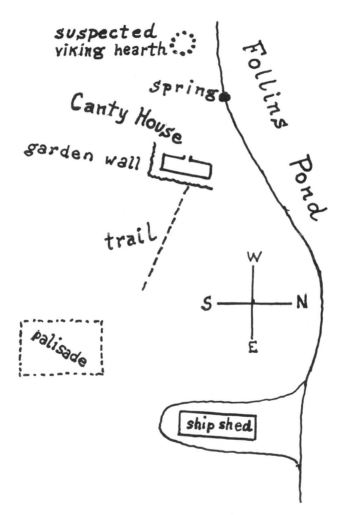

TRAIL TO SPRING AT LEIF'S SHELTERS

stances out of three. The name *Helluland* was as applicable to Baffin Island as it was to northern Newfoundland on its eastern side. When Karlsefni came to the island of Newfoundland, he gave it another name because he had already used the name Helluland, and the part of Newfoundland he saw did not call for that name. When he reached the southern shore of Nova Scotia, where some of his crew who had no doubt been on a previous voyage to Vinland recognized the place where Leif had named Markland, Karlsefni applied the name Markland to all the wooded land he had coasted by, all the continuous land from the northern tip of Labrador to southern Nova Scotia. He thus tremendously extended the concept of Markland.

"they sailed along the coast for a long time, and came to a   K 9
cape. . . . with long beaches and sand dunes. They . . . found the keel of a ship"

From Nova Scotia at or beyond the place where Karlsefni was informed that Leif had landed and named Markland, Karlsefni followed Leif's sailing directions and crossed the ocean gap south of the Bay of Fundy and the Gulf of Maine "to a cape." The keel Karlsefni found was of course the old broken keel which Thorvald Erikson had erected as a beacon. The "long beaches and sand dunes" identify Keel Cape as Cape Cod.

They called the beaches on Cape Cod "Astonishing Strands" because they were so much longer than any beaches Norsemen had found anywhere else.

"Beyond these Astonishing Strands, the country was indented with   K 10
bays, into one of which they sailed"

The bay they entered was between the first Astonishing Strands and the second such strands.

The second stretch of Astonishing Strands   K 11

In connection with other geographical observations, there can be no question that the second Astonishing Strands were the eastern half of the north shore of Long Island.

"he set the Gaels on shore and ordered them to run southward"   K 12

From Karlsefni's orders we learn that the second Astonishing Strands were on a north shore. They could not have been the 115 miles of sand beaches on the south shore of Long Island, for there the Gaels could not have run southward. The only extensive north shore beyond Cape Cod is the north shore of Long Island.

When the Gaels returned, one brought a bunch of grapes, and the other a sample of a kind of vegetable new to the Norsemen. One variant of the saga describes it as wheat of a new and cultivated kind, *nýsáid*—"new sown," new to the vikings and sown by man. It was not wild wheat. The sample of "wheat" considered important enough to bring to Karlsefni as a product of the land is distinguished in the saga from the observation a year later of wild "self-sown" wheat. If what one of the Gaels brought Karlsefni was a stalk of seed-headed grass or wild wheat, it would have seemed silly. In context, an ear of Indian corn makes sense.[10] The Gaels had found the Indian corn "sown"—growing in a cultivated field. Undoubtedly they had robbed a corn patch of the Setauket tribe. Both products they brought to Karlsefni's ship show that the exploration from that north shore occurred late in the summer or early in the autumn.

K 13   "the coast was indented with bays"

The only north shore which has the two features—long sand beaches and many bays—each section extensive enough to be memorable, is the north shore of Long Island.

K 14   "They sailed to a fjord. There lay an island around which flowed very strong currents"

The Zoëga *Concise Dictionary of Old Icelandic* defines *straumr* as "a stream, current, race of the sea, tide, river."

To a ship coming from Long Island Sound through the East River into Upper New York Bay, there is an island at the entrance to the bay. This is Governors Island, called by the early New

---

[10] Maize was almost certainly of American origin. While it is possible and indeed probable that maize had spread outside America by A.D. 1400, it was unknown and "new" to eleventh-century Norsemen. See M. D. W. Jeffreys, "Pre-Columbian Maize in Southern Africa," *Nature*, vol. 215 (1967), pp. 695–97; and also George F. Carter, "Origin and Diffusion of Maize," *Geographical Review*, vol. 58 (July 1968).

Netherlanders "Nootten Island" or "Nutten Island" because of the walnut trees that grew on it. Today Governors Island is more than twice the size of what it was formerly. Shallows on its south side have been filled in so that the polo grounds and beyond are all new land. Originally, the island was no larger than the ground which rises to the hill on which there is a fort, an abbreviated golf course, and officers' houses. Governors Island is only half a mile from the south end of the Hudson River.

Captain George H. Seeth, onetime president of the New York Harbor Pilots' Association, has told me the speed of the currents around Governors Island. Those in the East River run up to six knots. The currents ran faster than that through the appropriately named Hell Gate previous to the blasting away of rock obstructions. The current on the western side of Governors Island is less at flood, but it is six knots at ebb, when the flow of the Hudson is added to the tide. Karlsefni's men could not row a merchant ship as fast as six knots, and very seldom could they make headway with sail against a current of that speed. Powerful modern towboats with heavily loaded barges to be conveyed through the East River and around Governors Island time their passage to coincide with the direction of the tide and seldom fight against it. It is now being proposed that the currents in the Hudson be harnessed to supply New York City with electric light.

The observation regarding the many birds' eggs on Current Island was of course not made during the autumn of Karlsefni's arrival there, but in the following spring.

"Stream Fjord."   K 15

The Hudson River is the only fjord on the eastern seaboard of North America to the south and west of Mt. Desert Island.

"There were mountains thereabouts"   K 16

Anyone who has seen the Hudson River knows the applicability of this description.

"northward beyond Astonishing Strands and Keel Cape to explore   K 17
Vinland"

Hitherto it has been generally assumed that Thorhall the

Huntsman sailed away from the Karlsefni Expedition with the intention of returning home. It would not have been in character for him to have done so. If he had, he would have been called a deserter and coward. The saga clearly indicates that he intended to expore Vinland beyond the fjord where former explorations eastward had been terminated by Thorvald Erikson's death.

K 18   "sailed southward . . . for a long time"

In view of Karlsefni's purpose, which was to find a place for settlement of the colony far enough south of Stream Fjord to avoid any more winter hardships, it seems certain that he must have sailed beyond the coasts of New Jersey and Delaware, and at least as far as Maryland or Virginia or the Carolinas.

K 19   "a river that flowed . . . to water [*vatn*] and thence to the sea."

The saga mentions first the principal fact of the voyage: that Karlsefni came to where a river flowed down into water and thence to the ocean. The first meaning of *vatn* in Icelandic is "water" (literally, "wetness") without qualification. A secondary meaning is "fresh water," from which the word as here used has been frequently translated, or should we say mistranslated, as "lake." In the context, "lake" is inadmissible. The river itself had a tidal flow. Therefore, what the river flowed down into could not have been a freshwater lake. We must take the first meaning of *vatn* here as water, a wide water, a water passage where the tide meets a river current, an arm of the sea at the lower end of a river, an estuary, like Chesapeake Bay.

K 20   "There were large sandbanks"

After mentioning the river but before the naming of Hóp, the saga, in mentioning sandbanks, tells us what Karlsefni and his followers experienced as they approached the river and before they entered it.

K 21   "one could enter only at flood tide"

Dr. Luna B. Leopold, chief hydrologist for the United States Geological Survey, wrote me on August 19, 1965: "A small stream coming into a tidal area, whether an estuary or the open ocean, will tend to have built across its mouth a sandbar due to littoral drift. Under most circumstances I would agree that the vikings would have found bars at the mouth of most rivers and that if the river is relatively small, their boats would have crossed only at high tide."

Sandy Hook is vestigial to a bar which formerly extended across Lower New York Bay. The man-made Ambrose Channel allows deep-draft ships to pass this bar.

"Karlsefni sailed in there and called it *Hóp*."   **K 22**

Where was Hóp? It was somewhere at a considerable distance south of Stream Fjord. But the continent south of New York Harbor is a huge territory. In so large a region as all of Dixie, what hope could anyone have of pinpointing Hóp?

One published theory placed Hóp in Maryland, on the western shore of Chesapeake Bay, a few miles south of Annapolis. This theory, however, failed to meet all the geographical requirements. Most notably, it did not meet the requirement established by the statement that Karlsefni's men saw canoes of the Skraelings "out beyond the bay." How could anyone see canoes beyond the width of the Chesapeake?

The search for Hóp was encouraged by the realization that since sailing directions and geographical observations in the sagas had been an accurate guide to actual geography everywhere to the north and east of Current Island, there seemed to be promise that geographical observations in the saga telling of Hóp would be a similarly accurate guide to something to the south of Current Island. If so, the precise location of Hóp would be found by taking two simple steps. The first was to list all the geographical requirements for Hóp stated or implied in the saga. The completed list contained seventeen requirements. With so large a number, success in the search became mathematically certain; for the chances were overwhelming that there could be only one site on this planet that met so many requirements. The second step, therefore, was to examine all United States Geological Survey contour maps of riverbanks at a considerable distance south of New York Harbor until the site of Hóp was found. The search was great fun while it lasted, but it took only a few days.

There followed, however, the need for on-the-ground investigation.

For assistance in field research on a visit to the area, there was need of someone knowledgeable in the sagas and enthusiastic enough to be an encouraging companion on the back roads, over the meadows, and up and down hill through the woods. Whenever such a need has arisen during many years of study of viking sites, it has invariably happened that a "disciple" has offered himself as a timely volunteer. For the James River excursion it was Virginia-born Richard L. Mearns, who had been in the United States Navy, had corresponded on many matters relating to the vikings, and had twice visited at my home. He could read Old Icelandic well enough to raise challenging questions as to the meaning of words in the text of *Eirik's Saga*. The moment Rick Mearns heard of what was afoot, he expressed eagerness to drive in his "Bug" (Volkswagen) from where he worked in Rochester, New York. We met in Richmond on October 23, 1965.

The Westover quadrangle map showed a few scattered houses in the area we were to search. But the map was twelve years old. Since the area was only seven miles east of the industrial city of Hopewell in Prince George County, we feared that a housing development might have destroyed all possibility of seeing what the original terrain had been in Karlsefni's time, the summer and autumn of 1012 and the following winter. When we drove into the area of the quadrangle map, however, we were immensely relieved to see there had been no housing development. There were only two new houses in all the area, which had at one time been the estate of Edmund Ruffin, and included the shores of Tar Bay and Coggins Point eastward to Powell Creek. The Ruffin mansion on the bluff at the middle of Tar Bay shore had burned in 1964. It was a sad shell of brick walls. Boxwood hedges ten feet tall attested to the former magnificence of the manor. We ran into history. From that bluff on January 10, 1781, Baron von Steuben had observed the fleet of Benedict Arnold after its raid on Richmond as it retreated down the river. In the War Between the States, D. H.

Hill from the tip of Coggins Point had bombarded McClellan's camp on the north side of the river on July 31, 1862.

"vines on the hills"   **K 23**

We were entranced with the expansive vistas from the bluffs near the bay and from the point. We became intimately acquainted with the peanut fields on the Coggins Point farm. In the woods and the bluffs, we saw vines spiraling to the tops of trees, as Karlsefni did. Some of these immense vines had stems as thick as the trunks of small trees. None had thorns like the vines on Cape Cod.

"Every brook"   **K 24**

Karlsefni's campsite was necessarily near fresh water sufficient for his followers and their livestock. Since brooks were mentioned, it was presumably near a brook.

"Where the tide rose highest" and "when the tide fell"   **K 25**

Mr. Dale F. Jones, Surface Water Specialist for Virginia, wrote me on June 8, 1965: "The tidal flow probably brought salt to the fall line at Richmond at various times, but the exact point where the James becomes brackish and where it would remain fresh depends upon the time of the year and the quantity of flow of fresh water." A foreman at the gravel pits on the east side of Powell Creek said to Rick and me, "I never saw the river so blue and the creek so green." Usually both are mud color, but there had been very little rain in 1965 to wash mud into the river.

"they dug pits in the flats"   **K 26**

The map on page 107 shows the position of mud flats.

"holy fish were in the pits"   **K 27**

All translators of *helgir fiskar* ("holy fish") hitherto have given the word "halibut," since *hali* means "holy." The "butt" (blunt shape of head) is a name applied to all flatfish: flounder, plaice, sole, turbot, and halibut. In the Zoëga Icelandic dictionary, English to Icelandic volume, "halibut" is *flythra*. In the companion volume, Icelandic to English, *flythra* is "flounder." Dr. Kristján Eldjárn, director of the Icelandic Museum, wrote me on December 20, 1965: "I do not think we can ever be sure what exactly these 'helgir fiskar' seen and caught by the Vinlandfarers, were. . . . It seems to me extremely likely that the various kinds of fish were mixed up both in the Viking Age and at other times." Mr. Robert L. Edwards, of the Fish and Wildlife Service of the United States Department of the Interior, wrote me on November 5, 1965: "It is doubtful that halibut, in the last several thousand years at least, were ever abundant, or even occurred in the Chesapeake Bay country. Cape Cod pretty much represents their southern limit." Karlsefni's Icelanders presumably caught some American flounder, which grow to five pounds, and one species to twenty-six pounds, and mistook them for halibut, or knowing very well that they were not halibut, called them holy fish.

Local men told us of the kinds of fish they catch: in the spring, herring and salmon in the creek; eels at Eelbank Point; bass, perch, and bream in the brook; catfish, rock pike, and striped bass in the river.

K 28   "They had their livestock with them"

The enclosed area which contained the livestock at the campsite at Hóp was measured by Rick on one of his company's machines designed to measure irregular map areas.

K 29   "rowed away southward beyond the point"

See the map, and note the relation between Coggins Point, Windmill Point, and Three-Mile Reach.

K 30   "There came no snow at all"

United States Weather Bureau reports at Norfolk and at Richmond (averaged together for Coggins Point which is meteorologically halfway between them) show in the past forty years a total of 105 measurable snowfalls. Of these, fifty-nine, more than half, were of less than two inches. The number of months in which "T" ("Trace, an amount too small to measure") was recorded was sixty-four. A weather bureau observes at all hours. It never sleeps, as Karlsefni's men did. Slight falls of snow occur during the colder hours—in the evening, at night, in early morning. At Coggins Point, many such would have melted away by the time the vikings rose for winter breakfast. The climate was somewhat warmer a thousand years ago. There are three possibilities at Hóp: (1) There was literally no snow of measurable quantity; (2) A little snow fell but was melted away by the time Karlsefni's followers woke up; (3) A little snow was observed, but not enough to meet the meaning of "snow" in the minds of Greenlanders and Icelanders, to whom snow meant confinement indoors and especially the need of sheltering livestock in barns with fodder that had been previously stored.

"their livestock lived by grazing"   **K 31**

There are large areas of marsh grass between Coggins Point and Powell Creek. Where the marsh grass is two to four feet tall, a snowfall of two inches or so would have been ignored by the livestock and by Karlsefni's men. The seed heads of the march grass could have caused the vikings to think of it as self-sown or wild wheat.

"skin boats"   **K 32**

The boats of the savages in the James River were not "skin boats." It is equally certain they were not birchbarks. Paper birch trees, *Betula papyrifera* (white birch, canoe birch, silver birch) grow in Canada and the northeastern corner of the United States, and not south of northern Pennsylvania. Dugouts were the only kind of boats described and presumably the only kind seen in Virginia by the earliest post-Columbian visitors. Captain John Smith wrote: "Their fishing is much in boats. These they make of one tree by burning and scratching away the coales with stones and shels, till they have made it in the form of a Trough."[11] The boats of the Indians who came to Karlsefni's camp were almost certainly dugouts. We can say this with assurance in spite of the fact that

---

[11] Smith, Captain John, *Travels and Works of Captain John Smith*, pp. 76, 77.

Karlsefni's men called them "skin boats," the only kind of small native boats in the viking experience. Such a mistake would be incredible were it not clear from the saga that Karlsefni's men never had an opportunity to examine the boats. On the occasion of the first visit, they did not get near the boats, for the Skraelings rowed toward the vikings, stared at them, and "then" (after staring at them from on board the boats) "came up on the land" for closer staring. Obviously, some of the Skraelings waded ashore while others for safety precautions held their boats away from shore. There was mutual distrust, and both sides kept their distance. All that the vikings observed on that occasion were the facial features of the Skraelings, which were of sufficient novelty to draw their attention away from the boats. On the second visit, when they traded, there was less staring but continued timidity. The trading was suddenly broken off when Karlsefni's bull came out into the clearing near the shore and bellowed. The saga says that the Skraelings then "ran out to their boats." The boats were "out"—away from shore. On the occasion of the battle, the vikings of course had no opportunity to inspect the boats.

K 33   "out beyond the bay"

As the Skraeling boats appeared around Coggins Point, they looked "like coals flung out beyond the bay." This simile, the most vivid in all the sagas, precludes any theory that the settlement site could have been on the shore of a bay so large as the Chesapeake, because so large a bay would be too wide for canoes "out beyond" it to be visible. Tar Bay is two miles wide, and its middle shore is one mile from the river channel. The bay was formed geologically by a horseshoe bend of the river cutting into high ground.

Some have supposed that the "staves" the vikings heard being revolved on the approaching canoes were paddles, striking the water and making a noise like flails, with the Indians chanting or making grunts of effort in unison. My friend William L. Smyth of Winsted, Connecticut, makes the interesting suggestion that the staves may have been bull-roarers which made a whooshing sound.

Hitherto it has been widely assumed that the staves were objects associated with primitive magic. A possible clue may lie in Captain John Smith's description of Virginia Indian medicine men: "In their hands, they had every one a Rattell. . . . The manner of their devotion is sometimes to make a great fire, . . . and all to sing and dance about it, with rattles and shouts together, 4 or 5 houres."[12]

"a great ball-shaped object almost the size of a sheep's belly"   **K 34**

Mr. Smyth was the first to suggest that the weapon flung by the Skraelings was a hornets' nest.

"certain cliffs"   **K 35**

Captain John Smith observed the Tar Bay bluffs. After mentioning "the river of Apamatuck [Appomattox]," he wrote, "Next more to the East . . . a little farther is a Bay wherein falleth 3 or 4 prettie brookes and creekes that halfe intrench the inhabitants."[13] In addition to the mile-long brook, two creeks empty into Tar Bay, and there is also one marshy inlet too small to be called a creek. Captain Smith's word "intrench" aptly describes how deep ravines make a defensive position of the Tar Bay Bluffs.

"According to the telling of some, Bjarni and Gudrid"   **K 36**

"Gudrid" is the name given in one version of the saga. The name "Freydis," given in another version, is an obvious error. Both variants make it absolutely certain that Freydis had accompanied Karlsefni and Snorri (undoubtedly in the ship she shared ownership of with her husband) to Hóp where she spent the winter and was the heroine of the battle "in the spring."

"When they had traveled a long way"   **K 37**

The traveling was "with land on the port side" along the coast to the north from Keel Cape and later to the east. The words "a long way" are no clue as to how far, but the next statement in the saga makes it definite.

[12] Ibid., p. 66.
[13] Ibid., p. 50.

K 38   "a river which flowed . . . from east to west"

This statement tells how far Karlsefni had traveled—beyond Maine and New Brunswick and across the Bay of Fundy to the western side of Nova Scotia where he found the river he described.

K 39   "They steered into the mouth of the river and lay to by its southern bank"

Here is a geographical detail that applies equally to the two west-flowing rivers.

K 40   "Then they sailed away to the north"

If from Digby Gut, they sailed for about ninety miles to the north; and if from Apple River, for about thirty miles to the north.

K 41   "They thought they could see Uniped-Land"

The association with the death of Thorvald Erikson makes the identification clear. Some of the men in Karlsefni's ship had no doubt been in Thorvald Erikson's ship and they recognized the mountains of Mt. Desert Island as where their leader had been killed. Thorvald's body had been in the unconsecrated ground at Cross Cape for five years. The saga would no doubt have told us if Karlsefni had ventured into the fjord to recover the body, but he and his men sailed on past because they "were unwilling to risk their lives any longer."[14]

K 42   "the mountains which they now discovered"

Can the Presidential Range of the White Mountains of New Hampshire, which is sixty-eight miles inland, be seen from off the

[14] "It is hardly right to translate the noun *einfaetingr* by uniped. Its meaning at the time of this occurrence must have been merely the same as *einfaettr madr,* one-legged man. Later when foreign superstition about monstrous unipeds, as we find them depicted in medieval manuscripts, reached Iceland, the noun *einfaetingr* became associated with it, and then in the tradition the word came to be so interpreted 'here; moreover, it was added that the explorers thought they had got a glimpse of Einfaetingaland, the Land of the Unipeds, thus accepting the notion that there existed a race with this peculiarity. But this must be dissociated from the original story." Halldór Hermannsson, *The Problems of Wineland,* p. 24.

Maine coast? Most assuredly. Mt. Washington with altitude of 6,288 feet has a horizon visibility of seventy-nine miles. From its summit I have seen the ocean. Several peaks of the Presidential Range can be sighted from the decks of ships off Portland and off Old Orchard Beach.

"the mountains of Hóp"   K 43

Karlsefni would have explored with at least one ship to as far up the James River as a viking ship could go. Where the city of Richmond now is, shallows and the falls necessitated using an after-boat for further exploration. The after-boat, with only one-and-a-half-foot draft, could be partly lifted over shallows, or could be carried unloaded over a portage.

On the upper James at the site of Scottsville in Albemarle County in central Virginia, Karlsefni's small-boat exploring party would for the first time have the Blue Ridge in view. Rick Mearns sent me the findings of his personal observations, in a letter dated November 20, 1966:

> The James River flows in its flood plain significantly lower than the surrounding terrain. Mountains can be observed from hills near the river, but not from the river itself. I stood on hills near the river at Scottsville, Howardsville, Warminster, Wingina, Norwood, and Buffalo Station in that order, traveling upstream. Visibility varies widely from day to day. I know this from personal experience as a boy in Waynesboro. The distance across the Shenandoah Valley is 30–40 miles and from one side of the valley one could only occasionally see the mountains on the other side. This was not caused by fog or rain, but by a subtle haze which caused the mountains (blue at a distance) to blend in so well with the sky as to become invisible. So haze conditions played a very important role.
>
> Although the James River runs roughly parallel to the mountains in the area I visited, the mountains are much more prominent upstream, not because they are higher, but perhaps because there are less hills in the foreground obscuring the view.
>
> It is difficult to say at what point the vikings would have been able to conclude that they saw a *chain* and not just an isolated

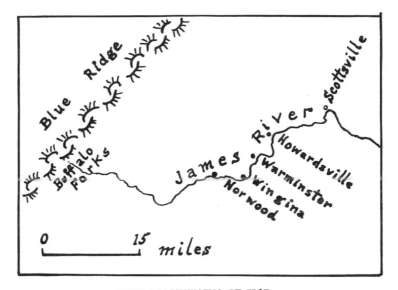

THE MOUNTAINS OF HÓP

mountain or two. I'd say they had to go to the point where they saw an impressive panorama of continuous mountains. If we assume an ascent of a hill every fifteen miles or so (progress was slow going upstream against the current), we can conclude with reasonable certainty that the discovery was made somewhere near Scottsville; nothing more, in my opinion. You may want to consider the possibility that the vikings climbed hills infrequently, devoting their efforts to river travel instead. In this case they would have traveled so far upstream that the mountains could be observed from the flood plain at a point where the course of the river headed directly toward the mountains. This would be in the Lynchburg area.

"formed one mountain chain"   K 44

Karlsefni's conclusion that he had discovered a mountain chain was correct. The mountains around Stream Fjord are a continuation of the Blue Ridge of Virginia which enters New York State from New Jersey and extends to and across the Hudson and continues into Massachusetts, Vermont, and New Hampshire.

"a land over against their land"   K 45

The two Skraeling boys kidnapped from Markland and later taught to speak Norse, told of "a land over against their land." If you are unwilling to accept Newfoundland as that land, you may find yourself forced to assume that American Indians in birchbarks sailed out into the Atlantic Ocean across to Ireland or wherever and back and had thus acquired their knowledge of "a land over against" theirs.

"farther from the sea on the bank of a lake"   F 1

From the point of view of those at Leif's Shelters, which were only a third of a mile from the west end of Follins Pond, "farther from the sea" must have referred to a lake farther from the sea than the one where Leif's Shelters were. Any theory as to the location of Leif Erikson's campsite in Vinland must take cognizance of the existence of another such lake. In being farther from the sea, the lake would be either farther up the waterway or farther to the west. But the Helgi-Finnboge campsite was near enough to Leif's

Shelters for Freydis to walk to it from Leif's house in a few minutes. On the other hand, it was far enough so that the two parties
met only for sports contests in the early winter on some ground between the two campsites and after quarrels arose, kept apart and
out of sight of each other. The Helgi-Finnboge campsite was de-
cidedly more than a stone's throw or a halloo distance away from
Leif's Shelters.

Would it be possible to find the Helgi-Finnboge campsite?

F 2, F 3   Helgi-Finnboge house and ship shed

In an endeavor to find these two sites, a thorough search of
the west end of Follins Pond was made in 1947 and 1948, and
thereafter many persons combed that area without finding any surface markings indicative of the Helgi-Finnboge campsite.

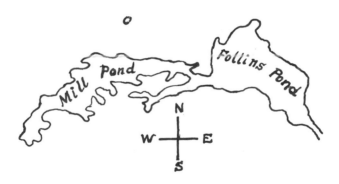

THE LAKE "FARTHER FROM THE SEA"

There had been a search of most of the south shore of Mill Pond, which lies to the west of Follins Pond and is tidal, and is farther up the Bass River waterway, and farther from the sea both in direction and in travel distance. With the sea level two to three feet higher in Leif's day, there were some recessions in the shore of Mill Pond from the present shoreline, but not so in two places along the south shore where there is a steep bank at the water's edge. There was one short section of the shore of Mill Pond in which the thickness of poison ivy and the tangle of thorny briers deterred one from penetration. Single contour lines on the Geological Survey map showed that the bank in that unsearched area was only a little over ten feet in height, and it seemed that Helgi and Finnboge would have chosen to build their house on the highest hill at the shore, the hill that rose to over thirty feet above the lake. Since that hill bore no surface indications of the site, it was assumed that the evidence sought had been obliterated during the construction of the house now on it.

The thicket of briers was entered in 1957 by Charles Boland of New Canaan, Connecticut, a man who had resided for several years in Iceland and had seen there house sites of the viking period. He found at the shore of Mill Pond a long, narrow rectangular hollow that seemed to him to resemble viking house sites in Iceland. After a newspaper reporter interviewed Boland over the telephone, the published story erroneously placed his activities in another town, where Boland happened to be lodging. He counted this error fortunate since it held off the public and diverted attention from Mill Pond. Three years later, Boland informed me that he had seen a house site on the shore of Mill Pond. He proposed to show me where it was, but when the time came other commitments made it impossible for him to go with me to the Cape.

In June 1960, a former student of mine, George McGrath, an ex-army man, went with me to Mill Pond. With a machete we cut our way through dense briers, which in one place were so thick it took us twenty minutes to hack our passage through them for one hundred feet. George learned why the vikings called it Vineland. We realized the aptness of the saga phrase, which said the Helgi-Finnboge party "trimmed up everything well around there" or "put it well in order." Observing where the shoreline of Mill Pond had been when the sea level had been two to three feet higher, we aimed for the only spot where logic and a contour map said the Helgi-Finnboge house site could have been. After pushing laboriously through the thorny tangle, we found the rectangular hollow in that precise spot we had reasoned it must be.

The hollow is a perfect rectangle, and is slightly more than forty-three feet in length and over eighteen feet in width inside. It is just the right size for the number of persons in the Helgi-Finnboge company to have slept on platforms six feet deep along the sides with a corridor six-and-a-half feet wide between the platforms. The platforms, probably about eighteen inches above the floor, served as seats in the daytime. They could have had stone or wood foundations with poles across, covered with mats of plaited salt grass on which were laid animal skins. Space beneath the platforms was undoubtedly used for storage.

The easiest way out from the site, which had taken us a strenuous hour to reach, seemed to be toward the west along the top of the bank some fifty yards back from the present lake shore. By this route we came upon a path which took us out to the road in three minutes.

There had to be two building sites, one a dwelling and the other a ship shed. The house site would be acceptable only if a ship-shed site existed in proximity to it. George and I had seen nothing of such a site to the west of the house site in our departure from the area. If the ship shed had existed, the evidence of it would be in the bank which had been at the shore in Leif's day, and somewhere to the east of the house site, the one area that had not been inspected.

A friend, John C. Mobyed, who planned to spend his vacation on Cape Cod in September, volunteered to search the woods to the east of the house site. He went into the woods on two separate days, wearing old clothes which got torn to shreds. He telephoned the exciting, but expected news. He had found an excavation which was in a proper position in relation to what had been the shore to have been the site of the ship shed. However, he said it was "about four hundred feet" to the east of the house site, and that distance, considering visibility in a forest wilderness, seemed too great to be accepted. The Icelanders would have wanted their ship shed to be no more than a stone's throw from their house, where they could keep an eye on it and reach it in a few seconds to protect it in an emergency.

When John returned from his vacation, he marked off along a city sidewalk the distance as he remembered it, between house and ship-shed sites. His estimate this time seemed to be less than 150 feet. The actual distance was later found to be only 130 feet.

An archaeological investigation was arranged for November 1960, at which time seventeen members of the Massachusetts Archaeological Society dug into both hollows. An alignment of some stones and some soil discoloration indicative of timberwork showed that there had been "some sort of construction" just above the hardpan floor in the presumed dwelling site, and along what would have been the edges of sleeping platforms. Nails would most certainly be found in any colonial or postcolonial house or barn site, and because no nails were found, the investigators reached a conclusion concurred in by all. They said, "Whatever these sites are, they are not colonial."

Since they were not colonial or postcolonial, and since the evidence was also clear that they were not excavations left by cranberry-bog builders who had sought sand,[15] it was reasonable to accept them as precolonial.

A description of the Mill Pond sites will be found in *The Viking Explorers,* pp. 159–64.

Here is a listing of all the factors that enter into identification of the Helgi-Finnboge sites:

They are far from the sea, farther than Follins Pond, both in direction and in travel distance.

They are in what had been the bank of the lake when tide levels were two to three feet higher.

They are approachable from Leif's Shelters over high ground.

---

[15] That they were not left by cranberry-bog builders is evidenced by their perfect rectangularity ☐ and ☐ by the fact that neither is in a bank that is dominantly sand, and by the fact that there had been some "construction" at the base of the hollow of the presumed dwelling site.

Aerial photographs show a trail for part of the distance, and while that could be a modern hunters' trail, it could also be the one Freydis used.

The distance from Leif's Shelters is slightly over one mile, a distance that fits perfectly with implications in the saga story.

The two sites at Mill Pond are in acceptable proximity to each other.

They are rectangular, in house and in ship-shed shapes.

They are correctly oriented, the presumed ship shed end-on to water, and the presumed house site with its long sides parallel with the shore, so that its door at the end of one long side faced the lake.

The excavated hollow end-on to water was just wide enough to accommodate a viking trading ship.

The house-site hollow was just wide enough for two sleeping platforms and a corridor between them.

A transverse ridge of stones in the house site was good evidence that there had been a partition wall.

The floor of the house-site hollow was about six and a half feet below the top of the bank, a reasonable depth for a dwelling.

The interior length of the house-site hollow to the west of the center of the ridge of stones was precisely what was needed for sleeping space for thirty-five people: twenty-five inches for each of seventeen persons on each long platform, and at the west end of the corridor a bed, indicated by F in the diagram, for one of the leaders, probably Finnboge, who "lay innermost." The seven-foot space to the east of the ridge of stones was probably a storeroom, and the doorway, where Freydis stood without speaking until Finnboge asked her what she had come for, was in the middle of the partition wall.

Carbon is instrumental in facilitating the growth of bacteria which supply plants with food. In excavating house sites archaeologists have learned to look for the hearth at the site of the largest tree. In the Mill Pond house site the largest tree was growing about five feet to the east of the precise middle of the hollow. This would have been a most logical position for the Helgi-Finnboge hearth.

The two Mill Pond sites are precisely where the saga would place the Helgi-Finnboge buildings in relation to Leif's house at Leif's Shelters.

Several archaeological possibilities beckon us when we consider what Freydis must have done to conceal evidence of her crime. Since her arrival in Greenland with a large shipload of timber and other good things would be an incentive to others to make profitable voyages to Leif's Shelters, she had to prepare the scene in the area of Leif's Shelters to support the story she would tell when she got home. She had to make it appear that Helgi and Finnboge and their men had peacefully sailed away and had been lost at sea. To do this, she had to dispose of the corpses of her victims, and it is most likely that she had them buried in the woods at some little distance from their house, and that she left their mass grave unmarked. She had to dispose of the Icelanders' weapons, their axes, swords, and any objects that would be identifiable as theirs. The easy way was to have these objects thrown into the water of Mill Pond. Also, she had to dispose of her husband's ship which was in the shed at Leif's Shelters and which, according to the story she would tell, was left for the Icelanders. She would certainly not have taken it from Follins Pond into Mill Pond. She no doubt kept some ropes and maybe some sailcloth from it. But the ship itself with its anchor, figurehead, and identifiable gear had to disappear. To burn the ship might leave evidence of what had happened to it. To take it down the Bass River and far out into Nantucket Sound to destroy it would not be the easy way. The easy way, and the safe way, was to launch the ship in Follins Pond, and load her with rocks, and tow her out to the deepest part of Follins Pond, and have holes cut in her planking, and let her sink. The ship would have filled and sunk on even keel.

The bottom of Follins Pond is not gravel, but sand and mud. The rock-laden hull would settle until her gunwales were flush with the bottom, or maybe a few inches under. Mr. Paul L. Erhardt of Bridgehampton, New York, thinks a grapnel dragged over the deepest portion of Follins Pond should catch her gunwales. Divers could then identify her size and shape. A ship sunk in Lake Champlain during the War of the American Revolution was lo-

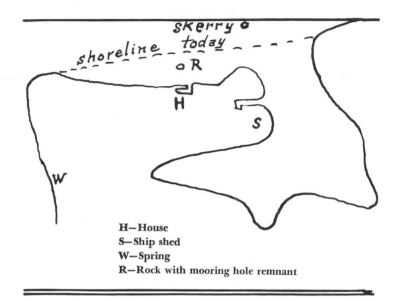

H—House
S—Ship shed
W—Spring
R—Rock with mooring hole remnant

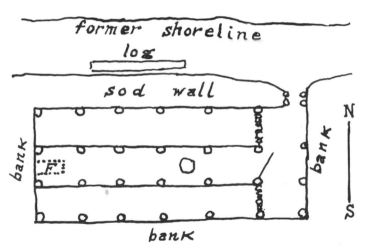

**HELGI-FINNBOGE CAMP AREA
AND DIAGRAM OF HOUSE**

cated after more than one hundred and fifty years and raised in a well-preserved condition. It would be expensive to raise a ship from beneath the bottom of a lake, even where there may be a depth of no more than ten feet. It would probably require a coffer-dam. But the discovery of a viking ship would be sensational and ample funds would doubtless be forthcoming. There is thus the exciting possibility that the ship which belonged to Thorvard, husband of Freydis, lies at the bottom of Follins Pond and may some-day be on display in a viking ship museum on Cape Cod.

We have now had eighty-nine identifications of sailing directions and geographical observations stated or implied in the sagas, including in the count several archaeological discoveries. Since each identification is placed in correct compass direction in relation to all others, as described in or deducible from the sagas, the pattern of the viking voyages to Vinland as told in the sagas would seem to be established. Is it too much to claim that the old Vinland puzzle has been solved?

Aside from carrying practical certainty of its own correctness, the pattern of so many geographical observations that fit the actual geography of the North American continent is proof positive that the Vinland sagas *could not have been invented*. No human beings could have fabricated so many details which fit the actual geography of a huge land they had not visited before. The pattern establishes that the sagas, the translation of which follows, are acceptable records of actual explorations.

PART THREE

The Vinland Sagas

THE VINLAND SAGAS

The sagas of the viking voyages to Vinland exist in manuscripts written in the fourteenth century, presumably copies of thirteenth-century manuscripts, which in turn were taken from orally transmitted tales.

Could tales handed down by word of mouth for centuries have come through into the written versions without error? We know how a saga began. When a distinguished leader returned home from a voyage to Vinland, he recounted to eager listeners what he most vividly remembered. His telling was repeated around the hearth-fires, where children learned it from the lips of their elders. The preservation of the precise text of a telling was not dependent upon any one person's memory, but upon the memories of all the community, who knew every syllable by heart and would instantly correct any individual's error. While boastful enhancements of the deeds of heroes may have been welcomed, seafaring people would not tolerate the slightest change in a sailing direction. Among such people, a verbal change of a geographical observation could not creep into such a narrative. Testimony to the accuracy of oral transmission of subject matter which the community valued is the fact that for centuries the Jews considered it sacrilegious to write any word of their religious prophecies, and so the Old Testament was handed down for centuries by word of mouth. Among the Dead Sea Scrolls is a text of Isaiah written down from oral transmission centuries apart from other similarly written texts of Isaiah, and the texts are identical. What preserved the sacred texts of the Hebrews could have preserved the tales of the viking voyages to Vinland.

The Vinland puzzle—where was Vinland, and where in that land did the vikings go?—has been dealt with in hundreds of books and articles. It would have been a very simple problem had there been only one saga. But the god of muddle entangled scholars in controversy by causing to be handed down two tellings: the *Graenlendinga Saga* that emanated chiefly from Greenlanders, and *Eirik's Saga,* which emanated from the experiences of an Icelander. In these rival tellings, prejudices which Icelanders and Greenlanders harbored against each other gave the god of enigmas many worshippers.

Since there seemed to be contradictions and the sagas seemed to discredit each other, many tried to simplify the Vinland problem by throwing away one of the sagas. Some considered *Eirik's Saga* more reliable because its manuscripts were older than that of the other saga. They closed their minds to the fact that in this case manuscript priorities were immaterial. They ignored the fact that both sagas had existed for at least two centuries before the earliest Icelandic manuscripts near the end of the twelfth century, or early thirteenth century. Which got written first could not have any bearing whatsoever upon the reliability of original tellings.

When Dr. Halldór Hermannsson of Cornell, an authority on Icelandic matters, gave the Icelandic texts of both sagas,[1] he said,

---

[1] Halldór Hermannsson, *The Vinland Sagas.*

"The two sagas, independent of each other, deal with the same events, but in a different way. . . . The details of their respective narratives, which are in places contradictory, must not be placed together to form a whole, but the version of the one, or the other, must be chosen as the more probable."[2]

Essentially, what Dr. Hermannsson was saying was that the Vinland problem could never be anything other than an entertaining but unsolvable guessing game. Perhaps the very synthesis which he decried would be the means of solving the puzzle. Would it be possible to fit all the sailing directions and geographical observations in both sagas into one pattern?

Professor M. L. Fernald encouraged the idea that it would be possible: "The matter-of-fact accounts of the voyages are so direct and without embellishment as to indicate that in the main they are trustworthy historical records."[3] Andrew Fossum said of the Vinland sagas, "If they are worth following, we should follow them closely and assume that they say just what they mean. . . . There are numerous details and names of places and descriptions of countries and coasts that can hardly be fictitious."[4]

Here are two conflicting opinions: that one saga must be preferred to the other because they contradict each other, or that both are geographically factual and can therefore be synthesized. Which shall we accept?

Anyone who believes that some sailing directions in the sagas can be followed literally and others can not dooms himself to failure as interpreter of the geographical realities. He will try to force the geography to his own preconception. In so doing, he will inevitably sail off course. Frankly, he should cast the sagas overboard and not profess to carry them along on his investigating voyage when he blithely steers to a destination of his own choosing. A fair description of such a theorist is contained in what a professor in a department of science has given me as his private reaction to a recent book in the viking field: "At one point the author accepts the

[2] Ibid., p. iv.

[3] M. L. Fernald, "The Natural History of Ancient Vinland and Its Geographical Significance," *American Geographical Society Bulletin* pp. 686–87.

[4] Andrew Fossum, *The Norse Discovery of America*.

sagas as sailing directions and as being accurate. In fact he gives an illustration as to how accurate a legend handed down by word of mouth for four hundred years among the Eskimo tribes can be. Then he goes on to analyze, reinterpret and rearrange the sagas, where there are to him apparent discrepancies in such a way as to prove his thesis."

My assumption has been that there are no geographical contradictions and that both sagas are geographically accurate in all details, and therefore equally reliable in respect to the geography, and that the two can be synthesized.

The sagas are stories of great human interest, masterfully told.

The *Tale of the Greenlanders,* or *Graenlendinga Saga,* originally came largely from Leif Erikson's lips. It was written in Iceland about the year 1385, a copy from an earlier manuscript, by order of Jon Hakonarson, whose descendants preserved it on Flatey (Flat Island) in an Icelandic fjord, so that it has also been known as the *Flat Island Book (Flateyjarbók).* The manucript has been in the Royal Library in Copenhagen, listed by number 1005.

The other saga came largely from the lips of an Icelander, Thorfinn Karlsefni, and is called *The Saga of Erik the Red,* or *Eirik's Saga.* This is in various manuscript versions in the Arnamagnean Library in Copenhagen. These were written before 1334. One variant is known by its number 557, the writer of which gave his name as Hauk Erlendsson, and is generally called the *Skalholtsbók,* and is referred to by the letter S. A variant known as 544 was at least partly written by a hand identified as Hauk Erlendsson's. For this reason the name *Hauksbók* has been applied to both variants, but herein the name *Hauksbók* or the letter H is used only in reference to 544.[5]

---

[5] The texts of *Skalholtsbók* 557 and *Hauksbók* 544 are printed in parallel columns in Sven B. F. Jansson's *Sagorna om Vinland.* Jansson names sixteen scholars who argued the relative status of H and S, and which of the two they thought was nearer to the original source. They had a field day, as though the search for Vinland was a matter of winning a victory in a literary controversy. They forget that it was a problem in geography.

The number of lines in S is 7,843, and in H it is 7,852. Since one variant is only nine lines longer than the other, it might be supposed that S and H are closely parallel. But in various sections of the story there are great differences in length. At any one point we naturally follow the text of the variant which at that point gives the greater number of details; or more accurately stated, we welcome all the details in both variants of *Eirik's Saga*.

Readers of my books on the vikings have often requested that I give my translation of the Vinland sagas. Why mine? There have been four reputable English translations which many readers have assumed to be reliable. They are: B. F. DeCosta, *The Pre-Columbian Discovery of America by the Northmen, illustrated by translations from the Icelandic sagas* (Albany, 1868, 1890, and 1901); A. M. Reeves, N. L. Beamish, and R. B. Anderson, *The Norse Discovery of America* (1906); Gwyn Jones, *The Norse Atlantic Sagas* (Oxford University Press, 1964); and Magnus Magnusson and Hermann Pálsson, *The Vinland Sagas* (1965).

Are these translations unsatisfactory? What claim do I make for the superiority of my translation?

The question of the comparative values of translations usually appears in discussions of translations of poetry. For example, there have been many translations of Ovid, and for any one poem preference has been given to the translation which makes the strongest appeal as English poetry. Consider the unrivaled achievement of Edward FitzGerald's translation of the *Rubáiyát*, which some think is better than the original.

As for poetry in the Vinland sagas, we have four samples of Skaldic verse. I have used the Reeves-Beamish-Anderson translation of Thorhall's first ditty because I do not see how it can be improved. As for my translations of the "Poem of the Ocean Combers" and Thorhall's second ditty, I am confident they will hold their own in comparison with any others.

As to the prose of the Vinland sagas, can any more be asked than that a translation should give precise meaning in idiomatic English? Are all reasonably careful translations of equal value?

Definitely not; for the sagas of the Vinland voyages present a special problem. The only translation that can be acceptable is one that enables us to trace the voyages. Rather obviously, therefore, the translator must be a person who is intimately familiar with the geography of North America. This is not to say that only an American can qualify as ideal translator of those sagas, but an American with extensive firsthand knowledge of the geography of the continent has an advantage over a European who has merely gazed upon the geography from across the ocean.

If a translator is himself confused as to sailing directions and the geography, will his translation help or hinder readers who seek to trace the voyages?

Let us look briefly at the previous English translations.

In Leif's description of what he saw when he landed in Newfoundland, the Icelandic words *aein hella* carry the two ideas of stone (or rock) and flatness. I submit that my translation, "a level stonefield," is a correct description of the ten-mile area Leif saw between the sea and the far-distant ice mountains. The Reeves-Beamish-Anderson translation, though in awkward English, is acceptable: "Large ice mountains were seen far away, but like one stonefield was all to the ice mountains from the sea." This translation has the merit of mentioning the great distance between the mountains and the sea. The Gwyn Jones translation is misleading: "The background was all great glaciers and right up to the glaciers from the sea as it were a single slab of rock." Anyone who looks for a slab of rock several miles long is likely to lose Leif's trail. The translation by Magnusson and Pálsson echoes Gwyn Jones: "The hinterland was covered with great glaciers, and between glaciers and shore the land was like one great slab of rock."

Which translation will best guide us to the fjord Thorvald entered? DeCosta says Thorvald sailed to the fjord "in a northerly direction on an east coast." Reeves, Beemish, and Anderson say Thorvald sailed "to the east of the land and into the firth-mouth that was next to it." Gwyn Jones says: "east along the land and into the mouth of the next fjord they came to." Magnusson and Pálsson say Thorvald and his men "found themselves at the mouth of two fjords." It is difficult if not impossible to visualize two fjords having one mouth. There are no such two fjords on the East

Coast of North America. The Icelandic words *inn j fiardar kiafta* mean "into the mouths of a fjord," and the fjord in New England has four mouths.

In the description of Karlsefni's Hóp, the Gwyn Jones translation says the dwellings were "up above the lake," with "some near the mainland and some near the lake." In context, the phrase "near the mainland" makes no sense. The Magnusson and Pálsson translation says, "sailed into the estuary and named the place Hope (Tidal Lake)." If this is not a misprint it is atrocious. Hóp does not mean "hope." From the saga we learn that Karlsefni's Hóp was up a river; it was not at a "lake."

The Cleasby and Vigfusson *Icelandic-English Dictionary* says *furtha (furda)* originally meant "spectral," with an "ominous" appearance. It hinted at the miraculous, and so previous translators have used the terms "Wonder Strands" or "Marvel Strands," suggestive of the mysterious and magical. My translation, "Astonishing Strands," is within the compass of the meaning in the saga, for the surprise to the Norsemen was merely that the strands were far more extensive than any they had ever seen. The vikings surely had intelligence enough to understand that strands "so long to sail by" were natural, and not works of magic.

My translation of *Graenlendinga Saga* is of the Icelandic text in photographed pages (with pages of the Icelandic text in modern lettering) of the original vellum manuscript of *The Flatey Book,* with reproductions by royal Danish sanction, published by the Norroena Society in 1908. My translation of *Eirik's Saga* is based upon the Icelandic texts of the *Skalholtsbók* and *Hauksbók* in Sven B. F. Jansson's *Sagorna om Vinland.*

My translations allow the sagas to guide the reader in geographical detection. They are not translations made to fit a geographical theory, but made with awareness of the actual geography, after years of mulling over the alternatives. The theory that has directed my translating is that both sagas are accurate geographical guides. Archaeological discoveries have vindicated both the theory and my translation.

We all make mistakes. Those mistakes which I have perpetrated but have eliminated from my translation fortunately did not affect geographical observations. The one that came closest to touching geography was my stiff-necked persistence for several years in translating *hamra nauckurra* as "a certain cliff" (singular), instead of the correct "certain cliffs," but now the plural beautifully illustrates the geographical precision of the sagas, for the term points to what local residents today call "bluffs." I have voided errors like the one made in the nineteenth century by Benjamin Franklin DeCosta, who, at the point where Leif's ship was grounded in a sound at the mouth of a river in Vinland, translated *tha langt til siofar at sia fra skipinu* as "a long way between the ship and the water." This led everyone astray, for it brought to mind mud flats, and so theorists for a generation or more looked everywhere for mud flats and got stuck in them wherever they found them. The correct translation is, "It was a long distance to look to the ocean from the ship."

In translating the sagas, the spelling of names is a nightmare. Paul Schach, translator of the *Eyrbyggia Saga* (University of Nebraska Press, 1959), says in his Preface, page vii: "The treatment of Icelandic names is a notoriously difficult task. Absolute consistency in either translating all names or leaving them all in their original forms is unattainable." I have retained the spelling of names as given in the *Graenlendinga Saga* and, to avoid confusing the reader, have made the names in *Eirik's Saga* conform to the spellings in the *Graenlendinga*.

GRAENLENDINGA SAGA

ERIK THE RED AND GREENLAND

The father of Erik the Red was a man named Thorvald. Because
of manslaughter, he and Erik left their home in Jaederen, Norway,
and sailed to Iceland. By then Iceland had been extensively settled, and therefore the best choice they had for a homesite was in
Drangar at Hornstrands.[6] Thorvald died there. Erik the Red then
married Thjodhild[7] and moved south to Haukadale near Vat-

[6] Undesirable for residence since on an exposed coast.
[7] Thjodhild's family held land in Haukadale.

nshorn, calling his farm Erikstead. They had a son named Leif.

Erik was banished from Haukadale for manslaughter, after slaying Eyolf and Foul and Hrafn the Dueller. He went to Oxen Island in Breidafjord. He loaned the posts and boards of his sleeping platform to Thorgest of Breidabolstead, but when he demanded the return of the boards and was denied them, quarreling and fighting broke out, as described in *Eirik's Saga.*[8] Those who sided with Erik were Styr Thorgrimsson, Eyjolf of Svin Island, Thorbjorn Vifilsson, and the sons of Thorbrand of Alptafjord. Those who stood with Thorgest were Thorgeir of Hitardale, and the sons of Thord Gellir.

The Thorsness Lawthing sentenced Erik to outlawry.[9] He prepared his ship in Erik's Bay, and when ready to put to sea, Styr and others accompanied him out beyond the islands. Erik told them he was going to search for the land that Gunnbjorn, son of Ulf Krage, had sighted when he was driven off course to the west and discovered the Gunnbjorn Skerries. If he found this land he said he would return to visit his friends.

He put to sea beyond Snaefellsjökul. He sighted land and came to what he called Mid-jökul, now called Blaserk (Black Sark). Thence he sailed southward along the coast, looking for habitable land.[10] He spent the first winter on Eriksey[11] which lies near the middle of the Eastern Settlement. The following spring he sailed into Eriksfjord[12] and selected a site for his farmstead. That summer he explored the western uninhabited region and named many landmarks[13] there. He spent the second winter in Erik's Holme at Hrafnsgnipa. (The third summer he sailed all the

---

[8] *Eirik's Saga,* emanating from Iceland, gives more information concerning Erik's troubles in Iceland, but no details of the settling of colonists in Greenland.

[9] Outlawry for three years.

[10] Pasturelands or grassy areas.

[11] A large island in Breidafjord on the southwest coast of Greenland.

[12] Now called Tunugdliarfik. Erik found the land farthest in from the sea in several fjords most desirable for dairy farming.

[13] Islands, headlands, and fjords.

way north to Snaefell and into Hrafnsfjord, at the head of which
he reckoned he was farther in from the sea than the head of Eriksfjord; and then he turned back and spent the third winter on
Eriksey, off the mouth of Eriksfjord.) [14]

The following summer he sailed back to Iceland and landed
in Breidafjord. He called the land that he had discovered Greenland, for, he said, "Men will be more readily pursuaded to go there,
if the land has an attractive name." Erik was in Iceland during the
winter, but the following summer he went out to settle the land.
He resided at Brattahlid in Eriksfjord. Well-informed men say
that in that same summer in which Erik set out to settle Greenland, thirty-five ships sailed out of Breidafjord and Borgarfjord,
and fourteen arrived there. Some were driven back and some cast
away. That was fifteen years before Christianity was legally established in Iceland. In that same summer Fredrick the Bishop and
Thorvald Kodransson went away. The following men who went
out with Erik took land in Greenland: Herjulf at Herjulfsfjord,
his dwelling at Herjulfsness; Ketil at Ketilsfjord; Rafn at Rafns-
fjord; Sölve at Sölvedal; Helgi Thorbrandsson at Alptafjord;
Thorbjorn Glora at Siglefjord; Einar at Einarsfjord; Hafgrim at
Hafgrimsfjord and Vatnehverf; Arnlög at Arnlögsfjord; but some
went to the Western Settlement.

LEIF SAILS TO NORWAY (I)

When sixteen winters had passed since Erik the Red built
(byggia) Greenland,[15] Erik's son Leif sailed from Greenland to
Norway. He came to Nidaros (Trondheim) in the autumn, when
King Olaf Tryggvason had come from Halogaland. Leif laid his
ship in to Nidaros and went at once to visit King Olaf. The king
expounded the faith to him and other heathen men. Leif found no

[14] The sentence in parentheses is from *Landnámabok*. Erik endured the full term
of his outlawry by staying out of Iceland for three full years.

[15] This brief section is out of chronological order and should come after Bjarni's
sighting of new lands.

difficulty in accepting the faith. He and all his shipmates were christened. Leif abode with the king all winter and was well treated.

BJARNI SIGHTS NEW LANDS

Herjulf was the son of Bard, who was the son of Herjulf, a kinsman of Ingolf, the first settler in Iceland.[16] Ingolf gave to the Herjulf family land between Vog and Reykjaness. Herjulf dwelt first at Drepstok. His wife was called Thorgerd, and their son, Bjarni. Bjarni had a shrewd eye for trading. He had in his youth an inclination for voyaging. He prospered and won the respect of his fellows. Every winter he was either abroad or with his father. He was soon the owner of a trading ship. One season before Bjarni returned from Norway, Herjulf his father decided to accompany Erik the Red to Greenland as a colonist, and he broke up his home. On the ship with Herjulf was a Christian man[17] from the Sudreyr (Hebrides) who composed the "Poem of the Ocean Comb-ers" *("Hafgerdinga Drapa"*: *haf* means "sea"; *gerdinga* means "fences," "walls of white water," "breakers"; *drapa* means lines with words accented by striking chords of accompanying instrument). There is this stanza in it:

> I pray to the tester of monks,
> Make smooth my voyages in shortest course;
> May the Master of heaven and earth
> Hold the sky above me steady.[18]

---

[16] Floki was the first settler in Iceland. Ingolf was the first settler in the southern section of Iceland where Herjulf resided.

[17] This was a Christian traveler (or missionary?) to Greenland fifteen years be-fore Leif Erikson introduced Christianity to that island.

[18] Since this poem was popular enough to be preserved, it seems safe to assume that it gave expression to a vivid experience. Here is a literal translation of the quoted stanza:

> My pray I monk tester
> Unhindered voyages in a straight course;
> Of the hawk may he hold the hood of the earth
> The hall's master over me seat.

In the first two lines the meaning is clear, but the other two lines challenge

Herjulf settled on Herjulfsness. He was a most highly regarded man. Erik the Red dwelt at Brattahlid, and was the most esteemed man there. Everyone bowed to him. These were Erik's children: Leif, Thorvald, and Thorstein, and Freydis who was called his daughter. She was married to a man named Thorvard. They dwelt at Gardar, where the bishop's seat is now. She was very proud, but Thorvard was a little man; the principal reason she had been given to him was for his wealth. The people in Greenland were heathen at that time.

That same summer, when his father had sailed away in the spring, Bjarni arrived with his ship at Eyrar (Eyrarbakki). He was much surprised to hear of the move his father had made. He would not unload his ship and when his shipmates asked him what he intended to do, he replied that it was his purpose to keep to his custom and to spend the winter with his father. He told his shipmates he would take the ship to Greenland if they would go with him. They all replied that they would follow him wherever he decided to go. Then Bjarni said, "Our voyage into the Greenland Sea may be regarded as foolhardy, since none of us has ever been there."

Nevertheless, they put to sea when they had provisioned their ship; and after three days' sail when the land was no longer visible, the fair wind failed and changed into north winds and fogs, and they knew not where they were carried. This uncertainty lasted many days. When the sun came forth again, they were able to establish direction from the heavens, and they hoisted sail and sailed for a day before they sighted land. They wondered what land it could be. Bjarni doubted if it were Greenland. Bjarni's shipmates

---

imagination. There was great confusion of word order in Skaldic poetry. A monk is a landsman not accustomed to ocean voyaging. God tests him through the hardships and perils of the sea. On a tossing ship he looks up above the mast and has the illusion of seeing the clouds or sun or stars swinging, and he prays that the sky will be held motionless on its seat *(stalli)* like a hooded hawk on its master's wrist, so that it will not be flying back and forth overhead. If we mistakenly insist that a huntsman held a hooded bird not on his wrist but on his hand, we make the stanza say: "hold God's hand over me"—and for a conventional figure sacrifice the sea meaning.

asked whether he wished to sail to the land, but he proposed
that they merely sail close to it, and as they did so, they soon per-
B 1   ceived that the land was mountainless and wooded, with low hillocks. Leaving the land on their larboard with their sail swung
B 2   over toward it, they sailed for two days before they sighted another
land. They asked Bjarni whether he thought this was Greenland,
but he said this was no more like Greenland than the first, because
he had been told that in Greenland there were mountains with
very large glaciers. When they drew near this land, they saw it was
B 3   extensively forested and appeared level. The fair wind then failed,
and the crew thought it prudent to land, but Bjarni refused. The
men protested that they needed wood and water, to which Bjarni
replied that they had no lack of either. His shipmates criticized
him for this assertion. He bade them hoist sail, which they did,
and turning the prow from the land they sailed out upon the high
B 4   seas, with southwesterly winds of gale strength. After three days'
B 5   sailing they sighted a third land which was high and mountainous
with glaciers. When Bjarni was asked whether he wished to land,
he said he did not, because this land looked unprofitable. Without
lowering their sail, they coasted along this land and perceived that
B 6   it was an island. They left this land astern, and sailed on with the
same fair wind. The wind rose mightily and Bjarni commanded
them to reef, to slacken speed for the sake of the ship and the rig-
B 7   ging. They now sailed for four days. Then they sighted a fourth
land, and this time Bjarni said, "This is most like Greenland, according to my information, and here we may steer to the land."
This they did, and came to land in the evening, below a cape
where there was a boat; upon this cape dwelt Bjarni's father, Herjulf, for whom the cape was named Herjulfsness. Bjarni now
joined his father. He gave up voyaging and remained with his
father as long as Herjulf lived, and made his home there after his
father died.

BJARNI VISITS NORWAY

Next to be told is that Bjarni Herjulfsson sailed from Greenland to visit Earl Eric (ruler of Norway after King Olaf's death).

The Earl received him well. Bjarni told of his voyage and the lands he had sighted. Many thought he lacked curiosity, since he could not tell anything about these lands. He was somewhat slandered on this account. Bjarni became the Earl's Man, and went out to Greenland the next summer. Now, there was much talk of land-seeking.

LEIF ERIKSON VOYAGES TO THE NEW LANDS

Leif Erikson went to visit Bjarni Herjulfsson, bought his ship, and hired a crew of thirty-five men. Leif begged his father Erik to lead the expedition. But Erik excused himself, saying he was too old and was no longer able to endure the hardships of the sea as of yore. Leif said he might be a better commander of the kinsmen and so Erik yielded to Leif. When they were ready, Erik rode from his house to the ship, though it was only a little way. The horse stumbled, and he fell off and hurt his foot. Erik declared, "It is not my fate to find more lands than this where now we dwell. You, my son, and I may no longer follow together."

Erik went home to Brattahlid, and Leif went to the ship with his thirty-five men. They had with them Tyrker the Southerner. They made ready the ship and put to sea. They found first the last land Bjarni had sighted. They sailed to the land, anchored, put out   **L 1** a boat, and went ashore. They saw no grass, but large ice moun-   **L 2** tains in the distance. From the sea to the ice mountains all was one level stonefield. To them the land seemed worthless. Then Leif said, "Unlike Bjarni, we have stepped ashore on this land, and I will now give it a name. I call it *Helluland* [Flat Rock Land]."   **L 3**

Afterward they returned to the ship and sailed away on the open ocean. They found another land, and again sailed to it and cast anchor, put out the boat, and went ashore. This land was level   **L 4** and completely wooded, with broad stretches of white sand. Wher-   **L 5** ever they went the shore region did not slant steeply. Then Leif said, "This land shall have a name in keeping with its nature. I call it *Markland* [Forestland]."

After that they went back to the ship as fast as possible and from there sailed on the ocean with a wind that blew from the

northeast. They were out of sight of land for two days. Then they
L 6   saw land and sailed to it, and came to an island which lay to the
north of the land. They went to the highest point on that island to
L 7   look around. It was a fair day. They found dew on (or "in") the
grass, and when they wet their fingers with the dew and brought
their fingers to their mouths, they thought they had never tasted
anything so sweet. Afterward they went to their ship and sailed
L8, L9 into a sound that lay between the island and that cape which extended to the north from the land. They steered in to the west of
the cape.

It was very shallow there at ebb tide and their ship was
L 10 grounded. From there it was a long distance to look to the ocean
from the ship. Yet they were so eager to go ashore that they could
not wait for the tide to rise under the ship, but ran a boat to the
L 11 land, into a river that flowed down from a lake. As soon as the tide
rose under the ship, they took the boat and rowed to the ship and
conveyed the ship up the river and to the lake where they cast anchor. They carried their sleeping bags ashore and built temporary
L 12, L 13 shelters. Later on, when they decided to remain there that winter,
L 14, L 15 they built a large house. (The essential ship shed would be taken for
L 16 granted by seafaring folk.) Salmon abounded in the river and
in the lake, and larger salmon than they had ever seen. There were
such good land qualities thereabouts that it seemed to them there
L 17 might be no lack of cattle fodder in the winter. There came no
frost in winter, and there was only slight withering of the grass.
The days and nights were more nearly of equal length than in
Greenland or Iceland. On the shortest day the sun touched the ho-
L 18 rizon at Eyktarstad, and rose at Dagmalastad.

When they had finished building their house, Leif said to his
fellows, "Now I will let our company be divided into two parts,
and I will let them explore the land; one-half of the company shall
remain at home, while the other half shall explore the land, but go
no farther away than they can return in the evening, and not be
separated." And they did so for a while. Leif alternately went out
with them and stayed at home in the hall (*skala*). Leif was a very
large and strong man, imposing in appearance, knowledgeable, and
moderate in all regards.

One evening came the tidings that a man was missing from

the company, and it was Tyrker the Southerner. Leif was very much toubled by this because Tyrker had been with his father and himself for a long time and had loved Leif much in his childhood. Leif severely blamed his companions and immediately ordered an expedition in search of him, taking twelve men with him. But when they had gone but a short way from the hall, Tyrker came to meet them. He was well received. Leif perceived at once that his foster-father was excited. He had a large forehead, and restless eyes, and small freckles on his face. Though he was a puny, insignificant-looking fellow, he was a leader in martial sports. Leif asked him, "Why are you late, my foster-father, and separated from your comrades?" For a long time Tyrker talked in his southern tongue, rolling his eyes and making wry faces, and they could not understand him. Then he explained in Norse, "I did not walk far beyond the others, but I have news for you. I have found withy vines [*vin vid*] and wine berries [*vin ber*]." "Is it truly so, foster-father?" Leif asked. "Most certain," said he, "for I was born where there is no lack of withy vines and wine berries."

      L 19
      L 20

After a night's sleep, Leif said to his shipmates, "From now on we have two things to do. Every day we shall either gather wine berries, or cut withy vines, and chop down trees to make a lading for my ship."

This they did, and it is said that their after-boat was filled with grapes. Now was hewn a lading for the ship.

When spring came, they made ready and sailed away. Leif named the land for its products. He called it *Vinland*.

LEIF RETURNS TO BRATTAHLID

Thereafter they went to sea and had a fair wind until they saw Greenland and moors under the glaciers. Then one of the men spoke to Leif, "Why do you steer the ship so much into the wind?" Leif replied, "I am taking care of the rudder, but of more than that besides, or what do you see that is remarkable?" The men answered that they saw nothing remarkable. "I do not know," said Leif, "whether I see a ship or a skerry." Now they saw it and said it was a skerry; but Leif saw sharper than they, for he saw men on the skerry. "Now I want to beat against the wind," said Leif, "so as to get near to them upwind and see if they want to be picked up by us, and whether they need our assistance. If they are not peacefully inclined, then we shall have the superior position, which they will not have."

They closed in to the skerry, lowered the sail, and dropped anchor. They put out the little boat which they had with them.

Then Tyrker asked, "Who is the leader of your party?" The leader said, "I am called Thorer, and am of northern kin. But what is your name?" Leif told his name. Thorer asked, "Are you the son of Erik the Red of Brattahlid?" Leif replied that he was, and said, "Now I make you this offer. I will take you all on my ship, and all the goods that the ship will hold." They accepted those terms.

Then they sailed to Eriksfjord with the lading, until they came to Brattahlid. They unloaded the ship, and then Leif invited Thorer and his wife Gudrid and three other men to dwell with him. He also provided dwellings for the other men, both Thorer's and his own. Leif had rescued fifteen men from the skerry. Thereafter he was called Leif the Lucky. He now had great wealth and was highly honored.

That winter there was much sickness among Thorer's men, and Thorer and a good part of his crew died. Erik the Red also died that winter.

Now there was much talk of the Vinland voyage of Leif. Thorvald, his brother, held the opinion that the country had not been sufficiently explored. Leif said to Thorvald, "You shall go out with my ship, brother, if you will go to Vinland. However, I want the ship to go first for the wood which Thorer had on the skerry." And so it was done.

THORVALD ERIKSON EXPLORES IN VINLAND

On Leif's advice, Thorvald prepared for the voyage with a crew of thirty men. They provisioned the ship and put to sea, and there is nothing to be said of their voyage until they arrived in Vinland at Leif's Shelters. They shored the ship there and kept quiet that winter, catching fish for food. In the spring Thorvald ordered that the ship be made ready, and that some men should go in the after-boat to explore the western part of the land during the summer. These men found it a pleasing, well-wooded country, with forests near the salt water and the white sands. There were many islands and shoals. They found no dwellings of men or lairs of beasts. On one of the islands to the west, however, they did find a corncrib of wood. They found no other works of man. They returned to Leif's Shelters at harvesttime.

The next summer Thorvald went eastward with the merchant ship, and northward along the land. Then, off a cape, they had a hard storm, and were driven on shore there, breaking the keel under their ship. There they had a long delay while they repaired their ship. Then Thorvald said to his followers, "I desire that we erect the old keel here on this cape and call it Keel Cape [*Kialnar Nes*]," and this they did.

After this they sailed away from there, eastward along the land and into the mouths of a fjord that was near there, to a headland which extended out there and was covered with trees. There they berthed their ship and put out the gangplank to shore, and Thorvald and all his companions went up on the land. Thorvald then remarked, "Here it is fair, and here I should like to set up my residence." Then they went back to the ship, and on the sands within the headland saw three mounds. They drew close and perceived there were three skin canoes and three men under each. They divided their party and seized all but one, who escaped with his boat. They killed those eight men.

Thereafter they ascended the headland and looked about. They saw some hillocks within the fjord, and surmised that these were human habitations. Thereafter such great weariness befell them that they could not keep awake, and all fell asleep. Then came a call above them, such that they all awakened. The call said, "Awake, Thorvald, and all your men, if you would save your life, and go to your ship, you and all your men, and get clear of the land with all speed!" From the inner reaches of the fjord, countless skin canoes were coming.

The skin boats came at them. Then Thorvald ordered, "We will put the shields outboards and defend ourselves as best we may, but attack only a little." So they did, and the Shriekers shot at them for a while, and then afterward fled, as fast as they could.

T 1

T 2

T 3

T 4
T 5
T 6
T 7
T 8
T 9
T 10

T 11
T 12

T 13

Thorvald asked his men whether they were wounded in any way, and they replied, "None wounded." "I have received a wound in my armpit," Thorvald said. "An arrow flew between the side of the ship and the shield under my arm, and here is the arrow. If this leads to my death, I advise you to prepare to sail as soon as possible on your return passage, but carry me to that headland which seemed to me most habitable. It may be that a true word came out of my mouth, when I said I might dwell there for a while. There you shall bury me and set a cross at my head and at my feet, and call it *Krossanes* [Cross Cape] forever after."

T 14

Thorvald died and his men did everything that he had told them to do. Then they rejoined their comrades and exchanged such tidings as they had. They dwelt there that winter and gathered grapes and vinestocks for their ship. They prepared to return to Greenland the next spring and when their ship came into Eriksfjord they had much to tell Leif.

THORSTEIN ERIKSON IN THE WESTERN SETTLEMENT

Meanwhile in Eriksfjord, Thorstein had married Gudrid, Thorbjorn's daughter, who had been the wife of Thorer the Eastman as was mentioned before. Thorstein Erikson desired to go to Vinland for the body of his brother Thorvald. He prepared the same ship and selected a crew of twenty-five stalwart and tall men, taking his wife Gudrid with him. They sailed as soon as they were ready, and were soon out of sight of land. They were driven this way and that all the summer and lost all reckoning of their whereabouts. At the end of the first week of winter[19] they came to land at Lysufirth in the Western Settlement of Greenland. There Thorstein sought out and obtained houses for all his crew, but none for himself and his wife. The two of them were left in the ship for two nights. Christianity was then still young in Greenland.[20]

[19] Winter in Iceland and Greenland officially began in the middle of October.

[20] Hospitality had been an honored custom among the followers of the old Norse gods, but the heathen customs were breaking down under the first impact of Christianity, and had not yet been fully supplanted by Christian charity.

Early one morning men came to their tent. One of the men outside asked who was in the tent. Thorstein answered, "Two persons. But who are you who asks?" "Thorstein is my name, and I am called Thorstein the Swarthy. My errand here is to invite you, man and wife, to abide with me."

Thorstein replied that he would consult with his wife, but she bade him to decide and he accepted at once. "Then will I come for you tomorrow with horses, as I do not lack means to provide an abode for you both. But it will be without anyone else in the house, for only my wife and I live there since I like to go my own way. And I have a different belief from yours; yet I think the one you have is better." And so Thorstein the Swarthy came for them in the morning with horses, and they went with him to his house, and were well treated.

Gudrid was a sturdy and understanding woman who knew well how to behave among strangers. Early in the winter, sickness came to the crew of Thorstein Erikson and many died. Thorstein ordered coffins made for their bodies, and carried them to the ship to keep them there, for he said he would convey all the corpses to Eriksfjord the next summer. It was not long before sickness came to the house of Thorstein. His wife, whose name was Grimhild, was the first taken ill. She was most robust and strong as a man yet the sickness overpowered her; soon after that the sickness took Thorstein Erikson. They both lay ill at the same time. Grimhild, Thorstein the Swarthy's wife, died. When she was dead, Thorstein went out for a plank on which to lay the corpse. Gudrid then spoke, "Stay away only a short time, Thorstein, my good man." He answered, "So shall it be." Then Thorstein Erikson said, "Our housewife acts in a strange way, for now she raises herself up on her elbow, and stretches her feet out from the bedside, and grasps after her shoes."[21] Just then Thorstein the master of the house re-

[21] The account in *Eirik's Saga* is equally shocking, but more entertaining: "Thorstein Erikson sent word to his namesake that he should come to him, saying that all was not as it should be there, for the housewife was endeavoring to rise to her feet, and wished to get in under the bedcovers beside him. When he [Thorstein the Swarthy] entered the room, she was up on the edge of the bed. He thereupon seized her hands and held a poleax before her breast." Since a poleax had a point opposite its cutting edge and thus roughly had the form of a cross, it was potent against misbehaving corpses.

turned, and Grimhild lay down with a thud that caused every timber in the room to creak. Thorstein the Swarthy made a coffin for
Grimhild's body, and then carried it away and buried it. He was a
very large and strong man, but he had need of all his strength before he got her away from the house.

Now the sickness of Thorstein Erickson worsened, and he
died. Gudrid his wife was much grieved. She had been seated
on a stool beside the sleeping platform where Thorstein her husband had been lying. Then Thorstein the housemaster picked
her up in his arms from the stool and seated himself on another
platform on the opposite side of the room from Thorstein's body;
he spoke to her in many ways and consoled her. He promised that
he would go with her to Eriksfjord with the bodies of Thorstein
her husband and his followers. He said he would bring into the
household more persons to comfort and pleasure her. She thanked
him. Then Thorstein Erikson sat up and spoke, "Where is Gudrid?" Three times he said this, but she remained silent. Then she
said to Thorstein the housemaster, "Shall I give answer to his
speaking or not?" He bade her not to answer. Then Thorstein the
housemaster went across the floor and sat down on the stool, and
Gudrid sat on his knee. Thorstein the housemaster spoke, "What
will you, namesake?" said he. Thorstein Erikson answered after a
while, "This now I wish, for I am come to good resting places. But
there is this to foretell, Gudrid; you will be married to an Icelandic
man, and your life with him will be long, and many offspring
will come from you—handsome, illustrious, superior, lovable
[sweet], and winsome [fragrant].[22] You shall go from Greenland
to Norway and thence to Iceland, and make your home in Iceland.
There you shall dwell for a long time, and you shall outlive him.
You shall go abroad and to the South,[23] and return again to your
home in Iceland; a church shall be erected there, and you shall
live there and take the veil as a nun, and there you shall die." And

[22] This appraisal was obviously added by one of Gudrid's descendants.

[23] The supernatural voice which religious superstition later said had prophesied
through the dead lips of Thorstein Erikson mentioned Gudrid's travels to Norway
and to Rome ("South") but failed to mention what is to us her most interesting
traveling—to and within Vinland.

after this Thorstein sank back, and his corpse was laid out and carried to the ship.[24]

Thorstein the housemaster fulfilled his promises to Gudrid. In the spring he sold his lands and his livestock, and went to the ship with Gudrid and all his possessions. He put the ship in order and got a crew, and sailed to Eriksfjord where the corpses were buried at the church. Gudrid went to Leif at Brattahlid, but Thorstein the Swarthy made his home in Eriksfjord. He dwelt there as long as he lived, and was held to be a most honorable man.

THORFINN KARLSEFNI AT LEIF'S SHELTERS

That same summer a ship came from Norway to Greenland. The master of the ship was called Thorfinn Karlsefni. He was a son of Thord the Horsehead, son of Snorri, son of Thord. Thorfinn Karlsefni had a rich cargo, and stayed for the winter at Brattahlid with Leif Erikson. He soon fell in love with Gudrid and proposed to her, but she made Leif answer for her. Afterward she was betrothed to him, and they were wedded that winter. At the same time there was talk of a voyage to Vinland like those before. People urged Karlsefni to make this voyage, both Gudrid and others. He decided to make the voyage, and he hired ship soldiers, sixty-five men, plus five women. A compact was made by Karlsefni and

---

[24] According to *Eirik's Saga:* "Thorstein the master of the house, bade Gudrid lie down and sleep, saying that he would keep watch over the bodies during the night. This she did, and early in the night Thorstein Erikson sat up and spoke. Among other things he said, 'This is no proper usage which has obtained here in Greenland since Christianity was introduced here, to inter men in unconsecrated earth, with naught but a brief funeral service. It is my wish that I be conveyed to the church, together with the others who have died here.' He bade Gudrid beware of marrying any Greenlander. He directed her also to give their property to the church and to the poor. He then sank down again a second time. It had been the custom in Greenland, after Christianity was introduced there, to bury persons on the farmsteads where they died, in unconsecrated earth. A pole was erected in the ground, touching the breast of the dead, and subsequently, when the priests came thither, the pole was withdrawn and holy water poured in, and the funeral service was held there, although it might be long thereafter." The expression of prejudice against Greenlanders, and the description of the burial customs are obvious accretions presumably added by an Icelander, and perhaps by a priestly scribe.

his crew that they should share equally in everything of value that they obtained. They took with them all sorts of cattle, because they intended to settle in the country if they were able to do so. Karlsefni asked Leif for his buildings in Vinland, but Leif replied that he would lend Karlsefni the buildings, not give them. Afterward they put to sea and arrived safely at Leif's Shelters, and carried up their leather bags. Soon they had plenty of good food, for a large and excellent whale was driven ashore. They went to where it was and cut into it, and so had no shortage. The domestic animals were turned out to graze, but the males soon became frisky and wild. They had brought one bull with them. Karlsefni had trees cut down and shaped into timbers to make a shipload, and this wood was stacked upon a rock for drying. They gathered a supply of all the good things that the country produced, grapes and game and fish.

During the summer following their first winter, they became aware of the presence of the Skraelings, a great band of whom came out of the forest. The cattle were near at hand and the bull bellowed and roared mightily. This frightened the Skraelings and they fled with their bundles of gray fur and sable and all kinds of skin wares. They turned toward Karlsefni's abode and tried to enter the buildings, but Karlsefni and his men held the doors to keep them out. Neither side understood the language of the other. Then the Skraelings put down their packs and loosened them and offered their wares in trade, showing especial eagerness for weapons. Karlsefni forbade his companions to trade any weapons, but got the idea of having the women carry milk out to them. The moment the Skraelings saw the milk, they wanted nothing else. The trading concluded with the Skraeling's carrying their goods away in their stomachs, while they left their bundles of fur skins with Karlsefni and his men.

K 1   Following this occurrence, Karlsefni had a strong fence of palings erected around his abode and made all ready there. At this time Gudrid his wife gave birth to a male child, who was called Snorri.

Early in the second winter the Skraelings came again, in larger numbers, with the same wares as before. Karlsefni then told the women to trade milk as they had before, and nothing else. When the Skraelings saw the milk, they threw their bundles in over the palisade. While Gudrid was seated inside the doorway beside the cradle of her infant son, Snorri, a shadow fell upon the door and a woman in a narrow black kirtle entered. She was a short woman, with a band about her head, and light chestnut hair, pale skin, and such large eyes as had never been seen in a human head. The woman went to where Gudrid sat and asked, "What is your name?" "My name is Gudrid [*ek heiti Gudridr*]. But what is your name?" "*Ek heiti Gudridr*," said the woman.

The housewife Gudrid pointed with her hand to a seat beside her. But at that instant there was a great crash and the woman disappeared. One of the Skraelings had tried to seize some weapons and had been slain by one of Karlsefni's men. Instantly the Skraelings fled, leaving garments and goods behind them. No one save Gudrid had seen the woman.

"Now we shall have to plan against them," said Karlsefni, "for I think they will return a third time to attack us in great force. This is what we shall do. Let ten of our men go out upon this cape and show themselves, while the rest of us will slip into the woods and hew a clearing for our cattle. When the savages advance from the forest we shall take our bull and let him precede us." **K 2**

The site chosen for the battlefield lay between water and forest. Karlsefni's tactics worked. The Skraelings advanced to the chosen battle site. In the fight many Skraelings were killed. Among the Skraelings was a tall man, fair to behold (*vaem*, meaning "beautiful," "fine"), whom Karlsefni believed to be their chieftain. One of the Skraelings picked up an ax and examined it. Then he lifted it against a comrade and struck at him, and he was instantly felled. The tall man seized the ax, and after looking at it for a while, hurled it into the salt water with all his might. Then they all fled into the forest. Thus the battle ended. **K 3**

Karlsefni stayed there throughout the winter, but in the spring he decided to remain no longer but return to Greenland. He and his men made ready for the voyage and took with them great quantities of withies, berries, and skin wares. They set sail upon the ocean and arrived at Eriksfjord with the ship in good condition. They spent the winter there.

FREYDIS AND THE ICELANDIC BROTHERS

Now there was new talk of voyaging to Vinland, because men thought such an enterprise would bring profit and esteem. That same summer in which Karlsefni came from Vinland, a ship came from Norway to Greenland. The ship was steered by two brothers, Helgi and Finnboge, Icelanders from the Eastfjords. They stayed the winter in Greenland.

Now, Freydis, Erik's daughter, made a voyage from her home at Gardar to meet with the brothers Helgi and Finnboge. She proposed that they voyage to Vinland with their ship and go halves with her on all the profits that might be obtained. They agreed to this. She then went to visit her brother Leif and asked him to give her the buildings which he had in Vinland, but he gave her his former answer, that he would lend the buildings not give them. Such was the agreement between the brothers and Freydis that each of their ships should carry thirty fighting men, and five women besides. But Freydis immediately violated this and added five men and concealed them, so that the brothers were not aware of the deception. They had an understanding that their two ships would sail in consort, if circumstances permitted. And, though there was little distance between them, the brothers arrived somewhat before Freydis and had their belongings carried up to Leif's house. When Freydis came to land, her crew unloaded their ship and carried their possessions up to the house. Then Freydis remonstrated with the brothers, "Why did you bring your things in here?" "Because we supposed," the brothers replied, "that all the terms of our agreement would be kept." "It was to me Leif loaned the buildings," said she, "and not to you." Helgi declared, "We brothers bear you no ill will." So they carried their belongings out and built themselves a hall and placed that hall farther from the sea on

F 1

---

[25] The repetition of *skala* (meaning "shed," "shelter hall") does not refer to more than one *skala*, but there were two, for the brothers had to have two, one to dwell in and the other to cover their ship.

the bank of a lake (*gerdu ser skala ok settu thann skala*[25] *firr sionum a uazstrondu*), and put it well in order.

Meanwhile Freydis had trees cut down for her ship's cargo. As it drew toward winter, the brothers proposed that everybody engage in games and sports. This they did for a time, until the men began to maltreat each other and their meetings were broken off and the games stopped, and visiting ceased between the halls. Thus the winter dragged on for a long time.

Early one morning Freydis got out of bed and dressed herself, except for shoes. The weather was such that a mighty dew had fallen. She took her husband's cloak, threw it around her, and she walked to the door of the brothers' hall. A man had gone out a little before and had shut the door behind him only halfway. She opened the door and stood in the entrance for a while and was silent. Finnboge who lay at the farthest end of the hall was awake, and he asked, "What do you want here, Freydis?" She answered, "I want you to get up and go out with me. I want to talk with you." He did so. "How do you like everything hereabouts?" she asked. He replied, "I think well of this land's products, but I am illpleased with the enmity that is between us, of which I do not call myself the cause." She said, "Just as you say, and that goes for me too. So I have come to propose something. I desire to trade ships with you brothers, for yours is a larger ship, and I want to get away from here." He said, "That I may let do, if it pleases you well." With that understanding they parted. She went home, and Finnboge went back to rest. As she got into bed, she awakened her husband Thorvard with her cold feet. He asked her why she was so chill and wet. She spoke with great rage. "I have been," she said, "to the brothers, asking to purchase their ship, for I wish to buy the larger ship, but they took it so ill that they struck me and handled me roughly. But you, spineless man that you are, will not avenge my shame or your own! And this I have to learn while I am no longer in Greenland! I shall separate from you unless you avenge this!"

At this he could endure her upbraidings no longer, and he ordered the men to get up at once and take their weapons, and this they did. Then they went straightway to the hall of the brothers. They entered and seized the sleeping men and tied them up

F 2
F 3

tightly. Then they led them out one at a time, and as each came out, Freydis had him put to death. All the men were slain, and only the women remained, whom no one would kill. Then Freydis spoke up, "Hand me an ax!" When she had it, she went at the five women and left them dead.

After this damnable deed they returned to their own house, and it was apparent that Freydis believed everything had worked out well. She spoke to her companions, as follows, "If it be our lot to return to Greenland, I will take the life of any man who talks about what has happened. What we shall say is that they stayed on here when we left."

Early in the spring they loaded the ship the brothers had traded to its utmost capacity, with all the good things they could obtain. They sailed out on the ocean and after a good voyage, came into Eriksfjord early in the summer. Karlsefni was there at the time, for he had prepared his ship for departure and was waiting for a fair wind. It is said by many that never had a richer ship sailed from Greenland than the one he steered.

Freydis then went back to her home which had stood, meanwhile, unmolested. She gave great gifts to all the men who had been in her ship, to help persuade them to keep their mouths shut. And she sat in her abode. But all the men did not keep silent about their crime and wickedness, and the truth leaked out at last. It came to the ears of Leif, her brother, who thought that the story was one of unmitigated evil in every particular. And so Leif took three men who had been with Freydis and tortured them into confessing all that had happened. Their accounts tallied in all details.

"I am not disposed," Leif said, "to do that to my sister Freydis which she deserves. But I foretell of her and her husband, that their offspring will thrive but little." From this it followed that no one thereafter thought them capable of anything but evil.

KARLSEFNI RETURNS TO ICELAND

Now should be told that Karlsefni, his ship prepared, sailed out on the high seas. All went well, and he came to Norway hale and well fleshed. He remained there over the winter and sold his cargo, and both he and his wife enjoyed good friendship there, with the most worshipful people in Norway. The next spring he prepared his ship for Iceland, and when he was quite ready, and his ship lay waiting at the wharf for a fair wind, there came to him a Southerner, a native of Bremen in Saxonland. He wished to buy from Karlsefni the beakhead of his ship. "I will not sell it," he said. "I will give half a mark of gold for it," said the Southerner. Karlsefni thought this to be a good offer, and sold it. The Southerner went away with the ship's beakhead. Karlsefni did not know what species of wood it was. It was *mausur*,[26] brought from Vinland.

Karlsefni then sailed out on the high seas and arrived with his ship in the north country in Skaga Fjord. He shored his ship there for the winter. In the spring he bought Glaumbeiarland, and set up his home there, and dwelt there the rest of his life. He was a most worshipful man. From him and Gudrid his wife came many worthy descendants. When Karlsefni died, Gudrid took over the wardship of his property with her son Snorri, born in Vinland. When Snorri married, Gudrid journeyed abroad and went to the South (on a pilgrimage to Rome). She came back to the house of her son Snorri, who had built a church at Glaumboer. After that, Gudrid became an anchorite nun and lived there the rest of her lifetime. Snorri had a son called Thorgeir. He was the father of Ingveld, mother of Bishop Brand. Snorri, Karlsefni's son, had a daughter named Hallfrid. She was the mother of Runolf, the father of Bishop Thorlak. A son of Karlsefni and Gudrid was called Bjorn. He was the father of Thorun, the mother of Bishop Bjorn. Many people are descended from Karlsefni, and he has a great progeny. And Karlsefni has given the most exact account of the events of all these voyages, as it has now been put into words.

---

[26] *Mausur* wood has never been identified with certainty. Bole maple is perhaps the best conjecture.

EIRIK'S SAGA

(Including variants *Hauksbók* H544 and *Skalholtsbók* S557).

ERIK THE RED AND GREENLAND (II)

A man named Thorvald was the father of Erik the Red. He and Erik left their home in Jaederen because of manslaughter and went to Iceland. They took possession of land in Hornstrands and dwelt at Drangar. Thorvald died there, and then Erik the Red married Thjodhild and moved south to Haukadale, where he cleared land and dwelt at Erikstead, near Vatnshorn. Erik's thralls caused a landslide that destroyed the farm of a man called Valthjof, at Valthjofstead. In revenge, Eyolf the Foul, a kinsman of Valthjof's, slew the thralls at Skeidsbrekkur, above Vatnshorn. To avenge this, Erik killed Eyolf the Foul, and also Hrafn the Dueller, at Leikskaler. Geirstein and Odd of Jorvi, Eyolf's kinsmen, brought charges over his killing, and Erik was banished from Haukadale.

Erik then took possession of Brok Island and Oxen Island, and spent the first winter at Tradir, in South Island. He loaned the boards of his sleeping platform to Thorgest of Breidabolstead. Thereafter, Erik moved to Oxen Island, and dwelt at Erikstead. He then requested the return of his boards, but they were denied him, and so Erik went to Breidabolstead and seized them. Thorgest pursued him, and they fought a battle near the farmstead at Drangar. Two sons of Thorgest and several other men were slain there. Thereafter, both Erik and Thorgest maintained a force of fighting men at home. Those who sided with Erik were Styr Thorgrimsson, Eyjolf of Svin Island, Thorbjorn Vifilsson, and the sons of Thorbrand of Alptafjord. Those who sided with Thorgest were Thorgeir of Hitardale, Aslak of Langadala and his son Illugi, and the sons of Thord Gellir. The Thorsness Lawthing sentenced Erik and his men to outlawry. He prepared his ship in Eriks Bay, and Eyjolf of Svin Island kept him in hiding in Dimunar Bay while Thorgest and his men searched the islands for him.

Thorbjorn Vifilsson and Styr and Eyjolf accompanied Erik out beyond the islands, and they parted in great friendship. Erik said he would furnish them with the like protection (a similar safe abode) to his utmost capacity, if they ever had need of it. He told them he was going to search for the land which Gunnbjorn, son of Ulf Krage, had sighted when he was driven off course to the west and discovered the Gunnbjorn Skerries. He added that if he found this land he would return to visit his friends.

Erik put out to sea beyond Snaefellsjökul, and made his landfall near the glacier that is known as Black Sark. Thence he sailed southward along the coast looking for habitable land. He spent the first winter on Eriksey, which lies near the middle of the Eastern Settlement. In the spring he went into Eriksfjord, where he selected his homestead. That summer he explored the western uninhabited region and named many landmarks. He spent the second winter at Eriks Holme off Hvarf's Peak. The third summer he sailed all the way north to Snaefell and into Hrafnsfjord, at the head of which he reckoned he was farther in from the sea than was the head of Eriksfjord; and then he turned back and spent the third winter on Eriksey, off the mouth of Eriksfjord.

The following summer he sailed back to Iceland, and landed in Breidafjord. He spent the winter with Ingolf of Holmlatur. In the spring he fought a battle with Thorgest of Breidabolstead and was defeated. After that a reconciliation was arranged between them. That summer Erik set out to settle the land he had discovered. He named it Greenland, for he said, "Men will be more readily persuaded to go there, if the land has an attractive name." [Two sections that deal with Gudrid's father and with pagan witchcraft are omitted because they have no direct bearing on voyages to Vinland.]

LEIF ERIKSON'S VOYAGES (V)

Erik was married to a woman named Thjodhild, and had two sons by her: Thorstein and Leif. They were both promising young men. Thorstein remained at home with his father, and he was considered the most promising young man in Greenland at that time. Leif had sailed to Norway, where he was the guest of King Olaf Tryggvason. However, when he had sailed from Greenland in the summer, he was driven off course to the Hebrides. He and his men stayed there most of the summer, waiting for a fair wind. There Leif fell in love with a woman named Thorgunna. She was of noble ancestry and Leif had reason to learn that she was a woman who knew more than a little. When he was about to leave, Thorgunna asked him to take her with him. Leif asked if her kinsfolk would approve of it. She replied that she did not care. Leif said he thought it inadvisable to abduct a woman of such noble kin in a foreign country, "and we so few in numbers." "You may find you are making a mistake," Thorgunna argued. Leif replied, "I shall put it to the proof notwithstanding." "Then you must hear it," said Thorgunna. "I no longer have only myself to consider; for I am pregnant, and the responsibility is yours. I foresee that I shall give birth to a male child. Even though you abandon me, I shall

rear the boy. I shall send him to you in Greenland, when he is able
to take his place among men. It is my guess that you will not relish
having a son by me anymore than this our parting implies. Furthermore, I intend to come to Greenland myself eventually." Leif
gave her a finger ring of gold, a wadmal mantle made from the
wool of Greenland sheep, and a belt of walrus ivory. The boy, who
was called Thorgils, later arrived in Greenland. Leif publicly acknowledged his paternity. Some say that Thorgils came to Iceland
the summer before the Frod River Marvels, and that there was
something not quite right about him.[27]

In the autumn Leif and his men sailed from the Hebrides to
Norway. He was received by King Olaf Tryggvason, who esteemed
him greatly and considered him a very capable man. On one occasion the king inquired of Leif whether he intended to sail to
Greenland the next summer. Leif said it was his intention, if the
king were willing. Then said the king, "You shall go on a mission
for me, to preach Christianity there." Leif said that was a matter
for the king's decision, but that he himself believed it would be
difficult to be a successful missionary in Greenland. The king replied that there was no man better fitted for the task—"Your good
luck will see you through." "That can only be," said Leif, "if I am
supported by the grace of your protection." Leif set sail when he
was ready.

On the ocean he met with prolonged delays, and finally came
upon lands previously unknown. Fields of self-sown wheat grew
there, and vines, and trees including maples. They took home samples of all these. Some of the trees were large enough to use for
house-building. Leif found some shipwrecked seamen and took
them to his home and extended hospitality to all of them throughout the winter. He revealed great generosity and goodness in

[27] Another saga, called the *Eyrbyggia*, tells of Thorgunna, a woman from the
Hebrides, who came to Frod River in Snaefellsness in Iceland the year after Leif's
love affair. But she was a fity-two-year-old woman at the time, a witch, whose
evil magic caused supernatural occurrences, apparitions, and deaths. With such a
mother, Leif's son must have had something wrong with him. Rather obviously,
I think, this is what religious prejudice did to the Thorgunna who had bewitched
young Leif before he was saved by becoming a Christian.

bringing Christianity to the country and in rescuing these men. He was called Leif the Lucky.[28]

He landed in Eriksfjord and went home to Brattahlid, where he was warmly welcomed. He immediately began preaching the Christian faith throughout the country. He gave the people King Olaf Tryggvason's message, and showed them the value and the glory of this religion.

Erik held to his old faith, but his wife, Thjodhild, was immediately converted, and she had a church built not too near the hall. This was called Thjodhild's Church, and there she worshipped with many others who had accepted the new faith. After she was converted, Thjodhild refused to have sexual relations with Erik, a deprivation which greatly vexed him. [Except for material given in footnotes to the Thorstein Erikson section of the *Graenlendinga Saga,* the remaining pages of Section V of *Eirik's Saga* and all of Section VI, which deal with Thorstein Erikson and his death in the Western Settlements, are omitted since they are not pertinent to the exploration of Vinland.]

KARLSEFNI MARRIES GUDRID (VII)

A man named Thorfinn Karlsefni was the son of Thord Horsehead, who dwelt at Reyniness in Skaga Fjord in the north (of Iceland). Karlsefni's mother was called Thorunn. Thorfinn Karlsefni was very wealthy, of illustrious ancestry. He was a seagoing merchant and was looked upon as a very distinguished trader. One summer he prepared his ship for a voyage to Greenland. Snorri Thorbrandsson of Alptafjord joined him, and they had with them forty men. A man named Bjarni Grimolfsson from Breidafjord, with a partner named Thorhall Gamlason who was from the Eastfjords, also prepared their ship for a voyage to Greenland that same summer, with forty men.

When they were ready the two ships put to sea. It is not known how long they were on the voyage, but both ships reached

[28] The scribe of this interpolated paragraph packed four years of Leif Erikson's experiences into a single sailing season.

Eriksfjord in the autumn. Erik (Leif) [29] and some other settlers rode down to the ships, and there was much good trading. The ship captains invited Gudrid to help herself to whatever of their wares she desired. Then Leif, not to be outdone in generosity, offered the hospitality of quarters for the crews of both ships. The cargoes were stored in warehouses. Leif invited the four merchants to be his houseguests for the winter at Brattahlid.

Toward Yule, Leif began to be silent, and was less cheerful than he used to be. One time Karlsefni turned toward Leif and said, "Have you any sorrow, Leif, my friend? People think they see you less cheerful than you used to be. You have entertained us with the greatest splendor, and we are bound to return it to you with such service as we can command. Say now, what troubles you?" Leif answered, "You have accepted my hospitality with courtesy and good grace, and I cannot think that our relationship will bring you any discredit. On the other hand, I fear that when you are a guest anywhere else it will be said that you never passed a worse Yule than that which now approaches, when Leif entertained you at Brattahlid, in Greenland." "It shall not be so, Householder!" said Karlsefni. "We have in our ship both malt and corn. Take as much of it as you desire, and make ready a feast as grand as you wish!" This Leif accepted. And preparations were made for the feast of Yule. This feast was so good that people thought they had hardly ever seen such excellent and lavish fare in a poor land.

After Yule, Karlsefni approached Leif and asked for the hand of Gudrid, whom he regarded as being under Leif's care, for he thought her a lovable and capable woman. Leif replied that he would speak to her in favor of the suit. He said, "She is worthy of a good match. It may be that it is her destiny to marry you." He also said that he had heard good reports of Karlsefni. When Gudrid heard the proposal, she said she would accept Leif's advice. Not to make a long story of it, she followed his counsel, and there

[29] Emanating from Iceland, this telling uses the name "Eirekr," because Erik the Red had been an Icelander and was one of Iceland's heroes. What was meant was the man who was the head of the family of Erik the Red. Hereafter, the correct name will be given.

was another feast to celebrate. Yet another feast followed when their bridal was drunk. There was great joy at Brattahlid that winter.

KARLSEFNI SAILS TO STREAM FJORD IN VINLAND (VIII)

In Brattahlid people began to talk much about Vinland the Good, and said it should be explored *(leita)*. It was said that a voyage thither would be particularly profitable because of the fertility of the land. The talk went so far that Karlsefni and Snorri made ready their ship to explore the land in the spring. With them also went the before-named men called Bjarni and Thorhall with their ship. There was a man named Thorvard who was Erik the Red's son-in-law. He was the husband of Freydis, a natural daughter of Erik the Red. He also went with them. So did Thorvald,[30] the son of Erik. There was a man named Thorhall who was called the Huntsman. Thorhall had long been with Erik, serving him as huntsman in summer and steward in winter. He was a large fellow, strong, swarthy, and uncouth. He was habitually taciturn, but when he did speak he was annoyingly offensive. He always egged Erik on to the worst. He was forever an irritant. He had very little association with religious faith after it had come to Greenland. He was a bad Christian. Useful as a man who had wide experience with uninhabited places, he went on a ship along with Thorvard and Thorvald.

They had the ship which Thorbjorn (Vifilsson) had brought out from Iceland. When they joined Karlsefni there were mostly Greenlanders on board.[31] They had 160 men in all.

[30] Thorvald Erikson was deceased. There may have been another Thorvald in the family.

[31] The meaning is obviously not "mostly Greenlanders on board one ship" but mostly Greenlanders on board the whole expedition. This was the fact, for they had in all 160 men, in addition to women, and only two crews of 40 men each were Icelanders. The word "they" does definitely refer to the whole expedition. The "160 men" was literally "forty men and a hundred" *(tie manna ok hundrad)*, but the great or long hundred may be understood, consisting of twelve decades, or 120.

Karlsefni sailed first to the Western Settlement and from there to Bear Island and thence across the open sea southward for two days' sailing distance and saw land. They put over a boat and explored the country and (*Hauksbók* 544 says) found large flat rocks there, many of them twelve ells broad. (*Skalholtsbók* 557 gives the measurement more picturesquely: "many of the stones were so broad that two men could be stretched out on their backs on one rock with their soles touching.") Foxes were there. They gave **K 4** the land a name, and called it *Helluland*. Then they sailed with **K 5** northerly winds two days' sailing distance and again saw land. It **K 6, K 7** was well wooded, with many wild animals. There was an island off to the southeast of this land; because they found a bear there they **K 8** called it Bear Island (*Biarney*). They called the wooded land *Markland*. From there they sailed along the coast for a long time, and came to a cape. The land was off to the starboard, with long beaches and sand dunes. They rowed ashore and found the keel of **K 9** a ship on the cape, and thereafter called it Keel Cape. They called the beaches *Furdustrands* ("Astonishing Strands"), because they **K 10** took so long to sail by. Beyond these Astonishing Strands, the country was indented with bays, into one of which they sailed.

When Leif had visited King Olaf Tryggvason, the king had given him two Gaels, advising him to make use of them if speed were ever required, for they could run faster than deer. Of these two, the man's name was Haki and the woman's Haekia. Leif had loaned this couple to Karlsefni. When Karlsefni had sailed past As-**K 11** tonishing Strands, he set the Gaels on shore and ordered them to **K 12** run southward to scout out the nature of the land, and to return before the end of the third day. The Gaels when set ashore were each attired in a garment called *biafal (kiafal)*, open at the sides and sleeveless, with a hood at the top, and held between the legs with buttons and loops. Except for this they were naked. The ships lay at anchor while they were gone.

When the Gaels came running back down to the ships, one of them had a bunch of grapes, and the other an ear of a new kind of cultivated wheat. Karlsefni said he thought they had found land with good qualities. He then took them on board his ship and the **K 13** expedition sailed along where the coast was indented with bays.

They sailed to a fjord. There lay an island around which   **K 14**
flowed very strong currents, and so they called this island *Straum-*
sey—"Current Island." There were so many birds on it that one
could scarcely set a foot between the eggs.

They sailed in through the fjord, and called it Stream Fjord.   **K 15**
There they carried their cargoes from the ships and established
themselves. They had with them all kinds of livestock. They
searched the land to find out its products. There were mountains   **K 16**
thereabouts and the country was beautiful to behold. They
thought of nothing except exploration. There was tall grass. They
remained there during the winter. They had a severe winter, but
had not provided for this possibility during the summer, so they
suffered a lack of provisions, and the hunting failed.

Then they moved out [of the fjord] to the island, and expected at the same time to get provisions from hunting, but the
people suffered from a shortage of food, though their livestock
faired well there. They had already prayed to God to send them
some food, but it did not come as promptly as they hoped.

THORHALL THE HUNTSMAN DEPARTS (FROM VIII AND IX)

Thorhall the Huntsman disappeared, and the men went to
look for him. They searched for three days. On the fourth day
Karlsefni and Bjarni found Thorhall on the top of a cliff. He was
face up toward the sky, with both eyes and mouth and nostrils
agape, scratching and pinching himself and talking to himself.
They asked him what had brought him thither. He replied that he
had lived long enough not to need them to look after him. They
bade him come home with them, and he did so. Soon after this a
whale was washed up and they rushed to cut it up. No one could
tell what kind of whale it was, not even Karlsefni, who had great
knowledge of whales. When the cooks had boiled the meat, they
ate of it, and all were made ill by it.

Then Thorhall, approaching them, said, "Has not the Red-
Beard [Thor] proved more helpful than your Christ? This is my
reward for the verses which I composed to Thor, the Trustworthy.

Seldom has he failed me." When the people heard this they cast the whale down into the sea, and made their appeals to God. Then the weather improved, and they could row out to fish; thenceforward they had no lack of provisions.

That spring they went back to Stream Fjord and gathered provisions, game on the mainland, eggs on the island, and fish from the sea.

K 17

They now discussed where to go, and laid their plans. It is said that Thorhall wished to sail northward beyond Astonishing Strands and Keel Cape to explore Vinland, but Karlsefni wanted to proceed southward along the coast, for he thought that the conditions in the land would be better the farther south they went. He thought it advisable to explore both possibilities.

Thorhall prepared for his voyage out below the island. No more than nine men sailed with him. All the remainder of the company went with Karlsefni.

And one day when Thorhall was carrying water on board, he recited this ditty:

> When I came, these brave men told me,
>   Here the best of drink I'd get.
> Now with water pail behold me;
>   Wine and I are strangers yet.
> Stooping at the spring I've tasted
>   All the wine this land affords;
> Of its vaunted charms divested,
>   Poor indeed are its rewards.[32]

And when they were ready they hoisted sail, whereupon Thorhall recited this ditty:

> Let us go back [along] the broad sea
>   Where our countrymen are,

[32] I have retained the translation by Reeves, Beamish, and Anderson, because it captures the spirit of this lampoon. This ditty is as factual as any narrative passage in the saga, and there can be no doubt as to the meaning.

Let the dead taste the joy
  Of sandy Paradise,
While blizzard-shy
  Wind-raising warriors
Boil the meat left them providentially,
  And inhabit the lands of Astonishing Strands.[33]

Then they sailed away northward past Astonishing Strands
and Keel Cape, intending to cruise westward around the cape.
They encountered westerly gales and were driven ashore in Ireland, where they were grievously maltreated and thrown into slav-

---

[33] This Skaldic poem was most difficult to translate because it is loaded with
kennings—metaphorical compound words or phrases in every conceivable com-
plexity. In the Icelandic text, word positions are confusing, and one sentence is in-
tertwined with parts of another. I consulted Mr. Hallberg Hallmundsson, whose
mother tongue is Icelandic, and he re-created the natural word order, and only then
did a literal translation become possible. There is need of explanation of several
kennings. "Let us go back the broad sea" needs a preposition in English. The use
of "across" would run into contradiction with the saga narrative, but "along" or
"by" does not. Skalds in Iceland looked upon themselves as "exiles from their home-
land," as Lee M. Hollander says in *The Skald*. As used by Thorhall, "our countrymen" may refer to homefolk in Norway, or since his home was then in Greenland, it
could refer to homefolk in Iceland. In all probability, it does not refer to Greenlanders. There is nothing in this poem to suggest that Thorhall intended to cross
the broad sea to where his countrymen were. With the announced intention of
exploring the coast of Vinland northward, and with the prospect of sailing along
that coast in the ocean, he would feel closer to his homefolk than he had felt in
Stream Fjord where he had been out of sight of the ocean. The words *sand* and
himins are clear, but their combination makes a difficult kenning. Sand and
heavens—or sandy Paradise—is a sarcastic slur at the Christians who believed the
dead whale had been "left to them providentially." The adjective *byl styggvir,*
which means "shy or afraid of blizzards," is particularly apt in its obvious reference
to the snows and freezing cold which the members of the expedition had faced far
inside the fjord and from which they had fled to the mouth of the fjord. The
kenning *bellendr laufa vedrs,* "makers of sword weather," means "warriors." The
separate words in the kenning mean: *bellendr,* "bellowing"; *laufa,* "foliage"; *vedrs,*
"wind," "weather." I translate this kenning as "wind-raising warriors." Thorhall was
making an indelicate reference here to a noisy symptom of the food poisoning which
the Christians had suffered from eating the whale meat. A perfect and humorous an-
tithesis to "blizzard-shy" is "wind-raising." When read in context with the saga
narrative, Thorhall's second ditty is as memorable an achievement as we have from
any Skald of viking times.

ery. There Thorhall lost his life, according to what traders have related.

KARLSEFNI AT HÓP (X)

K 18   Now it is said that Karlsefni sailed southward along the coast with Snorri (Thorbrandsson) and Bjarni (Grimolfsson) and their people. They sailed for a long time until they came to a river that **K 19** flowed down from the land to water and thence to the sea. There **K 20, K 21** were large sandbanks and one could enter only at flood tide. Karl- **K 22** sefni sailed in there and called it *Hóp*.

There they found fields of self-sown wheat in the lowlands, **K 23, K 24** and vines on the hills. Every brook was full of fish. Where the tide **K 25, K 26** rose highest, they dug pits in the flats, and when the tide fell, holy **K 27** fish were in the pits. A great many animals of all sorts were in the woods. They remained there half a month and enjoyed themselves, **K 28** without keeping watch. They had their livestock with them.

Early one morning when they looked out they saw a great many skin boats, and staves being swung about on the boats with a noise like flails, and they were being revolved in the direction in which the sun moves. Then Karlsefni said, "What is the meaning of this?" Snorri Thorbrandsson answered him, "Possibly this is a peace signal, and so let us show them a white shield." This they did, and the strangers rowed toward them and stared with wonderment at those they saw before them, and then came up on the land. They were swarthy and ill-looking men, and had ugly hair on their heads. They had large eyes and broad cheeks. They stayed there for a while staring at those they saw before them, and then **K 29** rowed away southward beyond the point.

Karlsefni's party had built their shelters above the water, some near it and some farther off, and there they spent that win- **K 30, K 31** ter. There came no snow at all and their livestock lived by grazing. **K 32**   Early one morning in the spring they saw a great many skin **K 33** boats rowing around the point, looking like coals flung out beyond the bay, and staves being swung about on every boat. Then Karlsefni's men showed their shields, and they came together and began to trade. Those people especially desired red cloth, for which they exchanged fur skins and all-gray skins. They wished also to purchase swords and spears, but Karlsefni and Snorri refused them. In return for unblemished skins, the Skraelings would accept a span length of red cloth and bind it around their heads. Thus the trading continued. When Karlsefni's people began to run short of cloth, they ripped it into pieces so narrow that none were broader than a finger, but even then the Skraelings gave as much for it as before, or more. This continued until the bull that Karlsefni had ran out of the woods bellowing loudly. This terrified the Skraelings, so that they ran out to their boats and rowed away southward along the shore.

Nothing was seen of them for three weeks, but at the end of that time, such a great number of the Skraelings' boats appeared that they looked like a floating stream, and their staves were all revolving in a direction opposite to the course of the sun, and they were all whooping with great outcries. Then Karlsefni's men took red shields and held them up to view. The Skraelings leaped from their boats, and they met and fought. There was a heavy shower of missiles, for the Skraelings had war slings. Karlsefni observed that the Skraelings had a great ball-shaped object almost the size of a sheep's belly, and nearly as black in color, on the end of a pole, and this they flung from the pole up on the land above Karlsefni's men. It made such a terrifying noise where it struck the ground that great fear seized Karlsefni and all with him, so that they thought only of flight and of making their escape up along the riverbank. It seemed to them that the Skraelings were driving at them from all sides, and they did not make a stand until they came to certain cliffs where they resisted fiercely.

K 34

K 35

Freydis came out and, seeing that Karlsefni and his men were retreating, called out, "Why run from these wretched creatures, such worthy men as you are? It looks to me as though you might slaughter them like cattle. If I had a weapon, I believe I would fight better than any of you!" They heeded her not. Freydis wanted to join them, but fell behind, for she was pregnant. Nevertheless, she followed them into the woods, the Skraelings pursuing her. In front of her she found a dead man, Thorbrand Snorrason, whose skull had been split by a flat stone. His drawn sword lay beside him. She took it up and prepared to wield it in self-defense. Then the Skraelings came at her, and she uncovered her breast and slapped it with the naked sword. This sight so terrified the Skraelings that they ran down to their boats and paddled away. Karlsefni and his men joined her and praised her courage.

Although Karlsefni's men were outnumbered, only two were slain, but a great number of the Skraelings were. They now returned to their shelters, and bound up their wounds, and discussed what sort of men that great host had been that had seemed to sweep down upon them from the land side. It was realized that there could have been but one host, the one which came from the boats, and that the other had been a self-deception, an illusion.

The Skraelings had found a dead man with his ax lying beside him. They had taken up the ax and had struck at a tree, all and sundry trying it, and it seemed to them a treasure, for it bit well. Later on, one of them had taken it and had struck at a slab of rock so that the ax broke, and since it would not split stone, they thought it useless and threw it away.

KARLSEFNI COMPLETES HIS EXPLORATION (FROM XI AND XII)

It was obvious to Karlsefni's party that, although the surrounding country appeared attractive, they could live there only with fear and warfare, because of the native inhabitants. Accordingly, they sailed northward along the coast and found five Skraelings, clad in skins, asleep near the sea. Beside them were containers of animal-marrow mixed with blood. Karlsefni's men thought they were exiles, and slew them.

Afterward they came to a headland where there were many animals. The headland looked like a huge cake of dung and they took it as evidence that animals wintered there. Soon afterward Karlsefni and his followers arrived at Stream Fjord, where they had everything they needed.

K 36   According to the telling of some, Bjarni [Grimolfsson] and Gudrid had remained behind there with ten times ten men and had not gone farther, while Karlsefni and Snorri [Thorbrandsson] had sailed south with forty men, tarrying at Hóp no longer than two months and returning that same summer.

While most of the men remained behind, Karlsefni went with one ship to search for Thorhall. He sailed northward around Keel Cape and then bore off westward with land on the port side. It was all one wilderness there with almost no clearing anywhere. When they had traveled a long way they came to a river which flowed out of the land from east to west. They steered into the mouth of the river and lay to by its southern bank.

One morning Karlsefni saw on the far side of the clearing a glittering speck, and he and his men shouted at it. It stirred. It was a one-footed creature. It came bounding down toward where the ship lay.

Thorvald, the son of Erik the Red, sat at the helm. The one-footed creature shot an arrow into his intestines. Thorvald pulled out the arrow and said, "We have found here a rich country, for there is much fat around my paunch." Thorvald died of this wound soon afterward.

Then the one-footed creature ran off to the north, and Karl-sefni's men raced after it and saw it from time to time, until it hopped into a bay. Then Karlsefni and his followers turned back. One of the men recited this ditty:

> They say they chased   a creature resembling
> A one-footed man,   down to the shore;
> A fantastic freak,   it had strength to course
> Beyond a peak—   Hear it, Karlsefni!

Then they sailed away to the north. They thought they could see Uniped Land, but they decided not to risk their lives any longer. They concluded that the mountains which they now discovered and the mountains of Hóp formed one mountain chain, and this seemed to be so since both mountain regions were the same distance from Stream Fjord. They returned to Stream Fjord, and spent a third winter there.

K 37
K 38
K 39

K 40
K 41
K 42
K 43
K 44

The men quarreled frequently because of the women. Those without wives sought to possess the married women and this caused the greatest trouble.

The first autumn,[34] Snorri, the son of Karlsefni, was born, and he was three winters old when they departed.

When they sailed away from Vinland they had wind from the south and bore in upon Markland. They found five Skraelings there, a bearded man, two women, and two children. They seized the two boys, but the others got away and disappeared as though they had sunk into the earth. They took the two boys with them, and taught them their language, and baptized them. They said their mother's name was Vaethild and their father's Evega. They said that the Skraelings were ruled over by kings, one of whom was named Avalldamon and the other Avalldidida. They said that there were no houses, but people lived in caves or holes in the ground. They said there was a land over against their land, the inhabitants of which went about in white garments, uttered loud cries, and carried sticks with patches of cloth attached. People believed this must be White Men's Land. Finally they reached Greenland and spent the winter at Erik the Red's.

K 45

BJARNI GRIMOLFSSON'S HEROISM (XIII)

Bjarni Grimolfsson's ship was blown into the Greenland Sea (Irish Sea, in variant 544). They found themselves in waters infested with maggots, and before they knew it the ship was riddled beneath them and began to sink.

They discussed what they should do. They had an after-boat which had been covered with seal tar. Men say that the worms will not pierce timber that has been so covered. Most of the crew said that as many of them should get into this boat as it could hold. But they found that the boat would hold no more than half of the crew. Bjarni then said, "The men who are to go into the boat should be chosen by lot, not by rank." But all the men tried to get

[34] The *Graenlendinga Saga* more circumstantially places Snorri's birth in the autumn "following their first winter."

into the boat. The boat, however, would not hold them all, and so they adopted Bjarni's plan of drawing lots. Bjarni drew a lot to go into the boat with nearly half of the men. But when they were settled in the boat and about to cast off, a young Icelander who had remained in the ship and who had come out from Iceland with Bjarni, said, "Bjarni, are you going to leave me here?" "It must be," Bjarni replied. "That is not what you promised my father when I left Iceland with you. You told him that we should share the same fate." "So be it," said Bjarni. "We will exchange places. You come into the boat and I will get back into the ship; for I perceive you are eager to live."

Bjarni then boarded the ship and the boy took his place in the boat. And the boat sailed away until it came to Dublin in Ireland and there they told this tale. It is generally believed that Bjarni and the men with him were drowned in the worm-infested sea, for they were never heard of again.

KARLSEFNI IN ICELAND (XIV)

The next summer Karlsefni sailed with Gudrid to Iceland, and went to his home at Reyniness. His mother thought that he had not made a satisfactory marriage, and Gudrid was not at their house the first winter. But when his mother became convinced that his wife was a very estimable woman, Gudrid went to his house and they got along kindly together. The daughter of Karlsefni's son Snorri was Hallfrid, who was the mother (grandmother?) of Runolf's son, Bishop Thorlak. Karlsefni and Gudrid had a son called Thorbjorn. His daughter was called Thorun. She was the mother of Bishop Bjorn. Karlsefni's son Snorri also had a son called Thorgeir, who was the father of Ingveld, who was the mother of Bishop Brand. And closes there this saga.

PART FOUR
Appendix

what the 1440 Map of Vinland makes it reasonable to believe must have been explored.

The decision of the Karlsefni Expedition to abandon its attempt at a permanent settlement in Vinland was a sagacious retreat. Before the advent of firearms, the vikings were not equipped to cope with the great number of savages in North America. Records show that from 1003 to 1362—for more than 350 years—Vinland was visited by Norsemen, but we also have evidences in various places in Vinland of Norse settlements which were without direct link to the sagas.[1] These settlements were presumably eliminated by massacre or intermarriage.

It seems safe to assume that there was emigration from the Western Settlement of Greenland, where a worsening climate forced the folk to rely less on farm and dairy products and more on hunting and fishing. Those Greenlanders seem to have moved closer to the Eskimo way of living, and were not driven out by Eskimos, as seems clear from a reported investigation[2] which indicates that there had not been violence. Knowing of land to the southwest where food was more readily obtainable, the folk of the Western Settlement apparently moved away en masse. Mr. Thomas E. Lee, archaeologist at the Centre d'Etudes Nordiques of Université Laval, has said of the Greenlanders, "The people of a land lacking in building timber and fuel must have gone to those

---

[1] "There is no reason to assume that each and every Norse voyage from Greenland to North America is recorded in the sagas, nor must we assume that every settlement site is listed. If, as several investigators assert, Vinland was a 'familiar country' to the Norse in Greenland and Iceland, then there is reason to believe that voyages there were more numerous than the ones enumerated in the sagas." Matti Enn Kaups, Ph.D., "Shifting Vinland—Tradition and Myth," in *Terrae Incognitae*, vol. 2 (1970), p. 57. We can only surmise as to what records of other viking voyages to Vinland may have been lost. At least 80 percent of the Árni Magnússon Collection of old manuscripts was destroyed in a fire in Copenhagen in the eighteenth century. Many manuscripts in private ownership in Iceland may have suffered destruction because of long periods of poverty there. One of the most poignant exhibits in the Icelandic National Museum is a single vellum page from an unidentified manuscript cut in the shape of half a vest, with stitch holes and button holes, and showing heavy wear.

[2] Paul Nörlund, *Viking Settlers in Greenland and Their Descendants during Five Hundred Years.*

UNGAVA BAY, LABRADOR

shores (forested Markland) as a routine and commonplace proce-
dure, within the limits of the shipping available."[3] The only
correction needed here is that since Markland was part of Vinland,
Mr. Lee's findings are in what Karlsefni had proved to be part of
Vinland. His significant finds include several beacons along the
Arnaud River in the Payne Bay region on the west side of Ungava
Bay in northern Labrador.

Mr. Lee made his first discovery in Ungava in 1964. He has
found several sites of longhouses in the Ungava region, one of
them 115 feet long and 24 feet wide, with outcurving ends, and
four cross walls or stone partitions dividing it into rooms. This re-
sembles some in Iceland and the Hebrides, and suggests a date of
about 1100 to 1200. Another house was 81 feet long, with some
stones in its walls weighing 1,000 pounds. This dwelling had three
partitions. Mr. Lee has obtained a C^{14} dating of about A.D. 1050.
There were small fireplaces along the middle of this house,
while along the inner sides of the stone and turf walls there are
post molds, one of them 6 inches in diameter. These molds indicate that the house had a timber roof. But since this was fifty miles
from the nearest trees, and since no driftwood comes to the area,
the posts must have been brought by ship.[4]

The longhouses of Ungava Peninsula are definitely not of Eskimo construction, though later occupied by Eskimos. Mr. Lee
sees no reason to suppose them Irish. His conclusion that they
were built by the Norse is the more convincing in that in accompanying artifacts he finds an admixture of cultures: Dorset, Norse,
and Eskimo.[5] Corroborative of his conclusion are skulls of European type.[6] On the basis of photographs and measurements, Dr.
Carleton S. Coon, anthropologist at Harvard, has declared that
these are not Eskimo but are more nearly like the ancient Norse of
Iceland and Greenland. What Mr. Lee calls Pamiok Longhouse

[3] Thomas E. Lee, *Archaeological Discoveries, Payne Bay Region, Ungava, 1966*,
p. 138.
[4] Ibid., p. 140.
[5] Ibid., p. 135.
[6] Ibid., pp. 128–31.

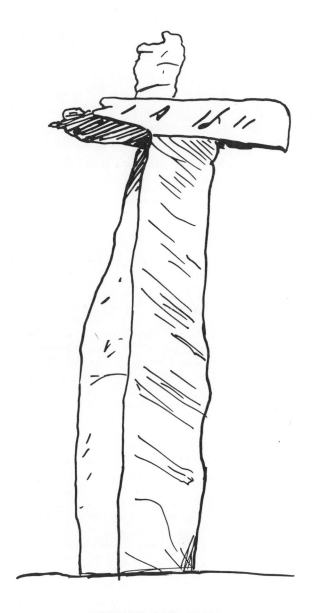

THORSHAMMER BEACON
UNGAVA, LABRADOR

No. 2 has sleeping platforms at its ends. Near it, not more than 250 feet from it, is a gully with a possible ship-hauling beach. A portion of a bow contemporaneous with the building on Pamiok is in all probability Norse, since the only other culture present was Dorset, and Dorset people are not known to have had the bow and arrow. Dr. H. Winterton, of the Physical Metallurgy Division, Department of Energy, Mines and Resources, Ottawa, has examined an iron ax from Pamiok and, from the composition of the iron and manner of manufacture (made by adding small strips of metal, with some cold hammering), believes it to be Norse.

Counting as separate those that are more than two miles distant from any other, there are six known Norse settlement sites in Ungava, and six others reported which have not yet been investigated. For further evidences, see Mr. Lee's *Archaeological Findings, Gyrfalcon to Eider Islands, Ungava, 1968.*

The findings at the northern tip of Newfoundland are relegated to a footnote because they are on land which was not part of Vinland.[7]

***

[7] At the northern end of the island Leif called "Helluland" and Thorfinn called "Biarney," archaeologists have found the sites of several dwellings and a smithy of sod or turf construction, with C^{14} datings pointing to A.D. 1000. This may be evidence of a viking settlement. Whatever importance historians ascribe to it, it is transcended by the evidence which indicates that there was considerable infiltration of the whole island by Norsemen. When the English first arrived, they observed that the aborigines of Newfoundland were "as white as French are" (Hakluyt); their hair was soft, European rather than Asiatic; they were much taller than any other American Indians, many over six feet, and some seven feet; they had stone weapons in the form of swords (Fracanzano di Montalboddo, *Paesi novamente ritrovati*, Venice, 1521. Chapter 126 is a letter from Piero Pasqualigo who described the Indians of Newfoundland); their boats or canoes were shaped "in the form of a new moon" (J. W. Damer Powell, "The Exploration of John Guy in Newfoundland," *Geographical Journal*, vol. 86, 1935, pp. 512–18, tells of a manuscript in Lambeth Palace Library written by John Guy, giving an account of his exploration of part of Newfoundland in 1612, with a description of the Indians there and a rough sketch entitled "the picture of the savages canoa"); their houses had gable-ended roofs; they wore hooded garments. In character and beliefs they resembled the vikings (John Gardner, five articles on Beothuk Indians of Newfoundland in *National Fisherman*, Feb. to June 1965). Patently, there had been widespread intermarriage of Norsemen with the aborigines of Newfoundland. The Zeno Narrative of the visit by Orkneymen to Newfoundland ("Estotiland")

THRUSTON TABLET, TENNESSEE

At Byfield on the Parker River south of Newburyport in Massachusetts are six runic inscriptions on large rocks, presumably grave markers. For photographs and suggested translations, see Olaf Strandwold, *Norse Inscriptions on American Stones*, pp. 19–24. What may be a more correct interpretation of Byfield No. 1 is what Mr. Alf Mongé says is a cryptographically given date, November 20, 1009. This date would make the settlement at Byfield contemporaneous with Thorvald Erikson's visit to Vinland and the Karlsefni Expedition and after. See pp. 122–27 in *Norse Medieval Cryptography in Runic Carvings*, by Alf Mongé and O. G. Landsverk; and also pp. 11–74 in *Ancient Norse Messages on American Stones* by O. G. Landsverk.

There is overwhelming evidence that a Norse settlement existed a hundred miles south of Byfield. At Newport, Rhode Island, the harbor is considered the best in New England. The evidences there leave us no alternative but to accept as fact that a settlement of Norsemen existed in and around Newport Harbor through the twelfth and thirteenth centuries. Among these evidences are many measurements which show that a round stone tower at the top of the hill above the harbor was built by masons who used the Norse linear measure; architectural features of the tower which show it was built as a combined church, fort, and watchtower;[8] the Mongé dating of the inscription on a stone in the wall of that tower twelve feet above the ground as A.D. 1116; the sailing of Bishop Erik (Henrico) Gnupson of Greenland to Vinland in 1117 to get acquainted with that other part of his diocese; the testimony

---

before 1398 and in 1398 is evidence of mixed cultures: native Indian, Irish, Norse, and several others, probably Breton, Basque, etc. "The inhabitants . . . possess all the arts like ourselves, and it is believed that in times past they have had intercourse with our people; for I saw Latin books . . . which they at the present time do not understand. . . . Their foreign commerce is with Greenland, with which they trade in furs, brimstone, and pitch. . . . We reached a quiet and safe harbor, in which we saw a very large number of armed people, who came running, prepared to defend the island. Sinclair now caused his men to make signs of peace to them, and they sent ten men to us who could speak ten languages, but we could understand none of them, except one who came from Islanda [Iceland]."

[8] Pohl, *The Lost Discovery*, pp. 187–94; and *Atlantic Crossings Before Columbus*, pp. 185–87.

of Dr. Johannes Brøndsted, curator of the Royal Copenhagen Museum, who said of the architecture of the Newport Tower: "This is in the style of the thirteenth to the fourteenth centuries";[9] the testimony of Bernardo Carli who was with Verrazano and who wrote in a letter to his father, August 4, 1524, a description of the Indians seen in and around Newport Harbor, "This is the most beautiful people and the most civilized in customs that we have found in this navigation. They excel us in size; they are of bronze color, some inclining more to whiteness"; a reference (Kensington Runestone) left by a churchman who was with a party exploring in 1362 "from Vinland" and therefore presumably from the region of the stone Norse church in Vinland; the existence in 1632 of "a rownd stone tower" across water from the eastern end of Long Island, and therefore presumably in the Rhode Island area, years previous to the founding of Newport;[10] and William Wood's seeing at the site of the future Newport an abandoned settlement of European origin which on his map of 1635 he called "Old Plymouth."

The date of the inscription in the wall of the Newport Tower was not the year when the tower was erected. The tower was built somewhere between about 1250 and 1325. There are good reasons for saying it could not have been earlier or later. Why then does the stone in the tower bear a much earlier date? The answer would seem to be that the parish at the site was established in 1116, or the first church there, presumably of wood, was dedicated there in that year, or the first priest commenced preaching there in that year. When, more than two hundred years later, a stone church was being built at the site, the parishioners with understandable piety incorporated into its wall a stone bearing the date of which they were proud.

Possible evidences that vikings ascended the Mississippi and its tributary, the Ohio River, are two runic inscriptions found in

---

[9] Dr. Johannes Brøndsted's comment on the architecture of the Newport Tower was expressed to the author, while standing in front of the tower.

[10] Plowden, "Commodities," in Pohl, *The Lost Discovery*, pp. 182–86; and *The Viking Explorers*, pp. 205–7.

West Virginia.[11] But these also are relegated to a footnote because they are on small tablets each weighing only a few ounces, and therefore portable, so that they might have been carried from the Great Lakes by Erie or Huron Indians, or from the eastern seaboard by Delaware or Shawnee Indians, or by Indian traders.

We look next at a pictographic record which has evoked a considerable literature and which appears to be a positive assertion that a ship which resembled a viking ship did ascend the Mississippi, the Ohio, and its tributary, the Cumberland River. In 1874 an inscribed tablet was found near Castalian Springs in Sumner County, Tennessee, in the water of a creek at Bledsoe Lick Mound-Builders site.[12] The tablet is 19 inches long, 15 inches

CHRIST CROSS AND THORSHAMMER
MOUNDSVILLE, WEST VIRGINIA

[11] One unearthed in the Indian mound at Moundsville is the so-called Grave Creek inscription, on a tablet 1⅞ inches long. It is marked with a combined Thorshammer and Christ Cross: ━━━━┼Ⓒ This symbol points to the time when the two religions were both active among Norsemen—the period between A.D. 1000 and 1050. The other inscription, the so-called Braxton inscription, is on a tablet 4⅜ inches in length and has a Christ Cross that suggests it is of about the same age as the Grave Creek inscription.

[12] Dr. Clyde E. Keeler and Ruth Verrill establish that the tablet was found in the creek near the excavated Bledsoe Lick Mound, and not in Rocky Creek as was formerly assumed. Keeler and Verrill, "The Viking Book Finale," *Georgia Academy of Science Bulletin*, p. 4.

wide, and about 1 inch thick. It is of local gray limestone, and it bears pictographs on both sides. On the principal face are seven human figures and a ship with various features that come close to identifying it as a viking ship. The tablet was acquired by General Gates Phillips Thruston, who was the first scholar to make an intensive study of it. It has ever since been called the Thruston Tablet. General Thruston presented it to the Tennessee Historical Society in 1878, and it is now in the Tennessee State Museum in Nashville. Its authenticity has not been questioned.

There are various interpretations of the Indian figures. Thruston saw the "two leading characters vigorously shaking hands in a confirmatory way."[13] Others see them as an almond-eyed Indian with an ax[14] threatening a ray-eyed warrior who has a square shield and spear. To the right of these are a well-dressed almond-eyed female with what appears to be a wampum belt (suggesting marriage), and she is meeting a round-eyed warrior who holds what could be a short sword horizontal in his left hand.

The idea that there had been a battle is supported by the dismembered body of a ray-eyed man at the extreme right, with the lower half of his body hung upside down and his heart placed in his hands. The idea of battle is also shown by the falling if not prone figure of a warrior holding a symbol of surrender—a bent spear.[15] It would seem this weapon must be of metal, since a wooden spear would not bend.

At the bottom of the tablet and of the same size as the warrior's square shield is another square, in this case not a shield but a small hut, within which is a ray-eyed chief smoking a long pipe, presumably a peace pipe. Smoke is rising from the pipe.

Three of the Indians are almond-eyed and three are ray-eyed or round-eyed. The eye shape of the seventh seems indetermina-

[13] G. P. Thruston, *Antiquities of Tennessee*, 1890, p. 91.

[14] Keeler and Verrill, "A Viking Saga in Tennessee?" *Georgia Academy of Science Bulletin*, pp. 2, 3, show that the ax is similar to a copper ax with shapes of a rabbit's head found in the Spiro Mound in Oklahoma; and they give a drawing of the Spiro ax.

[15] W. H. Holmes "The Thruston Tablet," *American Anthropologist*, pp. 161–65. Holmes perceived the weapon as a "gun."

ble. The men on the ship are round-eyed. Four lines of paint on the cheeks were a prevalent custom among the pottery makers of Tennessee and Arkansas. One of the almond-eyed warriors on the tablet has cheek decorations of four horizontal lines. Obviously picturing people of two types, the tablet would appear to represent a confrontation between Indians of ancestry intermarried with the type of men in the ship, and Indians of a more primitive type.

The head and headdress of the warrior with a square shield and a spear impinge upon the drawing of the ship, and this fact as well as differences in weathering seem to indicate that the ship was drawn at an earlier time. There is no certainty that the arrival of the ship and the confrontation were directly connected. The confrontation may have occurred centuries later.

Who were the ray-eyed Indians? We know that Bledsoe Lick was one of the population centers of prehistoric Indians. "When Middle Tennessee was first explored by the whites they found no Indians living here. . . . The territory was claimed as a common hunting ground by several tribes. But a long time before, so long that not even a tradition remains, it was . . . the home of a people well advanced in the arts of civilization. . . . That they remained long in this region is evidenced by their numerous remains, mounds, earthworks, stone and flint implements and fragments of pottery."[16]

The dominance of the Indian figures, costumes, etc., on both sides of the tablet testify to its having been engraved by an Indian of the Mississippi River Mound-Builder culture. "At the time the stone was found, no local white inhabitants were sufficiently aware of the nature of certain design elements such as the headdresses, to be able to depict them as they appear. . . . These specific figures had not yet appeared in any of the literature."[17]

The ship engraving presents revealing details. Hanging outside of the hull amidships is an anchor obviously made of metal,[18]

---

[16] Jay Guy Cisco, *Historic Sumner County, Tennessee* pp. 36–37.

[17] Malcolm Parker, "A Study of the Rocky Hill Pictograph," *Tennessee Archaeologist,* p. 13.

[18] Here, instead of an anchor, Keeler and Verrill see "a grappling or landing hook which would be of hard metal," "A Viking Saga in Tennessee?," op. cit., p. 5.

and similar in form and size to the anchor of the Oseberg ship in the Oslo Museum.[19]

Suspended from the side of the ship is what Keeler and Verrill see as a diamond-shaped fender. Further toward the stern is what may be a mooring line.

Superimposed over the stern end of the hull with most of it extending to the left out beyond the hull is something which Keeler and Verrill see as a wooden anchor of European form.[20] As an

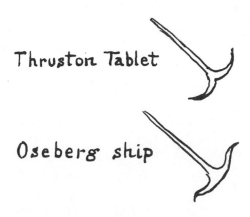

ANCHORS

[19] A. W. Brøgger and Haakon Shetelig, in *The Viking Ships,* say of the Oseberg ship's anchor that it "is too slight to hold even a small vessel like the Oseberg ship. The ship was also made fast ashore" (p. 98). They also say, "The anchor was dropped from the stern to keep the ship clear of land" (p. 136). They show anchors in photographs facing p. 98.

[20] Keeler and Verrill, "A Viking Saga in Tennessee?", op. cit., p. 3.

anchor, however, its size would be tremendous and out of proportion to the reasonably well-proportioned details in the drawing of the ship. It could be, and I think it is, the headdress of the warrior with ax.

The man on the ship nearest the prow wears a headpiece with horns. Just aft of the mast there appears to be a man whose head is encircled with rays, and if so, he presumably is the captain. The man at the stern has his arm extended behind him and holds a tiller handle.

Directly below the tiller post and slightly below the level of the oar holes is a round hole in the side of the hull. It intrudes into the top edge of the object which some see as a wooden anchor, but two-thirds of the hole is free and clear of that object. The hole is not part of that object. Brøgger and Shetelig describe how a steering oar at the stern on the starboard side was attached to the hull through a hole in the planking of a viking ship.[21] In line with the tiller post and the hole down toward the warrior's nose there seem to be faint vertical lines and an oval shape that may represent a steering oar.[22] If so, they were almost obliterated by the engraver who may have rubbed the area smooth before drawing the elaborate headdress.

There is a single mast forward of amidships, and a partly furled square sail of vertical strips. At the prow attached to the stem is a large circular object which Holmes thought "a conventional delineation of the sun."[23] Some have seen it as a delineation of the wind. It is more likely a romantically emphasized figurehead suggestive of a shape used on the Oseberg and other viking ships:

[21] Brøgger and Shetelig, op. cit., pp. 128–29. The attachment of the steering oar is illustrated on p. 128.

[22] In a letter to me, Keeler suggests the interesting alternative that there was no steering oar but a stern rudder, and if so, he thinks this would date the ship at A.D. 1180 or later. (See Brøgger and Shetelig, op. cit., p. 239.) This date brings to mind the fact that Prince Madoc of Wales sailed westward for the second time in A.D. 1190, and was never heard of again.

[23] Holmes, op. cit., p. 163.

FIGUREHEADS

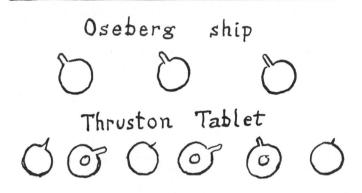

OAR HOLES

When the engraver drew the ship, did he have only a memory of a ship no longer there? Did he understand sailing and the rigging of a sailing ship? For answer, we note that he drew the two stays from near the middle of the yard to the prow figurehead—stays to strengthen the yard and mast when the sail was caught by a headwind. He drew the line from the near lower corner of the sail toward the stern. He showed the upper end of the corresponding line on the port side, though not in the proper direction. Since most of the length of the stays from the mast to the stern would be concealed by the sail, he seems to have avoided confusion by omitting all but a short length of them at the stern. He seems to have drawn a short length of the nearer one of these stays on the area of the sail before he remembered that it would not be visible behind the sail.

The engraver indicated something that was an ingenious feature of oar holes in viking ships. This was a slot to accommodate the oar blade. The width of an oar blade was greater than the diameter of an oar hole. The handle end of an oar was also of larger diameter than the hole, or was provided with a ring extension that would not permit the handle to be put through the hole, and so an oar could never be lost by slipping out through the hole. But the oar blade could be inserted into the hole and withdrawn from the hole from inside the ship. This was made possible by a slot along the upper half of the hole, where it would not weaken the bottom half of the hole against which the oar was worked.[24]

Unless proof can be adduced that all the features of the ship are also those of a late twelfth-century Welsh ship, it seems a safe conclusion that the Thruston Tablet is evidence of the arrival of a viking ship up the Mississippi, Ohio, and Cumberland rivers.

Positive evidences that vikings ascended the Mississippi are in a region made accessible by the first large river that flows into the Mississippi from the west—the Arkansas River. From it an exploring party could have ascended the Poteau River and Morris Creek to within a mile of Heavener in eastern Oklahoma. At Heavener are three runic inscriptions. At Poteau, ten miles north of Heavener, is another; there is also one at Tulsa; and another at Shawnee, which is 140 miles west of Heavener. It has been amply demonstrated that these are not hoaxes, but genuine inscriptions of great age.[25] None of the six has a translatable meaning in words.

Mr. Alf Mongé of Santa Rosa, California, shows that all the Oklahoma inscriptions are medieval cryptograms[26] giving these dates:

[24] Brøgger and Shetelig, op. cit., p. 134: "The slit is at that point in the circumference of the oar-hole which is least in contact with the oar during the normal process of rowing."

[25] Pohl, *Atlantic Crossings Before Columbus*, pp. 45–54; and *The Viking Explorers*, pp. 197–201.

[26] Mongé and Landsverk, *Norse Medieval Cryptography in Runic Carvings;* and Landsverk, *Ancient Norse Messages on American Stones.*

Heavener No. 1 — November 11, 1012
Heavener No. 2 — December 25, 1015
Poteau   — November 11, 1017
Heavener No. 3 — December 30, 1022/23
Tulsa   — December 2, 1022
Shawnee   — November 24, 1024

These dates are positive evidence of a viking settlement last-ing for more than a decade in the early eleventh century in Okla-homa. Other runic inscriptions with similar near dates have been discovered in the same general area of the continent, but details have not yet been released for publication. A runic inscription on a bank of the Arkansas River has been reported, but it awaits re-discovery.

Emphasis should be placed upon the date of Heavener No. 1. That earliest date, near the end of the year 1012, is particularly significant because (as I have shown near the beginning of the section "Thorfinn Karlsefni Completes His Explorations") the saga hints at a possible exploration by Karlsefni of the coast south of Hóp and presumably into the Gulf of Mexico during the first half of the sailing season of 1012. In our independent dating, Mr. Mongé and I clasp hands across the continent.

OKLAHOMA INSCRIPTIONS

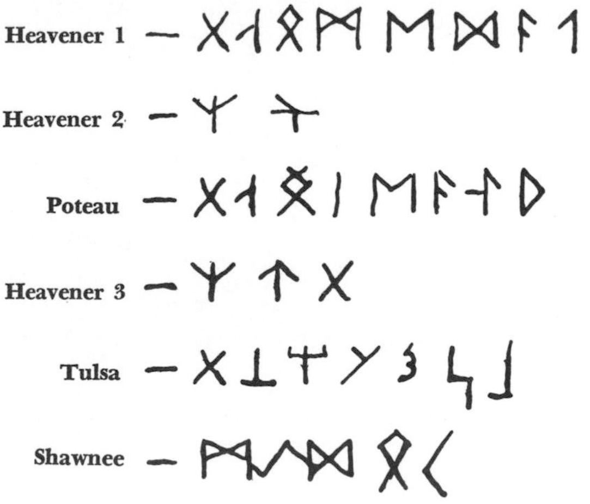

Heavener 1 — ᚷᚦᚠᛗ ᛗ ᛞ ᚠ ᚠ

Heavener 2 — ᛁ ᛏ

Poteau — ᚷᚦᛦᛁ ᛗᚠᛏᛞ

Heavener 3 — ᛁ ᛏ ᚷ

Tulsa — ᚷᛚᛏᛁᛦ ᛃ ᛐ ᛀ

Shawnee — ᛈᛁᛞ ᛦ ᚲ

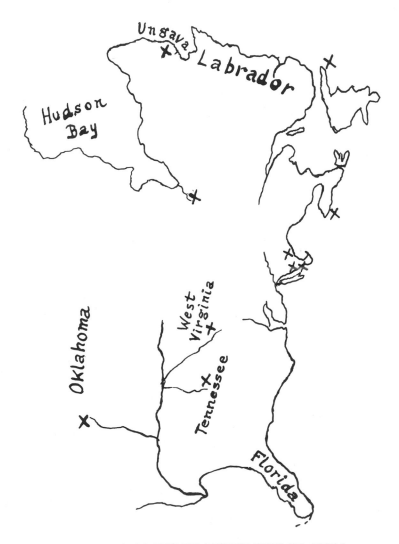

X—EVIDENCES WITH NO DIRECT LINK TO SAGAS

SELECTED
BIBLIOGRAPHY

Anderson, John R. L. *Vinland Voyage*. New York: Funk & Wagnalls, 1967.

Brøgger, Anton Wilhelm. *Winlandfahrten* (German translation). Hamburg: 1939.

———, and Shetelig, Haakon. *The Viking Ships. Their Ancestry and Evolution*. Translated by Katherine John. Oslo: 1953.

Carli, Bernardo. Letter to his father, Aug. 4, 1524, about Verrazzano's voyage along the Atlantic Coast of North America, 1524. *New York State Local History Source Leaflets*. Reprinted from Annual Report of the State Historian, by the University of the State of New York. Albany: 1916.

Cisco, Jay Guy. *Historic Sumner County, Tennessee*. Nashville: Folk-Keeling Printing Co., 1909.

Eyrbyggia Saga. Islenzk Fornrit, Vol. 4: Rcykjavik, 1935.

Fairbridge, Rhodes W. "Dating the Latest Movements of the Quarternary Sea Level." New York Academy of Sciences 11, vol. 20, no. 8 (April 1958), pp. 471–82.

——— "Recent World-Wide Sea Level Changes and Their Possible Significance to New England Archaeology." *Bulletin, Massachusetts Archaeological Society*, vol. 21 (April 1960), pp. 49–51.

Farley, Gloria. "The Vikings Were Here." *Heavener Ledger Print*. Heavener, Oklahoma, August 1968.

Fernald, M. L. "The Natural History of Ancient Vinland and Its Geographical Significance." *American Geographical Society Bulletin*, vol. 47 (Sept. 1915), pp. 686–87.

——— "Notes on the Plants of Wineland the Good." *Rhodora*, vol. 12, no. 134 (Feb. 1910), pp. 17–38.

The Flatey Book and Recently Discovered Vatican Manuscripts Concerning America as Early as the Tenth Century. London: Norroena Society, 1908. (Gives for each page a facsimile of Icelandic manuscript, the Icelandic text, Danish translation, and English translation.)

Flateyjarbók, manuscript, numbered 1005, fol. in Old Royal Collection in Royal Library of Copenhagen; will be in archives, Reykjavik, Iceland.

Floamanna Saga. Translated by Sigrid Undset in "A Saga of Greenland." *Bulletin, St. Ansgar's Scandinavian Catholic League of New York,* no. 41 (Feb. 1943), pp. 1–14.

Fossum, Andrew. *The Norse Discovery of America.* Minneapolis: Augsburg Publishing House, 1918.

Gams, Pius B. *Series episcoporum ecclesiae catholicae.* Ratisbon: 1873, p. 233ff.

Gardner, John. Five articles on Beothuk Indians of Newfoundland. *National Fisherman,* Feb. 1965, pp. 8–9; March 1965, pp. 8–9; April 1965, pp. 29, 34; May 1965, pp. 30–31; June 1965, pp. 31, 34–36, 51.

Gathorne-Hardy, Geoffrey Malcolm. *The Norse Discoverers of America. The Wineland Sagas Translated and Discussed.* Oxford: Clarendon Press, 1921.

Godfrey, William S. "The Newport Tower II." *Archaeology,* vol. 3, no. 2 (Summer 1950), p. 82–86.

————"The Newport Tower. A Reply to Mr. Pohl." *Archaeology,* vol. 4, no. 1 (Spring 1951), p. 54–55.

Gordon, Cyrus H. *Before Columbus: Links Between the Old World and Ancient America.* New York: Crown, 1971.

Hagen, Sievert Nielson. "The Kensington Runic Inscription." *Speculum,* vol. XXV, no. 3 (July 1950), pp. 321–56.

Hariot, Thomas. *A Brief and True Report of the New Found Land of Virginia.* London: 1588.

Hermannsson, Halldór. *The Northmen in America.* Islandica, vol. 2. Ithaca, N.Y.: Cornell University Library, 1909.

———— *The Problem of Wineland.* Islandica, vol. 25. Ithaca, N.Y.: Cornell University Library, 1936.

———— *The Vinland Sagas.* Islandica, vol. 30. Ithaca, N.Y.: Cornell University Library, 1944.

———— "The Vinland Voyages. A Few Suggestions." *Geographical Review* (Jan. 1927), pp. 107–14.

Holand, Hjalmar Rued. "A Fourteenth-Century Runic Inscription from Martha's Vineyard." *Scandinavian Studies,* vol. 21, no. 2 (May 1949), pp. 79–88.

———— *Explorations in America Before Columbus.* New York: Twayne, 1956.

————*Westward from Vinland.* New York: Duell, Sloan & Pearce, 1940.

Hollander, Lee M. *The Skalds.* Princeton: Princeton University Press, 1945.

Holmes, W. H. "The Thruston Tablet." *American Anthropologist,* vol. 4, no. 2 (April 1891), pp. 161–65.

Hornell, James. "The Role of Birds in Early Navigation." *Antiquity,* vol. 29 (Sept. 1946), pp. 142–49.

Hovgaard, William. Letter in *American-Scandinavian Review,* vol. 20 (April 1932), pp. 224–30.

———— *The Voyages of the Norsemen to America.* New York: American-Scandinavian Foundation, 1914.

Howley, James Patrick. *The Beothucks or Red Indians: The Aboriginal Inhabitants of Newfoundland.* London: Cambridge University Press, 1915.

Jansson, Sven B. F. *Sagorna om Vinland.* Stockholm Studies in Scandinavian Philology, vol. 5. Stockholm: University of Stockholm, 1954. (Gives *Flateyjarbók* text, and also *Hauksbók* 544 and *Skalholtsbók* 557 texts in parallel columns.)

Jelic, Luka. "L'Évangélisation de L'Amérique avant Christophe Colomb." *Congrès scientifique international des Catholiques, Compte rendu,* vol. 2, part 2 (1891); vol. 3, part 2 (1894). New Haven: Yale University Press.

Keeler, Clyde E., and Verrill, Ruth. "A Viking Saga in Tennessee?" *Georgia Academy of Science Bulletin,* vol. 19, no. 4 (Sept. 1961), pp. 78–82.

———— "The Viking Boat Finale." *Georgia Academy of Science Bulletin,* vol. 20, nos. 3, 4 (Sept. 1962).

Krogh, Knud J. *Viking Greenland.* Copenhagen: The National Museum, 1967.

Landsverk, O. G. *Ancient Norse Messages on American Stones.* Glendale, California: Norseman Press, 1969.

Lee, Thomas E., *Archaeological Discoveries, Payne Bay Region,*

Ungava, 1966. Centre d'études nordiques travaux divers 20, Quebec: Les Presses de l'université Laval, 1968.

—— *Archaeological Findings, Gyrfalcon to Eider Islands, Ungava, 1968.* Centre d'études nordiques travaux divers 27. Quebec: Les Presses de l'université Laval, 1969.

Liestøl, Aslak. "Cryptograms in Runic Carvings. A Critical Analysis." *Bulletin Minnesota History,* vol. 41 (Spring 1968), pp. 34–42.

"Magical Stones of the Sun." *Time,* 14 July 1967, p. 58.

Magnusson, Magnus, and Palsson, Hermann. *The Vinland Sagas.* New York: New York University Press, 1966.

Major, Richard Henry, ed. and trans. *The Voyages of the Venetian Brothers, Nicoló and Antonio Zeno, to the Northern Seas, in the XIVth Century.* Hakluyt Society Works, no. 50. London: 1873. (Italian text run with English translation.)

Marcus, G. F. "The Navigation of the Norsemen." *Mariner's Mirror,* vol. 39, no. 2 (May 1953).

Meinberg, Rev. Carl H. "The Norse Church in Medieval America." *Catholic Historical Review,* New Ser., vol. 5, no. 2 (July 1925), pp. 179–216.

Mongé, Alf, and Landsverk, O. G. *Norse Medieval Cryptography in Runic Carvings.* Glendale, California: Norseman Press, 1967.

Morse, Abner. Account of a paper read at Historic-Genealogical Society. *Historical Magazine,* series 1, vol. 6 (1967), pp. 123–24.

—— "Further Traces of the Ancient Norsemen in America; with Geological Evidences of the Location of Their Vinland." Dutton & Son; Boston, 1861.

Mowat, Farley, *Westviking. The New Quest for Vinland.* Boston: Little, Brown, 1965.

Munn, William A. *Location of Helluland, Markland, and Wineland, from the Icelandic Sagas.* Gazette Print: St. John's Newfoundland, 1914.

Nansen, Fridtjof. "The Norsemen in America." *Geographical Journal,* vol. 38 (Dec. 1911), pp. 557–75; discussion, pp. 575–80.

—— *In Northern Mists.* New York: F. A. Stokes, 1911.

Nörlund, Poul. "The Bishop's See of Ancient Greenland." *Discovery,* vol. 9 (1928), pp. 305–09.

————*Viking Settlers in Greenland and Their Descendants during Five Hundred Years.* London: Cambridge University Press, 1936.

————, and Russel, Aage. "Norse Ruins at Gardar. The Episcopal Seat of Medieval Greenland." *Meddelelser om Grönland,* vol. 76 (1930).

Oleson, Tryggvi J. *Early Voyages and Northern Approaches 1000– 1632.* New York: Oxford University Press, 1964.

Oxenstierna, Count Eric. *The Norsemen.* Edited and translated by Catherine Hutter. Greenwich, Connecticut: New York Graphic, 1965.

Packard, Alphaeus Spring. "Who First Saw the Labrador Coast?" *American Geographical Society of New York Journal,* vol. 20, no. 2 (1888), pp. 197–207.

Parker, Malcolm. "A Study of the Rocky Hill Pictographs." *Tennessee Archaeologist,* vol. 5, no. 2 (May 1949), pp. 13–17.

Pohl, Frederick J.

Articles in chronological order:

———— "Was the Newport Tower Standing in 1632?" *New England Quarterly,* vol. 18 (Dec. 1945), pp. 501–6.

———— Communication in *New England Quarterly,* vol. 19 (June 1946), pp. 283–85.

———— "Leif Ericsson's Visit to America." *American-Scandinavian Review,* vol. 36, no. 1 (March 1948), pp. 17–29.

———— "A Key to the Problem of the Newport Tower." *Rhode Island History,* vol. 7 (July 1948), pp. 75–83.

———— "The Newport Tower: An Answer to Mr. Godfrey." *Archaeology,* vol. 3, no. 3 (Autumn 1950), pp. 183–84.

———— "The Adventure of the Hasty Grave." *American-Scandinavian Review,* vol. 60, no. 1 (Spring 1952), pp. 15–24.

———— "Comments on the Follins Pond Investigation." *Bulletin, Massachusetts Archaeological Society,* vol. 14, no. 4 (July 1953), pp. 105–9.

———— "The Ship's Shoring at Follins Pond." *Bulletin, Massachusetts Archaeological Society,* vol. 16, no. 3 (April 1955), pp. 53–60.

———— "Can the Ship's Shoring at Follins Pond Be Radiocarbon

Dated?" *Bulletin, Massachusetts Archaeological Society,* vol. 17, no. 3 (April 1956), pp. 49–50.

────── "Further Comments on Mooring Holes." *Bulletin, Massachusetts Archaeological Society,* vol. 20, no. 1 (Oct. 1958), p. 15.

────── "Further Proof of Vikings at Follins Pond, Cape Cod." *Bulletin, Massachusetts Archaeological Society,* vol. 21, nos. 3, 4 (April–July 1960), pp. 48–49.

────── "Leif Erickson's Campsite in Vinland." *American-Scandinavian Review,* vol. 54, no. 1 (March 1966), pp. 25–29.

────── "The Vikings on Long Island." *Long Island Historical Society Journal,* vol. 6, no. 4 (Fall 1966), pp. 1–8.

────── "The Kingiktorsuak Inscription. A Posthumous Entry by Hjalmar R. Holand into the Cryptographic Controversy." *American-Scandinavian Review,* vol. 56, no. 4 (Dec. 1968), pp. 386–96.

────── "The Location of Southern Outposts." *American-Scandinavian Review,* vol. 57, no. 3 (Sept. 1969), pp. 250–259.

────── "Prince 'Zichmni' of the Zeno Narrative." *Terrae Incognitae,* vol. 2 (1970), pp. 75–86.

Books:

────── *Amerigo Vespucci, Pilot Major.* New York: Columbia University Press, 1944; reprinted by Octagon Books, 1966.

────── *The Lost Discovery.* New York: Norton, 1952.

────── *The Sinclair Expedition to Nova Scotia in 1938.* Pictou, N.S.: Pictou Press, 1950.

────── *The Vikings on Cape Cod.* Pictou, N.S.: Pictou Press, 1957.

────── *Atlantic Crossings Before Columbus.* New York: Norton, 1961.

────── *The Viking Explorers.* New York: T. Y. Crowell, 1966.

Reeves, Arthur Middleton. *The Finding of Wineland the Good.* London: 1890.

──────; Beamish, North Ludlow; and Anderson, Rasmus B. *The Norse Discovery of America* (translations and deductions). London: Norroena Society, 1906.

Robbins, Maurice. "An Editorial Comment (on the finding of the ship's shoring at Follins Pond)." *Bulletin, Massachusetts*

Archaeological Society, vol. 17, no. 3 (April 1956), p. 39.

Series espiscoporum, Grønland (Gardar). *Diplomatarium Norwegicum,* 17, B. (1913), pp. 280–86 and 358.

Skelton, R. A. *The European Image and Mapping of America,* A.D. *1000–1600.* Publication of The Associates of the James Bell Collection. Minneapolis: University of Minnesota, 1964.

———; Marston, Thomas E.; and Painter, George D. *The Vinland Map and the Tartar Relation.* Foreword by Alexander O. Vietor. New Haven: Yale University Press, 1965.

Smith, Benjamin L. "A Report on the Follins Pond Investigation." *Bulletin, Massachusetts Archaeological Society,* vol. 14, no. 2 (Jan. 1953), pp. 82–88.

Smith, Captain John. *Travels and Works of Captain John Smith.* Edited by Edward Arber. Edinburgh: J. Grant, 1910.

Steensby, H. P. "Norsemen's Route from Greenland to Wineland." *Meddelelser om Grønland,* vol. 56 (1917), pp. 151–202.

Strandwold, Olaf. *Norse Inscriptions on American Stones.* Magnus Björndal: Weehawken, N.J.: 1948.

——— *Norse Runic Inscriptions Along the Atlantic Seaboard.* Prosser, Wash.: privately printed, 1939.

Swanton, John R. "The Wineland Voyages." *Smithsonian Miscellaneous Collections,* Publ. 3906, vol. 107, no. 12 (Dec. 1947).

Thalbitzer, William. "Two Runic Stones, from Greenland and Minnesota." *Smithsonian Publications,* no. 4021 (Aug. 30, 1951).

Thruston, Gates P. *Antiquities of Tennessee.* Cincinnati: 1890.

Tornoe, J. Kr. *Early American History. Norseman Before Columbus.* Drammen, Norway: Universitetsforleget, Harold Lyche & Co., 1964.

Virginia Reader: A Treasury of Writings from the first voyage to the present. Edited by Francis Coleman Risenberger. New York: Dutton, 1948.

Zeigler, John M.; Tuttle, Sherwood D.; Tasha, Herman J.; and Giese, Graham S. "The Age and Development of the Provincelands Hook, Outer Cape Cod, Massachusetts." *Limnology and Oceanography,* vol. 10, supplement (Nov. 1965), pp. R298–R311.

INDEX